LEWIS ROWELL

THE
POSITIVE SCIENCES
OF THE
ANCIENT HINDUS

THE
POSITIVE SCIENCES
OF THE
ANCIENT HINDUS

BY
BRAJENDRANATH SEAL, M.A., Ph.D.

MOTILAL BANARSIDASS
Delhi Varanasi Patna Madras

© MOTILAL BANARSIDASS
Head Office : Bungalow Road, Delhi 110 007
Branches : Chowk, Varanasi 221 001
　　　　　　Ashok Rajpath, Patna 800 004
　　　　　　6 Appar Swamy Koil Street, Mylapore,
　　　　　　Madras 600 004

Reprint : Delhi, 1985

Printed in India by Shantilal Jain at Shri Jainendra Press,
A-45 Naraina, Phase I, New Delhi 110 028 and published by
Narendra Prakash Jain for Motilal Banarsidass, Delhi 110 007.

FOREWORD

THE following pages comprise a series of monographs on the Positive Sciences of the Ancient Hindus. In the present state of Indian chronology it is not possible to assign dates to the original sources from which the materials have been drawn. Practically the main body of positive knowledge here presented may be assigned to the millennium 500 B.C.—500 A.D. Colebrooke's account of Hindu Algebra, and Hœrnle's of Hindu Osteology, have made it unnecessary for me to write separate monographs on these subjects. The former, however, requires to be brought up to date. The progress of Indian Algebra (mainly in Southern India) after Bháskara, parallel to the developments in China and Japan, is a subject that remains for future investigation.

The chapter on the "Mechanical, Physical, and Chemical Theories of the Ancient Hindus" appeared in Dr. P. C. Ray's *Hindu Chemistry* (Vol. II.), and that on the "Scientific Method of the Hindus" as an appendix to the same work.

My direct aim in the present work is to furnish the historians of the special sciences with new material which will serve to widen the scope of their survey. The Hindus no less than the Greeks have shared in the work of constructing scientific concepts and methods in the investigation of physical phenomena, as well as of building up a body of positive knowledge which has been applied to industrial technique; and Hindu scientific ideas and methodology (*e.g.* the inductive method or methods of algebraic analysis) have deeply influenced the course of natural philosophy in Asia—in the East as well as the West—in China and Japan, as well as in the Saracen Empire. A comparative estimate of Greek and Hindu science may now be undertaken with some measure of success—and finality.

These studies in Hindu Positive Science are also intended to serve as a preliminary to my "Studies in Comparative Philosophy." Philosophy in its rise and development is necessarily governed by the body of positive knowledge preceding or accompanying it. Hindu Philosophy *on its empirical side* was dominated by concepts derived from physiology and philology, just as Greek Philosophy was similarly dominated by geometrical concepts and methods. Comparative Philosophy, then, in its criticism and estimate of Hindu thought, must take note of the empirical basis on which the speculative superstructure was raised.

I have not written one line which is not supported by the clearest texts. The ground trodden is, for the most part, absolutely new. Fortunately, the Sanskrit philosophico-scientific terminology, however difficult from its technical character, is exceedingly precise, consistent, and expressive. I may add that I have occasionally used (perhaps with a questionable freedom) scientific terms like isomeric, polymeric, potential, etc., in a broad sense, as convenient symbols to express ideas nearly or remotely allied.

BRAJENDRANATH SEAL.

CONTENTS

CHAPTER I.

THE MECHANICAL, PHYSICAL, AND CHEMICAL THEORIES OF THE ANCIENT HINDUS.

THE SĀṄKHYA-PĀTAÑJALA SYSTEM.

PAGES

Prakṛti, the Ultimate Ground—The Original Constituents and their Interaction — The Starting-point — Beginning of Evolution—Formation of Wholes or Systems—Collocation of Reals—The Formula of Evolution—The Conservation of Energy (and of Mass)—The Transformation of Energy—The Doctrine of Causation, a Corollary from the Conservation and Transformation of Energy—The Principle of Collocation—The Storing-up and the Liberation of Energy—Chain of Causation—Fixed Order—Time, Space, and the Causal Series—Space as Extension and Space as Position—The Causal Series—The Dissipation of Energy (and of Mass)—Their Dissolution into the Formless Prakṛti—The Evolution of Matter—The Genesis of the Infra-atomic Unit-potentials and of the Atoms—Cosmo-genesis, a Bird's-eye View—Chemical Analysis and Synthesis—Elements and Compounds . 1–56

CHEMISTRY IN THE MEDICAL SCHOOLS OF ANCIENT INDIA.

Physical Characters of the Bhútas—The Mahá-Bhútas—Mechanical Mixtures—Qualities of Compounds—The extant Charaka and Suśruta—Succession of Medical Authorities—Preparation of Chemical Compounds—Chemical Compositions and Decompositions—Organic Compounds — Poisons — Formation of Molecular Qualities in Chemical Compounds—Chemistry of Colours — Pariṇáma-váda versus Árambha-váda — Measures of Time and Space—Bháskarácháryya, a Precursor of Newton in the Conception of the Differential Calculus and its Application to Astronomy—Measures of Weight and Capacity—Size of the Minimum Visibile (Size of an Atom) . . . 56–85

CONTENTS

VEDÁNTIC VIEW.

PAGES

Máyá—Evolution of different Forms of Matter—Pañchí-karaṇa 85–92

THE ATOMIC THEORY OF THE BUDDHISTS . . . 92–93

THE ATOMIC THEORY OF THE JAINS.

General Properties of Matter—Atomic Linking . . 93–98

THE NYÁYA-VAISESHIKA CHEMICAL THEORY.

Theory of Atomic Combination—Chemical Combination—Mono-Bhautic Compounds—Hetero-Bhautic Compounds—The Theory of Dynamic Contact (Vish*tam*bha)—Oils, Fats, Milks—Mixtures like Soups, Solutions, etc.—Chemical Action and Heat—Light-Rays—Theory of Reflection, Refraction, etc.—Arrangement of Atoms in Space—The Foundations of Solid (Co-ordinate) Geometry—Three Axes of Váchaspati—Graphic Representation of the Constitution of a Bi-Bhautic Compound (with " complex contact ") . 98–121

CONCEPTION OF MOLECULAR MOTION (PARISPANDA) . 121–123

ADDENDA: EMPIRICAL RECIPES OF CHEMICAL TECHNOLOGY.

Searing of Rocks—Hardening of Steel—Preparation of Cements—Nourishment of Plants 124–128

CHAPTER II.
HINDU IDEAS ON MECHANICS (KINETICS).

Analysis of Motion—Motion considered in Relation to its Causes—Cause of Motion, or Force—The Concept of Vega—Causes of Pressure and of Impact—Illustrations of Combination of Forces—Composition of Gravity with Vega—Motion of a Particle in the Case of a Composition of Forces—Typical Cases of Curvilinear Motion—Vibratory Motion—Rotatory Motion—Motion of Fluids—Interesting Examples of Motion ascribed to Adriṣṭa—Measurement of Motion—

CONTENTS

Units of Space and Time—Component of Velocity—Notion of Three Axes—Relative Motion—Serial Motion 129–152

CHAPTER III.

HINDU IDEAS ON ACOUSTICS.

Analysis of Sound—Analysis of Vibratory Motion, *e.g.* of a bell (in air)—Echo—Pitch, Intensity, and Timbre—Musical Sounds—The Notes of the Diatonic Scale: Determination of their Relative Pitch—Musical Intervals 153–168

CHAPTER IV.

HINDU IDEAS ABOUT PLANTS AND PLANT-LIFE.

Classification of Plants—Elementary Ideas of Plant Physiology—Characteristics of Plant-Life—Sexuality—Consciousness 169–176

CHAPTER V.

HINDU CLASSIFICATION OF ANIMALS.

Classification of Animals—The Dietary Animals in Charaka and Suśruta—Snakes in Nágárjuna—Snakes in the Puránas—Umásváti's Classification of Animals—Recapitulation 177–201

CHAPTER VI.

HINDU PHYSIOLOGY AND BIOLOGY.

Metabolism—The Chemistry of Digestion—The Vascular System—The Nervous System in Charaka—The Nervous System after the Tantras—Psycho-physiology—Ganglionic Centres and Plexuses (Sympathetic-Spinal System)—Nerve Cords and Fibres—Automatic and Reflex Activity of the Organism—Fœtal Development after Suśruta—Heredity—The Sex Question—Life 202–243

CHAPTER VII.

HINDU DOCTRINE OF SCIENTIFIC METHOD.

Doctrine of Scientific Method—Test of Truth—Perception—Observation and Experiment—Results in the Different Sciences—Fallacies of Observation—Doctrine of Inference—The Chárváka View—The Buddhists, their Analysis and Vindication of Inference—Causality and Identity of Essence—How to ascertain Concomitance—Specific Cause and Specific Effect—Canon of the Method of Subtraction—The Joint Method of Difference (Pañchakáraṇí)—Proof of the Method—Doubt and its Limits—The Nyáya Doctrine of Inference—Definition of a Cause—Unconditional Antecedent—The Doctrine of Anyathásiddha—Elimination of the Irrelevant Factors—Nyáya Objection to the Method of Difference—The Nyáya Analysis of the Causal Relation Continued—Co-effects—Synchronousness of Cause and Effect—Plurality of Causes—The Nyáya Ground of Inference—Vyápti or Unconditional Concomitance—Ascertainment of Vyápti—Upádhi—Process of disproving suspected Upadhis—Tarka or Úha—Difference between the Nyáya Method and Mill's Joint Method of Agreement—Other Instances of Vyápti—Relation of Causality to Vyápti—Plurality of Causes—Scientific Methods as subsidiary to General Methodology and the Ascertainment of Truth—Hypotheses—Conditions of a Legitimate Hypothesis—Nirnaya or Verification of a Hypothesis—The Deduction Method—Navya Nyáya and its Significance in the History of Thought—Applied Logic—The Logic of the Particular Sciences—The Scientific Methods as applied to Therapeutics—The Scientific Methods as applied to Grammar and Philology—Conclusion . 244–295

Indexes
   A. Authorities
   B. Works
   C. Sanskrit Words
   D. English   297–313

THE POSITIVE SCIENCES

OF THE

ANCIENT HINDUS

CHAPTER I.

THE MECHANICAL, PHYSICAL, AND CHEMICAL THEORIES OF THE ANCIENT HINDUS.

I PROPOSE in this paper to give a synoptic view of the mechanical, physical, and chemical theories of the ancient Hindus. A chronological survey, even if the materials for it were available, would be here of little account. The origins of Hindu natural philosophy in the speculations of the Bráhmaṇas and the Upanishads, or in the mythology of the Puráṇas, do not come within the scope of the present exposition, which relates to the results of systematic thought as directed to the phenomena and processes of Nature. I have therefore confined myself to an account of natural philosophy as expounded in the principal systems of Hindu thought. The Sáṅkhya-Pátañjala system accounts for the Universe on principles of cosmic evolution; the Vaiseshika-Nyáya lays down the methodology of science, and elaborates the concepts of mechanics, physics, and chemistry. The Vedánta, the Púrva-Mímámsá, and in a less degree the Bauddha, the Jaina, and the Chárváka systems, make incidental contributions on points of special interest, but their main value in this regard is critical and negative. The principal authorities followed in this account—the Vyása-Bháshya on Pátañjali's Sútras, the Samhitá of Charaka, the Bháshya of Pra*s*astapáda, the Vártika of Udyotakara, and the V*ri*hat Samhitá of Varáhamihira —all centre round the Hindu Renaissance, the beginnings of the anti-Buddhist reaction in the fourth, fifth, and sixth centuries of the Christian era. Whenever I have made use of later authors, *e.g.* Kumárila, Śaṅkara, Śrídhara, Váchaspati, Udayana, Bháskara, Jayanta, Varavara, Raghunátha, Vijñána-bhikshu, etc., I have taken care to see (except where the opposite is expressly mentioned) that no idea is surreptitiously introduced which is not explicitly contained in the earlier authors.

The Sáṅkhya-Pátañjala System.

This system possesses a unique interest in the history of thought as embodying the earliest clear and comprehensive account of the process of cosmic evolution, viewed not as a mere metaphysical speculation but as a positive principle based on the conservation, the transformation, and the dissipation of Energy.

Prakriti: the Ultimate Ground.—The manifested world is traced in the Sáṅkhya to an unmanifested ground, Prak*ri*ti, which is conceived as formless and undifferentiated, limitless and ubiquitous, indestructible and undecaying, ungrounded and uncontrolled, without beginning and without end. But the unity of Prak*r*iti is a mere abstraction; it is in reality an undifferentiated manifold, an indeterminate infinite continuum of infinitesimal Reals. These Reals, termed Gu*n*as, may by another abstraction be classed under three heads: (1) Sattva, the Essence which manifests itself in a phenomenon, and which is characterised by this tendency to manifestation, the Essence, in other words, which serves as the medium for the reflection of Intelligence; (2) Rajas, Energy, that which is efficient in a phenomenon, and is characterised by a tendency to do work or overcome resistance; and (3) Tamas, Mass or Inertia, which counteracts the tendency of Rajas to do work, and of Sattva to conscious manifestation.

The ultimate factors of the Universe, then, are (1) Essence, or intelligence-stuff, (2) Energy, and (3) Matter, characterised by mass or inertia.

These Gu*n*as are conceived to be Reals, substantive entities—not, however, as self-subsistent or independent entities (प्रधान), but as interdependent moments in every real or substantive Existence.

Even Energy is substantive in this sense. The infinitesimals of Energy do not possess inertia or gravity, and are not therefore material, but they possess quantum and extensity (परिमाण—परिच्छिन्नत्व).

The very nature of Energy is to do work, to overcome resistance (रजश्चलम् उपष्टम्भकं), to produce motion. All Energy is therefore ultimately kinetic; even potential Energy (अनुद्भूतवृत्तिशक्ति) is only the Energy of motion in imperceptible forms.

The Original Constituents and their Interaction.—Every phenomenon, it has been explained, consists of a three-fold *arche*, intelligible Essence, Energy, and Mass. In intimate union these enter into things as essential constitutive factors. The essence of a thing (Sattva) is that by which it manifests itself to intelligence, and nothing exists without such manifestation in the Universe of Consciousness (समष्टिबुद्धि). But the Essence is only one of three moments. It does not possess mass or gravity, it neither offers resistance nor does work. Next there is the element of Tamas, mass, inertia, matter-stuff, which offers resistance to motion as well as to conscious reflection (तमः गुरु वरणकम्).

But the intelligence-stuff and the matter-stuff cannot do any work, and are devoid of productive activity in themselves. All work comes from Rajas, the principle of Energy, which overcomes the resistance of matter, and supplies even Intelligence with the Energy which it requires for its own work of conscious regulation and adaptation. (अन्यान्याभ्याम् अहङ्काराभ्यां स्वकार्योपजनने राजसाहङ्कारः सहकारी भवति । लोकाचार्य्ये-तत्त्वत्रय-अचित्प्रकरण ।)

The *Gunas* are always uniting, separating, uniting again. (अन्योन्यमिथुनाः सर्व्वे, नैषामादिसम्प्रयोगो वियोगो वा उपलभ्यते ।) Everything in the world results from their peculiar arrangement and combination. Varying quantities of Essence, Energy, and Mass, in varied groupings, act on one another, and through their mutual interaction and interdependence evolve from the indefinite or qualitatively indeterminate to the definite or qualitatively determinate. (एते गुणाः परस्परोपरक्तप्रविभागाः संयोगविभागधर्म्माणः

इतरेतरोपाश्रयेण उपाज्जितमूर्त्तेयः।—व्यासभाष्य।) But though co-operating to produce the world of effects, these divers moments with divers tendencies never coalesce. In the phenomenal product whatever Energy there is is due to the element of Rajas, and Rajas alone; all matter, resistance, stability is due to Tamas, and all conscious manifestation to Sattva. (परस्पराङ्गाङ्गित्वेऽपि असंभिन्नशक्तिप्र-विभागाः—व्यासभाष्य। अन्योन्याङ्गाङ्गिभावेन उत्पादितेऽपि द्रव्ये प्रकाशगुणः सत्त्वस्यैव क्रियागुणः रजसएव स्थितिगुणस्तमसएव—विज्ञानभिक्षु, योगवार्त्तिक on व्यासभाष्य, *ibid*. नैषां शक्तयः संकीर्य्यन्ते—वाचस्पतिमिश्र, तत्त्ववैशारदी on व्यासभाष्य, *ibid*.)

The nature of the interaction is peculiar. In order that there may be evolution with transformation of Energy, there must be a disturbance of equilibrium, a preponderance of either Energy or Mass-resistance or Essence over the other moments. The particular Gu*n*a which happens to be predominant in any phenomenon becomes manifest in that phenomenon, and the others become latent, though their presence is inferred by their effect. For example, in any material system at rest the Mass is patent, the Energy latent, and the conscious manifestation sub-latent. In a moving body, the Rajas, Energy, is predominant (kinetic), while the Mass, or rather the resistance it offers, is overcome. In the volitional consciousness accompanied with movement, the transformation of Energy (or work done by Rajas) goes hand in hand with the predominance of the conscious manifestation, while the matter-stuff or Mass, though latent, is to be inferred from the resistance overcome. (प्रधानवेलायाम् उपदर्शितसन्निधाना गुणानेवऽपि च व्यापारमात्रेण प्रधानान्नर्नीतानुमितास्तिताः—व्यासभाष्य।)

The Starting-point.—The starting-point in the cosmic history is a condition of equilibrium or equipoise consisting in a uniform diffusion of the Reals. The tendencies to conscious manifestation, as well as the powers of doing work, are exactly counterbalanced by the resistances of the inertia or Mass: the process of cosmic evolution (परिणाम) is under arrest. (सत्त्वरजस्तमसां साम्यावस्था प्रकृतिः—Pravachana, Sutra 61, Chap. I. साम्यावस्था अन्यूनानतिरिक्तावस्था अन्यूनाधिकभावेन असंहतावस्था अकार्यावस्था इति निष्कर्षः—विज्ञानभिक्षु, *ibid.*)

Beginning of Evolution.—The transcendental (non-mechanical) influence of the Purusha (the Absolute) puts an end to this arrest, and initiates the process of creation. Evolution begins with the disturbance of the original equilibrium. How this is mechanically brought about is not very clear. A modern expounder of the Sánkhya supposes that the particles of Sattva, Rajas, and Tamas possess a natural affinity for other particles of their own class, and that when the transcendental influence of the Purusha ends the state of arrest, the affinity comes into play, breaks up the uniform diffusion, and leads to unequal aggregation, and therefore to the relative preponderance of one or more of the three Gu*n*as over the others. Thus commences formative combination among the Reals, and consequent productive activity. (संहननम् आरम्भकसंयोगः न्यूनाधिकभावेन अन्योन्यं संयोगविशेषः—Sutra 66, Chap. I., प्रवचनभाष्य—विज्ञानभिक्षु । पृथिवीव्यक्तीनां पृथिवीव्यैनैव सत्त्वव्यक्तीनाम् एकजातीयतया एकता । खजातीयोपष्टम्भादिना वृद्धिह्रासादिकं च युक्तम् *ibid.*, Sutra 128, Chap. I.)

Formation of Wholes or Systems—Collocation of Reals.— Creative transformation accompanied with evolution of motion (परिस्पन्द) and work done by Energy (क्रिया) cannot take place without a peculiar collocation of the Reals (Gu*n*as). To form wholes or systems (समुदय) it is essential that one Gu*n*a should for the moment be preponderant and the others co-operant. And this cannot be without an unequal aggregation which overthrows the original equilibrium (गुणवैषम्य, न्यूनाधिकभाव)—in other words, without unequal forces or stresses coming into play in different parts of the system. (गुणविमर्हे—वाचस्पति । व्यक्तं सक्रियं परिस्पन्दवत् ... समुदयः समवायः । स च गुणानां गुणप्रधानभावमन्तरेण न सम्भवति । न गुणप्रधान-भावो वैषम्यं विना । न च वैषम्यमुपमर्द्योंपमर्दैकभावाट्टते ।—वाचस्पति, कौमुदी on Káriká 16.)

The Formula of Evolution—Differentiation in Integration. — Evolution (परिणाम) in its formal aspect is defined as differentiation in the integrated (संसृष्टविवेक). In other words, the process of Evolution consists in the development of the differentiated (वैषम्य) within the undifferentiated (साम्यावस्था), of the determinate (विशेष) within the indeterminate (अविशेष), of the coherent (युतसिद्ध) within the incoherent (अयुतसिद्ध). The evolutionary series is subject to a definite law which it cannot overstep (परिणामक्रमनियम). The order of succession is not from the whole to parts, nor from parts to the whole, but ever from a relatively less differentiated, less determinate, less coherent whole to a relatively more differentiated, more determinate, more coherent whole. That the process of differentiation evolves out of homogeneity separate or unrelated parts, which are then integrated into a whole, and that this whole again breaks up by fresh differentiation into isolated factors for a subsequent redintegration, and so on *ad infinitum*, is a fundamental misconception of *the course of material evolution*. That the antithesis stands over against the thesis, and that the synthesis supervenes and imposes unity *ab extra* on these two independent and mutually hostile moments, is the same radical misconception as regards *the dialectical form* of cosmic development. On the Sāṅkhya view, increasing differentiation proceeds *pari passu* with increasing integration within the evolving whole, so that by this two-fold process what was an incoherent indeterminate homogeneous whole evolves into a coherent determinate heterogeneous whole.

The different stadia in the order of cosmic evolution are characterised as follows :—

(1) The inconceivable, the unknowable, the formless, of which no character can be predicated (अलिङ्ग), including Prak*r*iti, or the Reals in a state of equilibrium.

(2) The knowable, the empirical universe, cosmic matter of experience, things as matter or stuff of consciousness (लिङ्ग), comprising Mahat, the intelligible Essence of the cosmos, evolved by differentiation and integration within the formless, characterless, inconceivable Prak*r*iti.

(3) Individual but still indeterminate stuff bifurcating into two series—Subject-experience and Object-experience, comprising on the one hand the indeterminate unity of apperception, or the empirical Ego, as the co-ordinating principle of the Subject-series (अस्मिता), and on the other hand

(though through the mediation of this subjective modification, अस्मिता or Ahaṅkára) the indeterminate material potencies, the subtle vehicles of potential Energy (तन्मात्र, सूक्ष्मभूत), the ultimate subtle constituents of the Object-series (the material world). The previous stadium, the cosmic matter of Experience (लिङ्ग, महत्), evolves within itself, by differentiation and integration, an individuated but still indeterminate stuff in two co-ordinated series, Subject and Object, though the latter is mediated through the former.

(4) Determinate stuff (विशेष) evolved within the indeterminate by further differentiation and integration, viz., in the series of Subject-experience, sensory and motor stuff; and in the Object-series, a corresponding atomic matter-stuff actualising the material potencies in the form of specific sensible Energies. The latter includes the different classes of Paramánus, the different kinds of atomic constituents of different kinds of gross matter (स्थूलभूत).

(5) Coherent and integrated matter-stuff, individual substances, characterised by generic and specific properties, which however are not rigidly fixed, but fluent, being subject to a three-fold change and constantly evolving. (अयुतसिद्धावयवभेदानुगतः समूहः द्रव्यमिति पतञ्जलिः—व्यासभाष्य, Sutra 44, Chap. III. सामान्यविशेषसमुदायो द्रव्यं—व्यासभाष्य, ibid. सामान्यविशेषात्मा अन्वयी धर्मी, ibid. धर्मिणो धर्मैलक्षणावस्थापरिणामः)

(6) And so the cosmic series moves on in ascending stages of unstable equilibrium (विसदृशपरिणाम) until the reverse course of equilibriation and dissipation of Energy (सदृशपरिणाम and साम्यावस्था), which even now constantly accompanies the evolution and transformation of Energy, completes the disintegration of the Universe into its original unmanifested ground, the unknowable Prak*r*iti.

The order of Cosmic Evolution according to the व्यासभाष्य (Sutra 19, Pada II.) is shown below in a tabular form :—

Prak*r*iti, the unmanifested unknowable ground
(गूढमव्यक्तमलिङ्गं)
|
Cosmic matter of experience (महत्, लिङ्गं)
|
SUBJECT SERIES (अविशेष). ⟶ OBJECT SERIES (अविशेष) : evolved in the cosmic matter of experience, but through the mediation of the individuated mind-stuff अस्मिता (Ahankára).

Individuated indeterminate mind-stuff (unity of apperception, empirical Ego (अस्मिता).

Individuated but indeterminate matter-stuff (subtile material potencies (तन्मात्र).

Determinate mind-stuff (विशेष), sensory and motor psychoses, etc. (ज्ञानेन्द्रिय, कर्मेन्द्रिय and मन:).

Determinate matter-stuff (विशेष), atomic and molecular constituents of gross matter (परमाणु—स्थूलभूत).

Coherent and integrated matter-stuff (अयुतसिद्धावयव: समूह: सङ्घात: द्रव्यं).

Individual substances, with generic and specific characters subject to constant change or evolution, *e.g.* inorganic objects composed of atoms or molecules (परमाणु), vegetable organisms (वृक्ष), animal organisms (शरीर). (अयुत-सिद्धावयव: सङ्घात: शरीरं वृक्ष: परमाणुरिति—व्यासभाष्य, Sutra 44, Pada III.)

तन्न तत् संसृष्टं विविच्यते क्रमानतिवृत्ते:, तथा षड्विशेषा: लिङ्गमात्रे संसृष्टा विविच्यन्ते, परिणामक्रमनियमात्, तथा तेषु अविशेषेषु भूतेन्द्रियाणि संसृष्टानि विविच्यन्ते, न विशेषेभ्य: परं तत्त्वान्तरमस्ति तेषान्तु धर्मैलक्षणावस्थापरिणामा व्याख्यायिष्यन्ते । (व्यासभाष्य, Sutra 19, Pada II.)

N.B.—The usual order given in the Sánkhya-Pátañjala compendiums is as follows :—Prak*r*iti, Mahat, Ahankára—and then the bifurcation, viz. 11 organs (sensory, motor and common sensori-motor) from Rájasic Ahankára, and Tanmátras from Támasic Ahankára—and finally the Paramánus of the Sthúla Bhútas. This is literally correct, but misses the significance of the doctrine of " differentiation within the integrated," according to which the Tanmátras are all evolved, through the medium of Ahankára, in the cosmic matter of Experience (Mahat).

The Conservation of Energy (and of Mass)—the Transformation of Energy.—The Gunas (Reals), though assuming an infinite diversity of forms and powers, can neither be created nor destroyed. The totality of the Mass (Tamas), as well as of Energy (Rajas), remains constant, if we take account both of the manifested and the unmanifested, the actual and the potential. But the individual products of the evolutionary process— the concrete phenomenal modes resulting from the combined action of the original Mass, Energy, and Essence—are subject to addition and subtraction, growth and decay, which are only due to changes of collocation, and consequent changes of state from the potential to the actual (in other words, from the future to the present and from the present to the past, in a time series)—changes which are illusorily ascribed to the Reals themselves. The different collocations of Mass and Energy give birth to the divers powers of things, the various forms of Energy which may be classed as like and unlike ; indeed, the course of Evolution from the Reals conforms to a fixed law, not only as regards the order of succession, but also as regards the appearance (and mutual relations) of like and unlike Energies. And this transformation is constantly going on—the course of Evolution is not arrested for a moment.

गुणास्तु सर्व्वधर्म्मानुपातिनः न प्रत्यस्तमयन्ते नोपजायन्ते व्यक्तिभिरेव अतीताऽनागतव्ययागमवतीभिः गुणान्वयिनीभिः उपजनापायधर्म्मेका इव प्रत्यवभासन्ते (व्यासभाष्य, Sutra 19, Pada II.) परिणामिनित्यता गुणानाम्। सर्व्वमिदं गुणानां सन्निवेशविशेषमात्रम् । (ibid., Sutra 13, Pada IV.) एते गुणाः तुल्यजातीयातुल्यजातीयशक्तिभेदानुपातिनः (ibid., Sutra 19, Pada II.) परिणामक्रमनियमात् (व्यासभाष्य, Sutra 19, Pada II.) क्रमान्यत्वं परिणामान्यत्वे हेतुः (Patañjali, Sutra 15, Pada III.) प्रकृतिः परिणमनशीला स्वयमप्यपरिणम्य नावतिष्ठते ।

The Doctrine of Causation, a corollary from the conservation and transformation of Energy—the Principle of Collocation—the Storing-up and the Liberation of Energy:—

The Sánkhya view of causation follows at once as a corollary from this doctrine of the conservation and transformation of Energy. As the total Energy remains the same while the world is constantly evolving, cause and effect are only more or less evolved forms of the same ultimate Energy. The sum of effects exists in the sum of causes in a potential (or unevolved) form. The grouping or collocation alone changes, and this brings on the manifestation of the latent powers of the Gunas, but without creation of anything new. What is called the (material) cause or sum of material causes is only the power which is efficient in the production, or rather the vehicle, of the power. This power is the unmanifested (or potential) form of the Energy set free (उद्भूतवृत्ति) in the effect. But the concomitant conditions are necessary to call forth the so-called material cause into activity. When the favourable combination or co-operation of concomitants is wanting, there is no manifestation of the effect. The question is—what is the aid which the concomitant conditions render to the determination (and production) of the effect existing in potency in its material cause? First there is the merely mechanical view as illustrated by some commonplace examples, *e.g.*, the manifestation of the figure of the statue in the marble block by the causal efficiency of the sculptor's art, or of the oil in the sesamum-seed by pressing, or of the grain of rice out of the paddy by the process of husking. In these cases the manifestation of an effect is only its passage from potentiality to actuality, a stadium in the process of evolution from possible (future) existence to actual (present) existence; and the concomitant condition (सहकारिशक्ति) or efficient cause (निमित्तकारण), the sculptor's chiselling, the pressing, the husking, is a sort of mechanical or instrumental help to this passage or transition. कार्य्यशक्तिमत्त्वमेव उपादान-कारणत्वम्। सा शक्तिः कार्य्यस्य अनागतावस्था एव। स एव विशेषः (उत्पत्तेः प्राक् कारणे विशेषः) अस्माभिः कार्य्यस्य अनागतावस्था इत्युच्यते। (विज्ञानभिक्षु-प्रवचनभाष्य, Sutra 115, Chap. I.) अभिव्यक्तिः वर्त्त-मानावस्था। कारणव्यापारोऽपि कार्य्यस्य वर्त्तमानलक्षणपरिणाममेव जनयति। यथा शिलामध्यस्थप्रतिमायाः टैङ्किकव्यापारेण अभिव्यक्तिमात्रं तिलस्थतैलस्य च निष्पीड़नेन धान्यस्थतण्डुलस्य च अवघातेन। (विज्ञानभिक्षु-प्रवचनभाष्य, Sutra 129, Chap. I.)

These mechanical examples of the Kapila-Sāṅkhya have the merit of simplicity, but the Patañjali-Sāṅkhya brushes them aside, and explains causation on the basis of the conservation and transformation of Energy advancing it as the liberation of potential Energy existing stored up in a Gu*n*a collocation (the sum of material causes), the liberation following on the action of the proximate efficient cause, or concomitant condition (निमित्तकारण).

The causal operation of concomitant conditions (efficient causes) lies only in this, that they supply a physical stimulus which liberates the potential Energy stored up in a given collocation. Everything in the phenomenal world is but a special collocation of the ultimate Reals (Energy, Mass, and Essence). The sum of (material) causes potentially contains the Energy manifested in the sum of effects; and in the passage from potency to actualisation, the effectuating condition (the concomitant cause), when it is itself accomplished, is only a step in the evolutionary series, which adds a specific stimulus, and renders determinate that which was previously indeterminate. When the effectuating condition is added to the sum of material conditions in a given collocation, all that happens is that a stimulus is imparted which removes the arrest, disturbs the relatively stable equilibrium, and brings on a liberation of Energy (उद्भूतवृत्तिशक्ति) together with a fresh collocation (गुणसन्निवेशविशेष). सर्व्वमिदं गुणानां सन्निवेशविशेषमात्रम् इति परमार्थतो गुणात्मानः (व्यासभाष्य, Sutra 13, Pada IV.) सतश्च फलस्य निमित्तं वर्त्तमानीकरणे समर्थं न अपूर्व्वोपजनने । सिद्धं निमित्तं नैमित्तिकस्य विशेषानुग्रहणं कुरुते । नापूर्व्वमुत्पादयति । (व्यासभाष्य, Sutra 12, Pada IV.).

Describing the production of bodies ("organic vehicles") for individual souls out of matter of Prak*r*iti, under the influence of their merit and demerit, as concomitant conditions, Patañjali points out that non-material concomitants like merit and demerit do not supply any moving force or Energy to the sum of material conditions, but only remove the arrest (the state of relatively stable equilibrium) in a given collocation, even as the owner of a field removes the barrier in flooding his field from a reservoir of water. This description is intended to represent the super-physical influence of non-material concomitants (or causes) like volition, merit and demerit, etc., but the causal operation of a material concomitant condition is essentially the same; there is the same reservoir of stored-up Energy in a given collocation, the same condition of arrest or relatively stable equilibrium, the same liberation of the stored-up potential Energy which flows along the line of least resistance; the only difference being that in the case of material concomitants the stimulus which removes the arrest is physical, instead of being transcendental as in the case of non-material causes like will, merit and demerit, etc.

The Vyása-Bháshya helps us to a clear mental representation of the details of this process:—As the owner of many fields can irrigate, from a field which is already flooded, others of the same or a lower level, without forcing the waters thereto with his hands, and merely by making an opening in the barrier or dyke, on which the waters rush in by their own force; or, further, as the same person cannot force these waters, or the earthy matters held in solution therein, into the roots of the rice plants, but only removes the obstructive grasses and weeds, on which the fluids of their own power enter the roots;—such is the action of an effectuating condition (निमित्त) added to a sum of material causes or conditions.

निमित्तम् अप्रयोजकं प्रवृत्तीनां वरणभेदस्तु ततः क्षेत्रिकवत् । (Patañjali, Sutra 3, Pada IV.) न हि धर्मादि निमित्तं यथा क्षेत्रिकः केदारात् अपां पूरणात् केदारं पिप्लावयिषुः समं निम्नं वा निम्नतरं वा नापः पाणिनाप-कर्षति आवरणं तु आसां भिनत्ति तस्मिन् भिन्ने खयमेवापः केदारान्तरम् आप्लावयन्ति ।

Chain of Causation—Fixed Order.—The order of Evolution with the transformation of the Energies follows a definite law. The unalterable chain of causes and effects in the phenomenal world illustrates this fixed order. But though the cosmic order is one and fixed, it comprehends divers series arising from different combinations of the original Gu*n*as, which constitute subordinate or particular laws of cause and effect (क्रमान्यत्वं परिणामान्यत्वे हेतुः, Patañjali, Sutra 15, Pada III.).

What we call the qualities of things are only modes of Energy acting in those collocations. योग्यतावच्छिन्ना धर्मिणः शक्तिरेव धर्मः—स च फलप्रसवभेदानुमितसद्भावः । (व्यासभाष्य, Sutra 14, Pada III.) ते खल्वमी धर्मा वर्तमाना व्यक्तात्मानः, अतीताऽनागताः सूक्ष्मात्मानः सर्वमिदं गुणानां सन्निवेशमात्रमिति परमार्थतो गुणात्मानः । (व्यासभाष्य, Sutra 3, Pada IV.). And these various Energies are sometimes actual (kinetic), sometimes potential, rising to actuality, and sometimes sub-latent, subsiding from actuality into sub-latency. In fact, the original Energy is one and ubiquitous, and everything therefore exists in everything else, *potentialiter* (सर्वं सर्वात्मकमिति), without prejudice to the generic and specific differences of things (जात्यनुच्छेदेन सर्वं सर्वात्मकं). Inorganic matter, vegetable organisms, and animal organisms are essentially and ultimately one (जलभूम्योः पारिणामिकं रसादिवैश्वरूप्यं स्थावरेषु दृष्टं तथा स्थावराणां जङ्गमेषु जङ्गमानां स्थावरेषु) so far as Mass and Energy are concerned, but the varied forms of Energy and the generic and specific qualities (or properties) of things, which are but modes of Energy, follow a definite unalterable law in the order of their appearance and succession, under conditions of space, time, mode, and causality, and hence all effects do not manifest themselves at once. देशकालाकारनिमित्तापबन्धात् न खलु समानकालम् आत्मनामभिव्यक्तिः (*ibid.*, Sutra 14, Pada III.) यो यस्य धर्मस्य समनन्तरो धर्मः स तस्य क्रमः । पिण्डः प्रच्यवते घट उपजायते इति धर्मपरिणामक्रमः । लक्षणापरिणामक्रमः घटस्य अनागतभावात् वर्त्तमानभावक्रमः, तथा पिण्डस्य वर्त्तमानभावात् अतीतभावक्रमः । (व्यासभाष्य, Sutra 15, Pada III.).

Time, Space, and the Causal Series.—A Tanmátra (infra-atomic particle of subtle matter) is conceived by our understanding to stand in three relations—(1) position in Space (देशावच्छिन्न), (2) position in the Time-series (कालावच्छिन्न), and (3) position in the Causal-series (निमित्तावच्छिन्न).

These three relations are the work of the intuitive stage of knowledge (निर्विकल्पप्रज्ञा) as opposed to the conceptual (सविकल्पप्रज्ञा). But this is not the pure relationless intuition of Reality (निर्विचारा निर्विकल्पप्रज्ञा), which may be termed intellectual intuition, but the intuition that imposes its forms on the Real substrate (सविचारा निर्विकल्पप्रज्ञा) or in other words empirical intuition. तत्र भूतसूक्ष्मेषु अभिव्यक्तधर्मकेषु देशकालनिमित्तानुभवावच्छिन्नेषु या समापत्तिः सा सविचारा इत्युच्यते । तत्रापि एकबुद्धिनिर्ग्राह्यमेव उदितधर्मविशिष्टं भूतसूक्ष्ममालम्बनीभूतं समाधिप्रज्ञायामुपतिष्ठते । (व्यासभाष्य, Sutra 44, Pada I.).

Infinite Time is a non-entity objectively considered, being only a construction of the understanding

(बुद्धिनिर्माण) based on the relation of antecedence and sequence, in which the members of the phenomenal series are intuited to stand to one another. These phenomenal changes as intuited by us in the empirical consciousness fall into a series, which the understanding conceives as order in Time. The Time-series, then, is a *schema* of the understanding for representing the course of Evolution. The *schema* of the understanding supervenes on the phenomenal world as order in Time, and hence in the empirical consciousness the Time-series appears to have an objective reality, and to form a continuum. As there is an ultimate and irreducible unit of extensive quantity (परिमाण) in the Gu*n*as or infinitesimal Reals of Prak*ri*ti, which are without constituent parts, so the moment may be conceived as the ultimate and irreducible unit of this Time-continuum as represented in the empirical consciousness. A moment therefore cannot be thought of as containing any parts standing in the relation of antecedence and sequence. If change is represented by the Time-series, a moment as the unit of time may be supposed to represent the unit of change. Now all physical change may be reduced to the motion of atoms in space, and we may therefore define the moment as representing the ultimate unit of such change—viz. the (instantaneous) transit of an atom (or rather a Tanmátra) from one point in space to the next succeeding point. Even an atom has constituent parts (the Tanmátras), and hence an atom must take more than one moment to change its position. The motion of that which is absolutely simple and without parts from one point in space to the next must be instantaneous, and conceived as the absolute unit of change (and therefore of time, क्षण). If this is held to be an irreducible absolute unit, it will follow that what we represent as the Time-continuum is really discrete. Time is of one dimension. Two moments cannot co-exist; neither does any series of moments exist in reality. Order in Time is nothing but the relation of antecedence and sequence, between the moment that is and the moment that went just before. But only one moment, the present, exists. The future and the past have no meaning apart from potential and sub-latent phenomena. One kind of transformation to which a thing is subject is that it changes from the potential to the actual, and from the actual to the sub-latent. This may be called the change of mark (लक्षणापरिणाम) as opposed to change of quality (धर्मपरिणाम) and the change due to duration or lapse of time (अवस्थापरिणाम). The present is the mark of actuality, the future the mark of potentiality, and the past of sub-latency, in a phenomenon. Only one single moment is actual, and the whole Universe evolves in that one single moment. The rest is but potential or sub-latent.

क्षणतत्क्रमयोर्नास्ति वस्तुसमाहार इति बुद्धिसमाहारः मुहूर्ताहोरात्रादयः । स खल्वयं कालः वस्तुशून्यो बुद्धिनिर्माणः शब्दज्ञानानुपाती लौकिकानां व्युत्थित-दर्शनानां वस्तुस्वरूप इव अवभासते । क्षणस्तु वस्तुपतितक्रमावलम्बी । क्रमश्च क्षणानन्तर्यात्मा । तं कालविदः काल इति आचक्षते योगिनः । न च द्वौ क्षणौ सह भवतः, क्रमश्च न द्वयोः सहभुवोरसम्भवात् पूर्वस्मादुत्तरभाविनो यदा-नन्तर्यं क्षणस्य स क्रमः । तस्मात् वर्त्तमान एवैकः क्षणः न पूर्वोत्तरक्षणाः सन्तीति तस्मान्नास्ति तत्समाहारः । ये तु भूतभाविनः क्षणाः ते परिणामान्विता व्याख्येयाः । तेनैकेन क्षणेन कृत्स्नो लोकः परिणाममनुभवति, तत्क्षणारूढाः

खल्वमी धर्माः । यथाऽपकर्षपर्य्यन्तं द्रव्यं परमाणुः एवं परमापकर्षपर्य्यन्तः कालः क्षणः । यावता वा समयेन चलितः परमाणुः पूर्व्वदेशं जह्यात् उत्तरदेशम् उप-सम्पद्येत स कालः क्षणः, तत्प्रवाहाविच्छेदस्तु क्रमः । (व्यासभाष्य, Sutra 52, Pada III.).

Vijñána-bhikshu points out that this does not amount to a denial of Time. It means that Time has no real (or objective) existence apart from the "moment." But the latter is real, being identical with the unit of change in phenomena (गुणपरिणामस्य क्षणत्ववचनात्). But even this is real only for our empirical (relative) consciousness (व्युत्थितदर्शन), which intuits the relation of antecedence and sequence into the evolving Reals (Gu*n*as), in the stage of "empirical intuition" (सविचारा निर्विकल्पप्रज्ञा). The "intellectual intuition" (निर्विचारा निर्विकल्पप्रज्ञा), on the other hand, apprehends the Reals as they are, without the imported empirical relations of Space, Time, and Causality.

Space as Extension and Space as Position.—Space must be distinguished as Desa (locus, or rather extension) and Dik (relative position). Space (Dik) as the totality of position, or as an order of co-existent points, is wholly relative to the understanding, like order in Time, being constructed on the basis of relations of position intuited by our empirical (or relative) consciousness. But there is this difference between Space-order and Time-order: there is no unit of Space as position (Dik), though we may conceive a unit of Time, viz. the moment (क्षण), regarded as the unit of change in the phenomenal or causal series (परमाणुक्रिया—गुणपरिणामस्य क्षणत्ववचनात्—योगवार्त्तिक, Sutra 51, Pada III.). Spatial position (Dik) results only from the different relations in which the all-pervasive Ákása stands to the various finite (or bounded) objects. On the other hand, Space as extension or locus of a finite body, Desa (देश: स्थित्याधार:), has an ultimate unit, being analysable into the infinitesimal extensive quantity inherent in the Reals (Gunas) of Prakriti. (गुणप्रकृते-रणुपरिणाम:—योगवार्त्तिक। एतेन नित्या दिगपि अप्रामाणिकी व्याख्याता, सामान्यतो दिग्व्यवहाराभावात्। पूर्ब्बादिव्यवहारस्य दिगुपाधिभिरेव सम्भवात्। सामान्यत: कालदिग्व्यवहारस्त्वेऽपि आकाशादेव तदुपपत्तेश्च। कालाच दिश्ययं विशेष: यत् काल: क्षणरूप इष्यते, दिक् तु सर्व्वैव नेष्यते।)

The Causal-Series.—The relation of Cause and Effect has been already explained. It only remains to add that the category of causality is mediated through the *schema* of order in Time. The empirical intuition first superimposes relations of antecedence and sequence on changing phenomena (the evolving Gunas or Reals), and the understanding out of these relations creates order in Time. The empirical intuition then intuits the phenomenal series of transformations of Energy in this Time-order, and in so doing imports the relation of cause and effect into the course of Nature. (कार्य्यकारणभावादीनां क्षणघटितत्वात्—योगवर्त्तिक, Sutra 51, Pada III.)

The Dissipation of Energy (and of Mass)—their Dissolution into the Formless Prakriti.—Cosmic Evolution (परिणाम) is a two-fold process, creative as well as destructive, dissimilative as well as assimilative, katabolic as well as anabolic (अनुलोमसर्गै and विलोमसर्गै, विसदृशपरिणाम and सदृशपरिणाम). In one aspect there is the aggregation (unequal aggregation) of Mass and Energy, with consequent transformation of Energy, resulting in the creation of inorganic as well as organic matter, and the genesis of worlds. The successive steps of this process may be described as (1) unequal aggregation with storing-up of Energy in a certain collocation, under a state of arrest (*i.e.* in a state of relatively stable equilibrium), (2) a stimulus removing the arrest and disturbing the equilibrium, and (3) liberation of the Energy, moving on to a fresh collocation, fresh aggregation, arrest, and equilibrium. The process of the world thus moves on from equilibrium to equilibrium, and the result of that process is the development of a coherent determinate heterogeneous whole (लिङ्ग, अविशेष, विशेष, अयुतसिद्धावयवसमूह, युतसिद्धावयवसमूह) in what is essentially an incoherent indeterminate homogeneous whole (अलिङ्ग).

But there is a second aspect of this evolutionary process. Unequal aggregations are unstable; there is a constant tendency in things to go back to the original stable equilibrium, the state of uniform equal diffusion of Reals. This process is called the resolution of like to like (सदृशपरिणाम), consisting in assimilation and dissipation, and being the exact opposite of the process of "differentiation in the integrated" which has evolved the Cosmos. The collocations of Mass, Energy, and Essence are always breaking up, and the Energy, as well as the Mass, however slowly, however imperceptibly, are being dissipated, *i.e.* dissolved into the original formless Prak*r*iti, a state of permanent equilibrium and arrest, from which there is, and can be, no return, except under the transcendental influence of the Absolute at the commencement of a new creative cycle. Not that there is a destruction of the Mass or Energy, but a dissipation or dissolution into a condition of equal uniform diffusion from which there is no return. This is not the phenomenon of kinetic Energy disappearing and becoming potential or sub-latent, for in such cases there is restitution or reconversion by natural means. When this reverse current of assimilation (and dissipation) prevails over the current of dissimilation (and integration), the Universe will disintegrate more and more, until it disappears in the formless Prak*r*iti, its unknowable source and ground. (*Vide* तत्त्वत्रय and कौमुदी.)

The Evolution of Matter (तान्मात्रिक सृष्टि).—The ultimate constitution of Matter is a question of the profoundest interest in the Sáṅkhya-Pátañjala system. Three stages clearly stand out in the genesis of Matter :—(1) the original infinitesimal units of Mass or inertia, absolutely homogeneous and ubiquitous, on which Energy does work, when the original equilibrium comes to an end (भूतादि—तामसाहङ्कार); (2) the infra-atomic unit-potentials, charged with different kinds of Energy, which result from the action of Energy on the original units of Mass (तन्मात्र); and (3) the five different classes of atoms, the minutest divisions of which gross matter is capable, but which are themselves complex Tanmátric systems (स्थूलभूतपरमाणु).

The first stadium, Bhútádi, is absolutely homogeneous and absolutely inert, being devoid of all physical and chemical characters (रूपादिभिरसंयुतं) except quantum or mass (परिच्छिन्नत्व, परिमाण); and this admits neither of addition nor of subtraction, can neither be created nor destroyed. The second stadium, Tanmátra, represents subtle matter, vibratory, impingent, radiant, etc., instinct with potential energy. These "potentials" arise from the unequal aggregation of the original Mass-units in different proportions and collocations with an unequal distribution of the original Energy (Rajas). (तन्मात्र-रूपादेः किं कारणम् इति चेत् खकारणद्रव्याणां न्यूनाधिकभावेन अन्योऽन्यं प्रति संयोगविशेष एव—खजातीयोपष्टम्भादिना वृद्धिह्रासादिकं च युक्तं।) The Tanmátras possess something more than quantum of Mass and Energy; they possess physical characters, some of them penetrability (अवकाशदान), others powers of impact or pressure, others radiant heat, others again capability of viscous and cohesive attraction. In intimate relation to these physical characters they also possess the potentials of the energies represented by sound, touch, colour, taste, and smell; but being subtle matter, they are devoid of the peculiar forms (विशेष) which these "potentials" assume in particles of gross matter like the atoms and their aggregates. In other words, the potentials lodged in subtle matter must undergo peculiar transformations by new groupings or collocations to be classed among sensory stimuli—gross matter being supposed to be matter endued with properties of the class of sensory stimuli, though in the minutest particles thereof the sensory stimuli may be infra-sensible (अतीन्द्रिय but not अनुद्भूत). (तस्मिंस्तस्मिंस्तन्मात्रा: ते च अविशेषिणः। ते च पदार्थाः शान्तघोरमूढाख्यैः स्थूलगतशब्दादिविशेषैः शून्या एकरूपत्वात्। तथाच शान्तादिविशेषशून्यशब्दादिमखमेव भूतानां शब्दादितन्मात्रत्वम्।)

The Tanmátras, then, are infra-atomic particles charged with specific potential energies. First, the "potential" of the sound-stimulus is lodged in one class of particles, Tanmátras which possess the physical energy of vibration (परिस्पन्द), and serve to form the radicle of the ether-atom (आकाशपरमाणु); then the potential of the tactile stimulus is lodged in another class of Tanmátras, particles which possess the physical energy of impact or mechanical pressure in addition to that of vibration, and serve to form the radicle of the air-atom (Váyu Paramá*n*u); next, the potential of the colour-stimulus is lodged in a third class of Tanmátras, particles which are charged with the energy of radiant heat-and-light, in addition to those of impact and vibration, and serve to form the nucleus of the light-and-heat corpuscle; then the potential of the taste-stimulus is lodged in other Tanmátras, particles which possess the energy of viscous attraction, in addition to those of heat, impact, and vibration, and which afterwards develop into the atom of water; and, lastly, the potential of the smell-stimulus is lodged in a further class of Tanmátras, particles which are charged with the energy of cohesive attraction, in addition to those of viscous attraction, heat, impact, and vibration, and which serve to form the radicle of the earth-atom.

षड्विशेषाः तद्यथा शब्दतन्मात्रं स्पर्शतन्मात्रं रूपतन्मात्रं रसतन्मात्रं गन्ध-तन्मात्रञ्च इत्येकद्वित्रिचतुष्पञ्चलक्षणाः शब्दादयः पञ्चविशेषाः । (व्यासभाष्य, Sutra 19, Pada II.) अहङ्कारात् शब्दतन्मात्रं ततश्चाहङ्कारसहकृतात् शब्दतन्मात्रात् शब्दस्पर्शगुणं स्पर्शतन्मात्रम् । एवंक्रमेण एकैकगुणवृद्ध्या तन्मात्राणि उत्पद्यन्ते । (प्रवचनभाष्य, Sutra 62, Chap. I.).

शब्दादीनां मूर्तिसमानजातीयानाम् एकः परिणामः पृथिवीपरमाणुः तन्मात्रा-वयवः । भूतान्तरेषु अपि स्नेहौष्ण्यप्रणामित्वाऽवकाशदानानि उपादाय सामान्यम् एकविकारारम्भः समाधेयः । (व्यासभाष्य, Sutra 14, Pada IV.) तद्यथा । गन्धतन्मात्रं वर्ज्जयित्वा चतुस्तन्मात्राणां स्नेहजातीयानां एकः परिणामः जल-परमाणुः तेषां च महाजलादिः । एवं गन्धरसौ वर्ज्जयित्वा औष्ण्यजातीयानां

चित्तन्मात्राद्या तेजोऽणुः तेभ्यः महातेजआदिः । एवं गन्धरसरूपाद्या वज्रीनात्
द्वाभ्यां वाय्वणुः तेभ्यः महावाय्वादिः । एवं शब्दतन्मात्राद्दहङ्कारांशसहकृतात्
आकाशाणुः तेभ्यः महाकाशादिः ।

विज्ञानभिक्षु remarks : अत्र दर्शने अयं सिद्धान्तः शब्दादितन्मात्रपञ्चके
काठिन्यस्नेहादिव्यङ्ग्याः पृथिवीत्वादिजातयः सन्ति । (योगवार्त्तिक, Sutra 14,
Pada IV.).

Before explaining the genesis of atoms it is necessary to say something about Ákása, which is the link between the infra-atomic particles (Tanmátras) and atoms (Paramánus). Ákása corresponds in some respects to the ether of the physicists, and in others to what may be called proto-atom (protyle). In one aspect Ákása is all-pervasive (विभु), and devoid of the property of impenetrability which characterises even the infra-atomic potential units (Tanmátras). In another aspect Ákása is described as having originated out of the mass, or inertia, in Prakriti (Bhútádi) when the latter became charged with the first potential (the sound-potential). Vijñána-bhikshu, in the Yoga-Vártika, boldly tackles the difficulty. Ákása, he explains, has two forms—original and derivative, non-atomic and atomic. The original Ákása is the undifferentiated formless Tamas (mass in Prakriti, matter-rudiment—Bhútádi), which is devoid of all potentials, and is merely the all-pervasive seat or vehicle of the ubiquitous original Energy (Rajas). This Ákása must not be confounded with vacuum, which is merely negative (आवरणाभाव—un-occupiedness), though it must be conceived as all-pervasive, occupying the same space as the various forms of gross matter (समानदेशकम्—अवकाशस्वरूपम् आकाशं—योगवार्त्तिक), and therefore devoid of the property of impenetrability (मूर्त्तान्तरासमानदेशत्वं—योगवार्त्तिक) which characterises atomic matter. But when the original equilibrium (साम्यावस्था) comes to an end, unequal aggregations form collocations in different groups and proportions of the three Gunas (न्यूनाधिकभावेन अन्योऽन्यं संयोगविशेषः संहननं—विज्ञानभिक्षु, प्रवचनभाष्य and योगवार्त्तिक). The transformation of Energy now begins—working on a collocation of mass (with Essence) (गुणान्तरोपसमृद्धं सदंशतः—विज्ञानभिक्षु, योगवार्त्तिक); it first gives rise to the sound-potential (शब्दजननयोग्याथैरूपेण परिणमति—विज्ञानभिक्षु), and the atomic Ākāsa (proto-atom, protyle) is but an integration of the original unit of mass charged with this vibration-potential. This vibratory (or rather rotary) ether-atom (आकाशाणु) is integrated, limited (परिच्छिन्न), and as such cannot occupy the same space with other (subsequently integrated) atoms. But this proto-atomic integration of Ākāsa (कार्य्याकाश) is formed everywhere, and, itself residing in the ubiquitous non-atomic Ākāsa (कारणाकाश—अवकाशरूपमाकाशं), forms the universal medium in which air or gas atoms, light-and-heat corpuscles, and other atoms move and float about.

वायोरावरणं । यदि हि अवकाशरूपम् आकाशं न स्यात् तदा मूर्त्तेद्रव्येषु स्यात्यादिषु अनन्तस्तेजआदिप्रवेशो न स्यात् (विज्ञानभिक्षु, योगवार्त्तिक, Sutra 40, Pada III.) आकाशं हि कार्य्येकारणरूपेण द्विविधम् । तत्र कारणाकाशं तमोगुणविशेषमत्येव व्यवह्रियते । तदानीम् आकाशताव्यञ्जकशब्दादिगुणविशेषाभावात् । तच्च कारणाकाशं गुणान्तरोपसमृद्धं सदंशतः आदौ शब्दजननयोग्याथैरूपेण परिणमते । ततश्च अणुसङ्घातेन पृथिवीवदेव महाभूताकाशम् अहङ्कारापेक्षया परिच्छिन्नं वायोरावरणम् उत्पद्यते (विज्ञानभिक्षु, योगवार्त्तिक, Sutra 40, Pada III.).

The Genesis of the Infra-Atomic Unit-Potentials (*Tanmātras*) *and of the Atoms.*—The subject of the genesis and the structure of the Tanmátras and the Paramá*n*us was a fascinating one to these ancient thinkers, and a wide divergence of views prevailed. I will here notice several typical views—those of the Vish*n*u Purána, Parásara, Patañjali, and a certain school of Vedántists reported in the तत्त्वनिरूपण.

I. A famous passage in the Vish*n*u Purána explains the genesis and the structure of the Tanmátras and of the Bhútas (Paramá*n*us) in the following manner:—

The first Tanmátra originated from the rudiment-matter (Bhútádi), the individuated but still indeterminate potential-less Mass in Prak*r*iti, under the action of Energy (उपष्टम्भतः परिणमयन्ति—प्रवचनभाष्य, Sutra 62, Ch. I.) by a process of disintegration and emanation (विकुब्बीर्णः—विष्णुपुराण—एकविकारारम्भः—व्यासभाष्य, Sutra 14, Pada IV. विकरणभावः विक्रीयेतास्वभावा व्यापिता इति यावत्, योगवार्त्तिक on Pátañjali's Sutra—मनोजवित्वं विकरणभावः etc.) in the menstruum, or surrounding medium of the unindividuated cosmic mass (Mahat, महतावृतः).

This first subtle matter, the first result of "Mass-disintegration" and Energy-transformation, is charged with the sound-potential, the potential of vibration or oscillation (परिस्पन्द). It is called the sound-potential (शब्दतन्मात्र).

This is typical of the genesis (and structure) of the other Tanmátras (kinds of subtile matter). In each of the remaining cases, an atomic Mass charged with actual specific energies (भूतपरमाणु) disintegrates and emanates, and thus evolves a form of subtile matter (a kind of Tanmátra) under the action of Energy, and always in the same menstruum or surrounding medium

—that of Bhútádi, the super-subtile. Each kind of subtile matter becomes charged with a new potential in addition to the potentials already evolved. The genesis of an atom, a Bhúta-Paramánu, is a quite different process. Here the unit-potential (Tanmátra) receives an accretion of Mass, and by a sort of condensation and collocation evolves an atom (Bhúta-Paramá*n*u).

The genesis and structure of the Tanmátras and the Bhúta-Paramánus are worked out below :—

1. The super-subtile inviduated Mass (rudiment-matter, Bhútádi), under the action of the original Energy (रज:) disintegrates and emanates (विकुरुते) in the menstruum or surrounding medium (समावरण) of Mahat cosmic super-subtile Mass, and evolves a form of subtile matter (तन्मात्र), which becomes charged with the sound-potential (vibration-potential, परिस्पन्द), and is called the unit of sound-potential (शब्दतन्मात्र).

2. This subtile matter, the Mass, charged with sound-potential, receives an accretion of Mass from the rudiment-matter (Bhútádi), and by condensation and collocation evolves the Ákáśa Bhúta, the atomic Ákáśa, the proto-atom charged with the specific Energy of the sound-stimulus (actual vibratory motion). (स एव भूतादि: शब्द-तन्मात्रात् खडितीयात् शब्दगुणकम् आकाशं ससज्जे । तथाच अहङ्कारशब्दतन्मात्राभ्यां मिलित्वा आकाशं सृज्यते—योगवार्त्तिक on the Vish*n*u Purána passage, Sutra 14, Pada IV.)

3. This proto-atom, the atomic Ákáśa, charged with its actual specific Energy, again disintegrates and

emanates, under the action of the original Energy and in the menstruum of the rudiment-matter (super-subtile Mass), and thus evolves another kind of subtile matter (Tanmátra) which becomes charged with the touch-potential (the potential of impact or mechanical pressure—प्रणामित्व, वहनशीलत्व) in addition to the sound-potential (vibration-potential—परिस्पन्द) and is called the unit of touch-potential (स्पर्शतन्मात्र).

4. Next, this subtile matter, the Mass charged with touch- (and sound-) potential, *i.e.* with the potentials of vibration and impact, receives an accretion of Mass again from the rudiment-matter (Bhútádi), and by condensation and collocation evolves the Váyu Bhúta, a kind of gaseous matter or air of which the atoms are charged with the actual specific energy of the touch-stimulus, *i.e.*, with actual energy of impact in addition to the actual energy of vibratory motion.

5. Next, the atom of Váyu, so charged with the actual specific energy of impact and vibration, again disintegrates and emanates, under the action of the original Energy, and in the same menstruum or surrounding medium of the rudiment-matter (super-subtile Mass—Bhútádi), and thus evolves another kind of subtile matter (Tanmátra), which becomes charged with the heat-potential (सौष्म्य—रूप, heat-and-light potential) in addition to the impact-potential and the vibration-potential, and is called the unit of colour-potential (रूपतन्मात्र).

6. Now this subtile matter, this radiant matter, charged with light-and-heat potential, and also with impact- and vibration-potential, receives an accretion of Mass again from the rudiment-matter (Bhútádi), and by condensation and collocation evolves the Tejas Bhúta, the light-and-heat corpuscle, which is charged with the specific Energy of the colour-stimulus, *i.e.* radiates actual heat and light (विकिरण) in addition to manifesting the energy of impact (impingency) and of vibration (or oscillation).
7. Next, this atom or light-and-heat corpuscle disintegrates, and emanates as before a form of subtile matter charged with the taste-potential (रसतन्मात्र), in addition to the three potentials already generated, and also with the physical potential of viscous attraction.
8. This subtile matter charged with the taste-potential and with the potential of viscous attraction condenses, and collocates as before into the water-atom, which manifests the actual specific energies of viscous attraction and the taste-stimulus.
9. The viscous water-atom charged with the actual specific energy of the taste-stimulus disintegrates, and emanates as before a form of subtile matter charged with the smell-potential in addition to the four potentials already generated and also with the potential of cohesive attraction.
10. This subtile matter charged with the smell-potential and with the potential of cohesive

attraction condenses, and collocates as before into the earth-atom, which manifests the actual specific energies of cohesive attraction and the smell-stimulus.

Vijñána-bhikshu, in the Yoga-Vártika, briefly summarises the Vishnu Purána process as follows :—

Bhútádi as radicle in conjunction with Mahat produces the sound-potential, which as radicle in conjunction with Bhútádi produces Ákása, which as radicle in conjunction with Bhútádi produces the touch-potential, which as radicle in conjunction with Bhútádi produces Váyu, which as radicle in conjunction with Bhútádi produces the colour-potential, which as radicle in conjunction with Bhútádi produces Tejas, and so on.

In this brief summary he does not bring out the force of विकुब्बाण: (the disintegrating process) and the distinction between the genesis of subtile and gross matter (Tanmátra and Bhúta).

यथा प्रधानेन महान्, महता स तथावृतः ।
भूतादिस्तु विकुब्बाणः सर्गे तन्मात्रिकं ततः ।
ससर्ज शब्दतन्मात्रात् आकाशं शब्दलक्षणं ।
शब्दमात्रं तदाकाशं भूतादिः स समावृणोत् ।
आकाशस्तु विकुब्बाणः स्पर्शमात्रं ससर्ज ह ।
बलवान् अभवत् वायुः तस्य स्पर्शो गुणो मतः । (विष्णुपुराण)

II. A famous passage in Parásara takes another view of the genesis and structure of the Tanmátras and the Bhúta-Paramánus. Krishnapáda, in the तत्त्वत्रयविवरण, represents the scheme as follows :—

The Tanmátras originate from one another in one

D

linear series, and each Bhúta originates in a separate line from its own Tanmátra :—

भूतादि	Bhútádi.
शब्दतन्मात्र	Sound-Tanmátra—as a radicle or centre surrounded or encircled by Bhútádi generates Ákása—
स्पर्शतन्मात्र	Touch-Tanmátra—as a radicle or centre encircled by sound-Tanmátra with Ákása-atom as a help generates Váyu—
रूपतन्मात्र	Colour-Tanmátra — as a radicle or centre encircled by touch-Tanmátra with Váyu-atom as a help generates Tejas—
रसतन्मात्र	Taste-Tanmátra—as a radicle or centre encircled by colour-Tanmátra with Tejas-atóm as a help generates Ap—
गन्धतन्मात्र	Smell-Tanmátra—as a radicle or centre encircled by taste-Tanmátra with Ap-atom as a help generates Prithivi.

The genesis of a Bhúta-Paramánu (atom) from the subtile matter of a Tanmátra is not here so simple as in the view of the Vishnu Purána. The latter speaks of condensation and collocation, but in the passage under reference a Tanmátra is supposed to act as a radicle, as the centre of a system, surrounded or encircled by Tanmátras of the immediately higher order in the medium of their own Bhúta.

Thus an atom of Ákása has the following structure :—

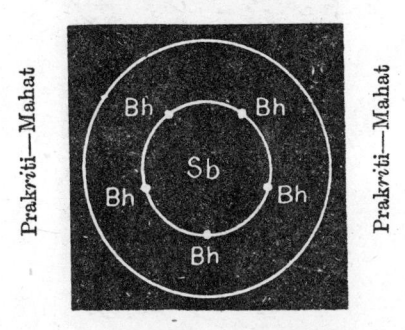

Prakriti—Mahat

AN ATOM OF ÁKÁSA.

Sb = Śabda-Tanmátra (vibration-potential).
Bh = Bhútádi.

An atom of Váyu is constituted as follows (this takes place within the surrounding medium of Ákása) :—

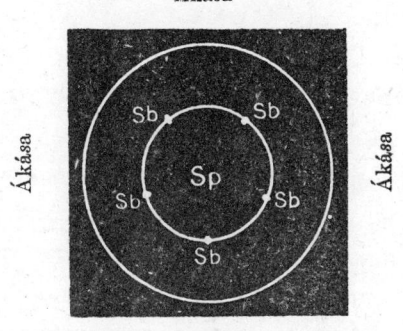

AN ATOM OF VÁYU.

Sp = Sparsa-Tanmátra (impact-potential).
Sb = Śabda-Tanmátra (vibration-potential).

An atom of Tejas (heat-and-light corpuscle) has the following structure :—

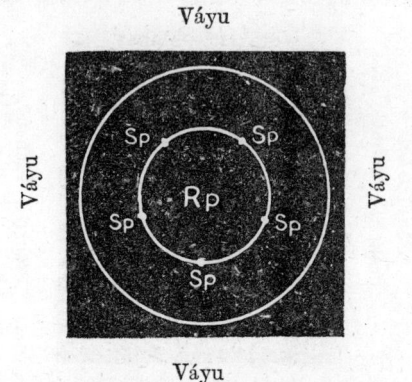

Váyu

Váyu   Váyu

Váyu

AN ATOM OF TEJAS.
Rp = Rúpa-Tanmátra (light-potential).
Sp = Sparsa-Tanmátra (impact-potential).

and so on.

A chemist will be disposed to push his chemical processes into the region of subtle matter. He may translate आवरण as a menstruum, and सहायक as a catalytic agent. In this case an atom of Váyu will be considered as generated from the impact-Tanmátra as a radicle, in the menstruum of vibration-Tanmátra, with Ákása-atoms as a catalytic agent.

अत्रायं क्रमः—भूतादेः शब्दतन्मात्रं जायते, शब्दतन्मात्रं भूतादिरावृणोति, ततः आकाशं जायते, ततः अस्मात् शब्दतन्मात्रात् स्पर्शतन्मात्रं जायते, स्पर्शतन्मात्रं शब्दतन्मात्रमावृणोति, एवं शब्दतन्मात्रावृतात् आकाशसहायकात् स्पर्शतन्मात्रात् वायुर्जायते, ततः अस्मात् स्पर्शतन्मात्रात् रूपतन्मात्रं जायते, रूपतन्मात्रं स्पर्श-तन्मात्रमावृणोति, एवं स्पर्शतन्मात्रावृतात् वायुसहायकात् रूपतन्मात्रात् तेजो जायते—and so on. अयं क्रमः तत्त्वत्रयविवरणे कृष्णपादैरुक्तः । वरवरमुनि, तत्त्वत्रयभाष्य (अचित्प्रकरण) ।

A slight variation of the above view is ascribed to a certain school of Vedántists in the तत्त्वनिरूपण.

The scheme may be represented as follows:—

A Bhúta-atom is evolved by integration (condensation and collocation, स्थूलावस्थारूप) from the corresponding Tanmátra (subtile matter). This is the same view as that of the Vish*n*u Purá*n*a.

The Tanmátras again evolve from one another in a lineal series, as in Pará*s*ara's view. But the process of this generation is somewhat more complex. A Tanmátra first disintegrates and emanates in a surrounding medium (a menstruum) of the Tanmátra just preceding it in the order of genesis, and, with the help of its own Sthúla Bhúta as a sort of catalytic, generates the Tanmátra next in order; *e.g.*, the infra-atomic impact-particles (स्पर्शतन्मात्र) disintegrate or emanate, in a surrounding "atmosphere" of the vibratory subtile matter (शब्दतन्मात्र), and then, with the help of their own atomic integration Váyu, gas, generate the Tanmátra next in order, the subtile matter of radiant light-and-heat (तेज:).

III. Patañjali's view, as expounded in the व्यासभाष्य and योगवार्त्तिक, is as follows:—

(*a*) The order of genesis of various forms of subtile matter (potentials):—

(1) Bhútádi, the rudiment-matter, original Mass, acted on by Rajas (Energy) produces the sound-potential (vibration-potential), अन्यान्याभ्याम् अहङ्काराभ्यां स्वकार्य्यंजनने राजसाहङ्कार: सहकारीभवति ।

(2) This subtile vibration-potential, as a radicle, with accretion of rudiment-matter (Bhútádi), condensing and collocating, and acted on by Rajas, generates the subtile touch-potential

(impact-potential), which is impingent as well as vibratory (oscillating).

(3) This subtile impact-potential, again, as a radicle, with accretion of rudiment-matter (Bhútádi), condensing and collocating, and acted on by Rajas, generates the subtile light-and-heat potential (रूपतन्मात्र) which radiates light and heat, in addition to being impingent and vibratory.

(4) Next, the light-and-heat potential, as a radicle, with accretion of rudiment-matter (Bhútádi), condensing and collocating as before, generates the subtile taste-potential, which is charged with the potential of the taste-energy and of viscous attraction, in addition to being vibratory, impingent, and radiant.

(5) Lastly, the subtile taste-potential as a radicle, with accretion of rudiment-matter as before, condensing and collocating, generates the subtile smell-potential, which is charged with the potential of the smell-energy, and also of cohesive attraction, in addition to being vibratory, impingent, and radiant.

(*b*) The order of genesis of the Bhúta-Paramáṇus (forms of atomic matter).

The five classes of atoms are generated as follows :—

(1) The sound-potential, subtile matter, with accretion of rudiment-matter (Bhútádi), generates the Ákása-atom.

(2) The touch-potentials combine with the vibratory particles (sound-potential) to generate the Váyu-atom.

(3) The light-and-heat potentials combine with touch-potentials and sound-potentials (*i.e.* with impact particles and vibratory particles) to produce the Tejas-atom.

(4) The taste-potentials combine with light-and-heat potentials, touch-potentials, and sound-potentials (*i.e.* with radiant, impingent, and vibratory particles) to generate the Ap-atom; and

(5) The smell-potentials combine with the preceding potentials (*i.e.* with particles of taste-energy and with radiant, impingent, and vibratory particles) to generate the Earth-atom.

The Ákása-atom possesses penetrability, the Váyu-atom impact or mechanical pressure, the Tejas-atom radiant heat-and-light, the Ap-atom viscous attraction, and the Earth-atom cohesive attraction.

Vijñána-bhikshu in one passage gives the following scheme of the genesis of the Bhútas :—

A radicle of sound-potential with rudiment-matter gives Ákása-atom (Bhútádi), a radicle of touch-potential with Ákása-atom gives Váyu-atom, a radicle of light-and-heat potential with Váyu-atom gives Tejas-atom, a radicle of taste-potential with Tejas-atom gives Ap-atom, and a radicle of smell-potential with Ap-atom gives Earth-atom. On this view, an atom

$$\text{of Ákása} = \text{Bh(Sb)}$$
$$\text{of Váyu} = \overline{\{\text{Bh(Sb)}\}}\,(\text{Sp})$$
$$\text{of Tejas} = \overline{\{\text{Bh(Sb)}\}\,(\text{Sp})}\,\text{Rp}$$

where Bh = भूतादि, Sb = शब्दतन्मात्र, Sp = स्पर्शतन्मात्र, Rp = रूपतन्मात्र, and so on.

Bhútas and Paramá*n*us—Cosmo-genesis and its successive stages :—

The "five Bhútas" stand for a classification of substances on the basis of their generic properties, resulting, as the Sáṅkhyas hold, from the structural type of their constituent atoms—a classification more physical than chemical, or properly speaking chemico-physical, unlike the purely chemical classification of the so-called elements of modern chemistry. A Paramá*n*u, again, is a type of atoms corresponding to each Bhúta class, and indeed one and the same kind of Paramá*n*u may comprehend atoms of different masses, if only these should agree in their structural type.

Cosmo-genesis: a Bird's-eye View.—Out of the all-pervasive rudiment-matter (Bhútádi) appeared Ákása (ether), first as a Tanmátra (subtile matter) charged with the potential energy of sound (vibration-potential), and then as an atomic integration of a mono-Tanmátric structure (the Ákása-atom—आकाशाणु) also ubiquitous and all-enveloping. In the next stage we find a new kind of Tanmátras, systems of the infra-atomic vibratory particles, so arranged as to manifest a new form of Energy, that of impact or mechanical pressure, and these Tanmátras (स्पर्शतन्मात्राणि) combining with the vibration-potentials (Ákása-Tanmátra) produced a new kind of atom, the di-Tanmátric Váyu-atom, which by aggregation formed a gaseous envelope composed of impinging (driving) vibratory particles (Váyu). Next appeared the third class of Tanmátras, infra-atomic systems of the impinging vibratory particles, which by their collocation developed a new form of Energy—the energy of radiant heat-ard-light. These Tanmátras (रूपतन्मात्राणि) combining with the potentials (Tanmátras) of vibration and impact, produced a new kind of atom—the tri-Tanmátric Tejas-atom, the light-and-heat corpuscle, which by aggregation enveloped the gaseous world in huge flames. In the next stage we have the fourth class of Tanmátras, new and complex infra-atomic systems of the radiant impinging vibratory particles, which evolved the energy of viscous attraction, as well as the potential energy concerned in the taste-stimulus. These Tanmátras (रसतन्मात्राणि) combining with the three previous ones, gave rise to another class of atoms, the tetra-Tanmátric Ap-atom, and the flaming gases were thus precipitated into cosmic masses of viscous fluid matters (Ap). Finally appeared the fifth class of Tanmátras, infra-atomic systems of the viscous radiant impinging vibratory particles which developed new forms of Energy—the energy of cohesive attraction, as well as the potential energy concerned in the stimulus of smell. These Tanmátras (गन्धतन्मात्राणि) uniting with the other four kinds of infra-atomic subtile particles, formed another class of atoms, the penta-Tanmátric Earth-atom. Thus the viscous fluid matters were condensed and transformed into the Earth-Bhúta, comprising the majority of the so-called elements of chemistry.

The Puránas, in their own fanciful way, conceive that, in the course of cosmic evolution, each succeeding Bhúta appeared within an outer envelope of its immediate predecessor, with a total mass (or volume?) a tenth less than that of the latter.

वियत् तत्राप्येकदेशगतो वायुः प्रकल्पितः ।
चिन्तयेत् वह्निमप्येवं मरुतो न्यूनवर्त्तिनं ॥
ब्रह्माण्डावरणेष्वेषां न्यूनाधिक-विचारणा ।
वायोर्देशांशतो न्यूनो वह्निवांयौ प्रकल्पितः ॥
पुराणोक्तं तारतम्यं दशांशैर्भूतपञ्चके ॥

(पञ्चदशी-भूतविवेक, Ślokas 72, 81, and 82.)

Examples of the different Bhútas :—

1. Ákása. This is ubiquitous.

2. Váyu. Various substances composed of di-Tanmátric atoms—kinds of Váyu—must have been formed in the gaseous envelope, in the second stage of cosmic evolution, out of the proto-atoms of Ákása ; but they have either suffered a fresh transformation into substances of a more complex atomic structure, or have dissipated into the mono-Tanmátric Ákása, out of which they took their rise. The one familiar example now surviving is atmospheric air. Water-vapour (वाष्प) is but water (Ap), and smoke, fumes, etc., but earth-particles in gaseous diffusion.

3. Tejas. Various classes of Tejas-corpuscles — substances with tri-Tanmátric atomic structure, *i.e.* two grades subtler than the ordinary elements of chemistry (which are of a penta-Tanmátric structure)—are even now known (तेजो भौमादिभेदेन बहुविधं । भौमं दिव्यं औदर्यं आकरजं—वरवरमुनि, तत्त्वत्रयभाष्य).

First, there is fire, or the light and heat emitted by the burning log of wood or lamp (अग्निः-दीपः-भौमं तेजः).

Now it is important to note that the flame of a burning log of wood (इन्धन) or of an oil-lamp is not pure Tejas, a pure mass of light-and-heat corpuscles. There is chemical union with Earth-particles (particles of the hard penta-Tanmátric substance) acted on by Energy; and then the Tejas-corpuscles, light-and-heat particles which are latent (absorbed) therein, come forth as flame (पार्थिवीपष्टम्भेन तदनुगतात् तेजसः अग्निर्भवति—विज्ञानभिक्षु, प्रवचनभाष्य, Sutra 110, Chap. V.). Then there is the light of the sun and the stars (दिव्यं सौरं आदित्यादि) which are flaming masses of molten viscous matters (जलमाचेन्धनं तेजः दिव्यं तच्च सूर्यादि—तच्चयभाष्य, अचित्प्रकरण) or of molten earthy matters (सूर्यादीनि सब्राणि तेजांसि पार्थिवद्रव्यसङ्गेनेव अवस्थिनानि—विज्ञानभिक्षु, प्रवचनभाष्य, Sutra 13, Chap. III.). There is also the lightning, which liberates a kind of Tejas latent in the aqueous particles and vapours, under the action of Energy, in the same way as an ordinary fire liberates the Tejas latent in the wood or other fuel. Next there are the stores of animal heat derived from the break-up of the nutritive material (औदर्यं). Lastly there comes the peculiar form of the Tejas Energy (radiant Energy) stored up in the metalliferous ores and igneous rocks which have been formed in the subterranean heat. Here earthy matters are mixed up, but the radiant Energy predominates in the composition of the metals (तेजआधिक्येन तैजसादिता सुवर्णादीनां—विज्ञानभिक्षु, प्रवचनभाष्य, Sutra 19, Chap. III.). Aniruddha, a late Sáṅkhya commentator, notes in reference to "igneous bodies" that the greater part of their mass is derived from the Earth Bhúta, though the Tejas particles determine the peculiar chemical combination which produces them; and this must also be his view of the composition of the metals (तत्र अपि (तैजसे शरीरे अपि) बहुतरपार्थिवावयवावष्टम्भकत्वं, अल्पत्वे चानुपभोगात्—अनिरुद्धवृत्ति, Sutra 112, Chap. V.).

4. Ap. This viscous fluid of a tetra-Tanmátric structure has but one pure example, viz., water, though the various organic acids, the juices of fruits and the saps of plants, are supposed to be transformations of watery radicles combined with different kinds of earthy accretions.

5. Lastly, the Earth Bhúta, the hard full-formed matter, with its penta-Tanmátric atoms, comprises by far the majority of the so-called chemical elements.

The question is,—how does one and the same Bhúta, of the same formal structure, comprise different kinds of elements, with different atomic masses and different characteristic properties? And the answer is not far to seek. The properties of a thing are only the energies that are manifested in the particular collocations of the three Gunas—Mass, Energy, and Essence; and a tri-Tanmátric or a penta-Tanmátric atom, *i.e.* an atom composed of three or five kinds of Tanmátras, may differ from another of the same class in respect of the number of constituent Tanmátras of any particular kind, as also of their collocation or grouping, and therefore in mass as well as in generic and specific characters.

The Sáṅkhya-Pátañjala conceives the properties (or energies) of substances to result from the grouping or the quanta of the Tanmátras, or the Gunas themselves, and hence any radical differences in substances of the same Bhúta class must characterise their atoms, though in an infra-sensible form. In the Nyáya-Vaiseshika, on the other hand, the atoms of the same Bhúta class are alike in themselves, homogeneous; and the variety of substances comprehended under the same Bhúta is ascribed merely to the different arrangements or groupings of the atoms (व्यूह) and not of their components, for components they have none.

As a typical and familiar instance of the variety of characteristic properties (or energies) that may result from variations in accompaniment or grouping, the Sánkhya-Pátañjala points to the various kinds of fruit acids and juices, all originating from one and the same Bhúta (water) with different accretions of earthy matters (भूविकाराः). In the same way, though we speak of only five classes of Tanmátras and atoms, the infinite variety of the world results from the infinitely varied collocations of the three original Gunas which underlie Tanmátra and atom alike. (सत्त्वरजस्तमसां व्यपकर्षैकाग्रतापन्नः संघातः परमाणुरिति—न्यायवार्त्तिक, उद्द्योतकर, reporting the Sánkhya view. अयुतसिद्धावयवः संघातः परमाणुरिति—व्यासभाष्य, Sutra 44, Pada III. परमाणुः सामान्यविशेषात्मा अयुतसिद्धावयवभेदानुगतः समुदायः —व्यासभाष्य, Sutra 44, Pada IV. योग्यतावच्छिन्ना धर्मिणः शक्तिरेव धर्मः—ibid., Sutra 14, Pada III. यो धर्मेषु अनुपाती सामान्य-विशेषात्मा सोऽन्वयी धर्मी—ibid., Sutra 14, Pada III.)

स्यादेतत्—कथं एकरूपाणां गुणानां अनेकरूपा प्रवृत्तिः—इत्यत आह परिणामतः सलिलवत् । यथा वारिदविमुक्तं उदकं एकरसं अपि तद्द्रव्यविकारान् आसाद्य नारिकेल-ताली-विल्व-चिरविल्व-तिन्दुकामलक-कपित्थ-फलरसतया परिणामात् मधुराम्ललवणतिक्तकटुकषायतया विकल्पते, एवमेकैकगुणसम्भवात्

प्रधानं गुणं आश्रित्य अप्रधानगुणाः परिणामभेदान् प्रवर्त्तयन्ति । तदिदमुक्तं प्रतिप्रतिगुणाश्रयविशेषात्, एकैकगुणाश्रयेण यो विशेषस्तस्मात् इत्यर्थः ।

(वाचस्पति—कौमुदी—on Káriká 16.)

If we take a unit of rudiment-matter (Bhútádi) for the unit of mass (*cf.* the mass of an electron with a charge of motion, etc.), and represent the first Tanmátra by t_1 such units, and if further t_2, t_3, t_4, t_5 units of mass (Bhútádi) be successively added at each accretion to form a fresh Tanmátra, then the second, third, fourth, and fifth Tanmátras will respectively contain $t_1 + t_2$, $t_1 + t_2 + t_3$, $t_1 + t_2 + t_3 + t_4$, and $t_1 + t_2 + t_3 + t_4 + t_5$ units of mass.

Also the Váyu-atom (bi-Tanmátric system) will contain $t_1 + (t_1 + t_2)$, *i.e.* $2t_1 + t_2$ units of mass; the Tejas-atom (tri-Tanmátric system) will contain $t_1 + (t_1 + t_2) + (t_1 + t_2 + t_3)$, *i.e.* $3t_1 + 2t_2 + t_3$ units; the Ap-atom (tetra-Tanmátric system) $t_1 + (t_1 + t_2) + (t_1 + t_2 + t_3) + (t_1 + t_2 + t_3 + t_4)$, *i.e.* $4t_1 + 3t_2 + 2t_3 + t_4$ units; and the Earth-atom (penta-Tanmátric system) $t_1 + (t_1 + t_2) + \ldots + (t_1 + t_2 + t_3 + t_4 + t_5)$, *i.e.* $5t_1 + 4t_2 + 3t_3 + 2t_4 + t_5$ units.

If t units of mass be added to the first Tanmátra to form the atom of Ákása, the latter will contain $t_1 + t$ units of mass.

In other words, the numbers representing the mass-units (Tamas) in the different classes of atoms (gross matter) will form an ascending series, viz. $t_1 + t$, $2t_1 + t_2$, $3t_1 + 2t_2 + t_3$, $4t_1 + 3t_2 + 2t_3 + t_4$, and $5t_1 + 4t_2 + 3t_3 + 2t_4 + t_5$.

Now if a follower of the Sánkhya-Pátañjala were

asked to account for differences among Paramá*n*us of the same Bhúta class, he would perhaps suppose t_1 to vary from a_1 to β_1, t_2 from a_2 to β_2, t_3 from a_3 to β_3, t_4 from a_4 to β_4, and t_5 from a_5 to β_5.

Therefore the mass-units contained in the Váyu-atoms of the different possible Váyu substances would be represented by $2a_1+t$, $2a_1+1+t$, $2a_1+2+t$, ... $2\beta_1+t$, in A. P. with unity as common difference, there being $2(\beta_1-a_1)+1$ possible Váyu substances.

The mass-units contained in the Tejas-atoms of the different possible Tejas substances would be represented by the series $3a_3+2a_2+a_3$, $3a_1+2a_2+a_3+1$, ... $3\beta_1+2\beta_2+\beta_3$, increasing in A. P. by unity as common difference, there being $3(\beta_1-a_3)+2(\beta_2-a_2)+(\beta_3-a_3)+1$ Tejas substances possible.

The mass-units contained in the Ap-atoms of the different possible Ap substances would form the series $4a_1+3a_2+2a_3+a_4$, $4a_1+3a_2+2a_3+a_4+1$,......... $4\beta_1+3\beta_2+2\beta_3+\beta_4$, there being $4(\beta_1-a_1)+3(\beta_2-a_2)+2(\beta_3-a_3)+(\beta_4-a_4)+1$ Ap substances possible.

The mass-units contained in the Earth-atoms of the different possible Earth substances would form the series in A. P., $5a_1+4a_2+3a_3+2a_4+a_5$, $5a_1+4a_2+3a_3+2a_4+a_5+1$,.........$5\beta_1+4\beta_2+3\beta_3+2\beta_4+\beta_5$, there being $5(\beta_1-a_1)+4(\beta_2-a_2)+3(\beta_3-a_3)+2(\beta_4-a_4)+(\beta_5-a_5)+1$ Earth substances possible.

Size (परिमाण).—As to size or volume, the Sáṅkhya accepts only two kinds—the infinitesimal, which is also without parts (अणु—निरवयव), and the non-infinitesimal, which consists of parts (महत्—सावयव). The latter varies from the excessively small (the so-called A*n*us, Tan-

mátras, and Paramánus) to the indefinitely great
(परममहत्—विभु,—*e.g.* Ákása).

The Gu*n*as alone are infinitesimal, with the exception of those ubiquitous ones that evolve into Ákása-atoms and Mind-stuff (आकाशाण, and अन्तःकरण); all the rest of the evolved products (whether subtile or gross matter) are non-infinitesimal.

Vijñána-bhikshu notes that all the Gu*n*as (Reals) cannot be ubiquitous. If this were the case, that disturbance of equilibrium, that unequal aggregation with unequal stress and strain with which cosmic evolution begins, would be impossible. The Gu*n*as, which give rise to Ákása and Mind-stuff, must be held to be ubiquitous, and this will suffice for the ubiquity of Prak*r*iti. (न च अस्मदृष्टेन गुणाख्यप्रकृतेः विभुत्वमेवावगम्यते इति वाच्यम् । अन्तःकरणाकाशहेतुगुणानां विभुत्वेन तदुपपत्तेः । सर्व्वगुणानां विभुत्वे सति आद्यपरिणामहेतुक्षोभसंयोगाद्यसंभवात्—योगवार्त्तिक, Sutra 51, Pada III.)

Chemical Analysis and Synthesis—Elements and Compounds.—What, then, is the equivalent in the Sánkhya-Pátañjala of the distinction between a chemical element and a chemical compound, or is there none? Did or did not this physical analysis and classification of things lead on to a classification based on chemical analysis and chemical synthesis? These are questions of singular interest, the answer to which will disclose some new points of view from which the ancient Hindu thinkers approached the problems.

Aggregates (समूहाः) may, in regard to their structure, be divided into two classes: (1) those of which the parts are in intimate union and fusion, being lost in the whole (अयुतसिद्धावयवाः समूहाः), and (2) mechanical aggregates, or collocations of distinct and independent parts (युतसिद्धावयवाः समूहाः).

A substance is an aggregate of the former kind, and may be divided into two classes: (1) the Bhútas and their "isomeric" modifications (भूत, भूतभेद, and भूतविकार), and (2) chemical compounds (मिलितद्रव्य, संहतभूतार्थै). Chemical compounds, again, may be subdivided into two classes: (1) those composed of atoms of the same Bhúta class, *i.e.* of different isomeric modifications of the same Bhúta, and (2) those composed of atoms of different Bhúta classes. In the first case, there is contact between "isomeric" atoms (सजातीय-संयोग), in the second case between heterogeneous atoms (विजातीय-संयोग). The first contact leads to intimate union (सङ्गः,—सङ्गाख्यः यः संयोगविशेषः तेनैव द्रव्याणां विकारो भवति—विज्ञानभिक्षु, प्रवचनभाष्य): the isomeric atoms by a peculiar liberation of Energy (सजातीयोपष्टम्भ—the action of similars on similars) are attracted towards one another, and being riveted, as it were, form the so-called material cause (उपादानकारण) of the compound product. The second kind of contact (that between unlike atoms of heterogeneous Bhútas) begins with a liberation of Energy (उपष्टम्भ), which breaks up each of the Bhútas; and taking particles (or atoms) of one as nuclei or radicles, groups particles of the rest round these radicles in a comparatively free or unattached condition. In this case, one Bhúta, that which serves to furnish the radicles, not necessarily that which is numerically or quantitatively predominant, gets the name of material

E

cause (उपादानकारण), and the others, which by their collocation cause the liberation of Energy (उपष्टम्भ, अवष्टम्भ, or विष्टम्भ), are called efficient causes (निमित्तकारण)—(एवमेकैकगुणसम्भवात् प्रधानगुणं आश्रित्य अप्रधानगुणाः परिणामभेदान् प्रवर्त्तेयन्ति—वाचस्पति, कौमुदी on Káriká 16). The illustrations given (viz. the Rasas as modifications of Ap, water, with Earth-accretions) show that this process applies not only to the Gunas, but also to the Bhútas. (यथा आकाशादेकरसं सलिलं पतितं नानारूपात् संस्षेघात् भिद्यते—गौड़पाद on Káriká 17. तत्र अपि (तैजसे शरीरे अपि) बहुतरपार्थिवावयवावष्टम्भात्, अल्पत्वे च अनुपभोगात्—अनिरुद्ध on Sutra 112, Chap. V. जातिसाङ्कर्य्यस्य अस्माकमदोघत्वात् सामग्रीसमवधाने अनेकैरपि इन्द्रियैः एकदा एकवृत्त्युत्पादने बाधकं नास्ति ।—विज्ञानभिक्षु, प्रवचनभाष्य ।)

Aniruddha goes so far as to hold that both "isomeric" and "heterogenic" combinations are real cases of constitutive contact. (आरम्भकसंयोग, *e.g.* भौतिकवायोर्देहारम्भकत्वम्—अनिरुद्ध on Sutra 113, Chap. V.). But in the later Sánkhya-Patañjala the current teaching denied this—बहूनामुपादानायोगात् (Sutra 102, Chap. V.), where विज्ञानभिक्षु notes—बहूनां भिन्नजातीयानां चोपादानत्वं न दृष्टमिति सजातीयमेवोपादानम् । इतरच्च भूतचतुष्टयमुपष्टम्भकम् ।

But besides these transformations of substance (द्रव्यान्तर-परिणाम) by "isomeric" or "heterogenic" process, ceaseless changes go on in the characters, the modality, and the states of substances—changes which are due to the unequal distribution of force (or of stress and strain —pressure) among the Gunas, which are in themselves constant. (धर्मलक्षणावस्थापरिणामाः न द्रव्यान्तरतः—यथा एका रेखा शतस्थाने शतं दशस्थाने दश, एकैकस्याने, यथा चैकात्वेऽपि स्त्री माता चोच्यते दुहिता च स्वसा चेति—गुणनित्यत्वेऽपि गुणानां विमर्देवैचित्र्यात्—व्यासभाष्य, Sutra 13, Pada III.)

"Even as the same figure '1' stands for a hundred in the place of hundred, for ten in the place of ten, and for a unit in the place of unit."[1]

Now the question is—in these mixed substances does the fusion take place by Paramáṇus or by larger masses (or lumps)? Now a Paramáṇu is defined to be the smallest portion of any substance which exhibits the characteristic qualities of that substance; in other words, it stands for the smallest homogeneous portion of any substance. It is not without parts, and there-

---

This conclusively proves that the decimal notation was familiar to the Hindus when the Vyása-Bháshya was written, *i.e.* centuries before the first appearance of the notation in the writings of the Arabs or the Greco-Syrian intermediaries. Váchaspati, who comments on the Vyása-Bháshya, composed his Nyáya-Súchí-Nibandha in वस्वङ्कवसुवत्सरे, *i.e.* Samvat 898 or 842 A.D. This cannot be Śaka 898, for apart from the decisive use of वत्सर, which by this time had come to signify the Samvat era, Vácaspati's commentator, Udayana, wrote the Lakshaṇávalí in Śaka 906—

तर्काम्बराङ्कप्रमितेष्वतीतेषु शकान्ततः ।
वर्षेषूद्यनखस्त्री सुबोधां लच्चणावलीं ॥

and Udayana, who wrote the Pariśuddhi on the Tátparyyatíká of Váchaspati, could not have been a contemporary of the latter, as will also appear from the invocation to Sarasvati in the opening lines of the Pariśuddhi. Váchaspati, then, preceded Udayana by 142 years, and must have been himself preceded by the author of the Vyása-Bháshya by a longer interval still, for Váchaspati ascribes the Bháshya to Veda-Vyása himself (वेदव्यासेन भाषिते भाष्ये व्याख्या विधास्यते). The internal evidence also points to the conclusion that the Bháshya cannot have been composed later than the sixth century—*cf.* the quotations from Pañchaśikha, Várshagaṇya, and the Shashṭhi-Tantra-Sástra, without a single reference to Íśvara-Kṛishṇa—which is decisive. I may add that I remember to have come across passages of a similar import in Buddhist and other writings of a still earlier date.

fore not indivisible. It is subject to disintegration. In a Bhúta or its isomeric modification, the Paramá*n*u, the smallest homogeneous component particle, is unmixed, and therefore corresponds to the atom of modern chemistry. In a mixed substance (मिलितद्रव्य, संहतभूतार्थं), whether it be an "isomeric" or a heterogenic compound, the qualities are due to the mixture, and therefore its Paramá*n*u (usually called Arambhaka Paramá*n*u), the smallest homogeneous particle possessing its characteristic qualities, must result from the mixture of the Paramá*n*us (in smaller or larger numbers as the case may be) of the component substances. In the Sá*n*khya view, then, the Paramá*n*u of a mixed substance (Arambhaka Paramá*n*u) corresponds to what we now call molecule. (अपकर्षपर्य्यन्तं द्रव्यं परमाणुरिति—व्यासभाष्य । लोष्टस्य हि प्रविभज्यमानस्य यस्मिन्नवयवे अल्पन्वतारतम्यं व्यवतिष्ठते स: अपकर्षपर्य्यन्तपरमाणु:—वाचस्पति, तत्त्ववैशारदी—Sutra 52, Pada III. नाणुनित्यता न निर्भागत्वं । पृथिवीपरमाणु: जलपरमाणुरित्यादिव्यवहारस्तु पृथिव्यादीनां अपकर्षकाष्ठाभिप्रायेणैव ।—विज्ञानभिक्षु, प्रवचनभाष्य, Sutra 88, Chap. V.) That the Paramá*n*us may form binary molecules (द्व्यणुक) in forming substances, is acknowledged by the Sá*n*khyas, as will appear from Gau*d*apáda: तथा अन्योन्याश्रयाश्च द्व्यणुकवत्गुणा: । (गौड़पाद, on Káriká 12). Even the Vai*s*eshikas, with their prejudice against "poly-Bhautic" or "heterogenic" combination, acknowledge that in "poly-Bhautic" compounds the different Bhúta substances unite by their Paramá*n*us (or atoms), though they rigidly insist that in such cases only one atom should be regarded as the "radicle" (उपादान or द्व्यारम्भक कारण) and the others as co-efficient causes (निमित्तकारण—उपष्टम्भक, *e.g.* प्रशस्तपाद—एवं समुत्पन्नेषु चतुर्षु महाभूतेषु महेश्वरस्या-

भिध्यानमाचात् तैजसेभ्योऽशुभ्यः पार्थिवपरमाणुसहितेभ्यो महदराडमुत्पद्यते (प्रशस्तपादभाष्य—where Srídhara notes पार्थिवा अवयवा उपष्टम्भकाः and Udayana तैजसानां परमाणुनां पार्थिवाणुसाहित्येन अराडस्य हिरण्मयत्वं विवक्षितं).

It was only in the mediæval Sáṅkhya-Pátañjala that under the influence of the Nyáya-Vaiseshika doctrine a radical difference was conceived to exist between the structure (or constitution) of a molecule composed of "isomeric" atoms, and that of one composed of heterogeneous atoms. In the former case there was believed to take place intimate union (सङ्ग), in the latter case only a grouping of comparatively free or loosely attached atoms round a radicle atom (व्यूहन), with liberation of Energy (उपष्टम्भ, अवष्टम्भ, or विष्टम्भ) and the setting up of unequal stress and strain (गुणवैषम्यविमहें—ईश्वरकृष्ण). At the same time it was of course admitted that this distinction does not apply to the forms of subtile matter (Tanmátra—सूक्ष्मभूत) which could unite in intimate fusion, whether homogeneous or heterogeneous. For example, the subtile body (सूक्ष्मशरीर) which is supposed to be the seat or vehicle of the conscious principle is acknowledged by Vijñána-bhikshu to be penta-Bhautic (पञ्चभूतात्मक); in other words, all the five Tanmátras serve as material causes, though the gross body (the animal organism) is stated to be only a "heterogenic" compound with the Earth Bhúta as radicle or base. (अधिष्ठानशरीरं च सूक्ष्मं पञ्चभूतात्मकं वक्ष्यते । तन्मात्रकार्यं यत् भूतपञ्चकं लिङ्गाधिष्ठानंशरीरम् —प्रवचनभाष्य, Sutras 11 and 12, Chap. III. स्थूलशरीरं पार्थिवमेव अन्यानि च भूतानि उपष्टम्भकानि—*ibid.*, Sutra 19, Chap. III.)

But in the original Sánkhya-Pátañjala it appears that the production of a new substance by mixture of unlike Bhútas (विजातीयसंयोग) was conceded as freely as in the Vedánta, and was conceived as in nowise differing from the formation of a compound of atoms of the same Bhúta class. The Sánkhya analysis of all change into transformations of Energy due to collocations of unchanging Gu*n*as, in other words the prevailing chemico-physical (or physical) point of view, naturally recognises no distinction between collocations of "isomeric" and those of heterogeneous atoms. At bottom they are all collocations of the Gu*n*as. Even Vijñána-bhikshu, who, as one of the latest expounders of the Sánkhya-Pátañjala, has been most affected by the Vaiseshika prejudice against "poly-Bhautic" combination (विजातीयसंयोग), urges that the qualities of a compound substance are not necessarily the result of similar qualities in the component elements. (सजातीय-कारणगुणस्यैव कार्य्येगुणारम्भकता इति तु तेषां (तार्किकाणां) अपि न नियमः।) Elsewhere he explains that, so far from the vital activity being independent, it is originated and maintained by the combined operation or fusion of the different sensory and motor reflexes of the living organism, and notes that the united operation of mixed (or miscellaneous) causes, where there is a fit collocation of matter, offers no difficulty to a follower of the Sánkhya-Pátañjala. (जातिसाङ्कर्य्यस्य अस्माकमदोषत्वात्, सामग्रीसमवधाने सति अनेकैरपि इन्द्रियैः एकदा एकवृत्त्युत्पादने बाधकं नास्ति—प्रवचनभाष्य, Sutra 32, Chap. II.) In the middle of the ninth century we find Vácháspati instancing some "heterogenic" or "poly-Bhautic" compositions as typical examples of evolutionary change

(परिणाम) and unhesitatingly accepting the substantive character of the products. In the Kaumudi he describes the various acids and juices of fruits as modifications of the same original water in the presence of different kinds of earthy accretions. The process is peculiar. The water-particle (or atom) serves as a radicle or centre of a system, and the different kinds of the Earth-Bhúta centering round this as a nucleus become the seat of forces, which bring in the development of new energies (and new qualities, *e.g.* tastes) in the water. (यथा वारिदविमुक्तं उदकं एकरसमपि तत्तद्भूतविकारान् आसाद्य नारिकेल-ताली-बिल्व-कपित्थादि-रसतया परिणामात् मधुराम्ललवणतिक्तकटुकषायतया विकल्पते । इति एकैकगुणसम्भवात् प्रधानगुणं आश्रित्य अप्रधानगुणाः परिणामभेदान् प्रवर्त्तयन्ति ।—कौमुदी on Káriká 16.) Váchaspati also points out that different substances may be transformed into one and the same substance (*e.g.* the production of salt by the cow, the horse, the buffalo, and the elephant, thrown into the salt-factory of Sambara in Rajputana, or of the flame of a candle by the combination of wick, oil, and fire). (परिणामैकत्वं बहूनामपि एकः परिणामः दृष्टः । तद्यथा गवाश्व-महिषमातङ्गानां रोमानिक्षिप्तानां एकलवणत्वजातीयलक्षणः परिणामः, वर्त्तितैलानलानां च प्रदीप इति ।— तत्त्ववैशारदी on व्यासभाष्य, Pada IV., Sutra 14.)

Earlier still, *i.e.* not later than the sixth century, the Vyása-Bháshya, noting that inorganic matter, vegetable substances, and animal substances do not differ from one another essentially in respect of their potential energies and ultimate constituents, points out that various bi-Bhautic chemical compounds of water and earth substances, in the shape of saps, acids, and juices, are found in plants in their different parts

(जलभूम्योः पारिणामिकं रसादिवैश्वरूप्यं स्थावरेषु दृष्टम्). In other words, bi-Bhautic compounds are here placed in the same category as compounds of substances of the same Bhúta class, for here the particles of both the Bhútas are regarded as forming the matter (material cause—उपादानकारण) of the smallest homogeneous portions of the compound substances.

N.B.—Váchaspati naturally interprets this to mean separate modifications of the two Bhútas.

The view of the earlier Sánkhyas, that atoms of different Bhútas may chemically combine to form molecules of compound substances as much as atoms of different modes of the same Bhúta, comes out clearly in Utpala's brief reference to the Sánkhya system in his commentary on Varáhamihira's V*ri*hat Samhitá. (हृभ्यः पञ्चभ्यः [तन्मात्रेभ्यः] पञ्चमहाभूतानि भवन्ति । तेभ्यः शरीरिणां शरीराणि । यतः पञ्चमहाभूतमयानि शरीराणि—Utpala, Chap. I., Śloka 7.)

Chemistry in the Medical Schools of Ancient India.

As a matter of fact, long before the fifth century, probably as early as the first century A.D., the prevailing schools of medicine and surgery which were based on the Sánkhya teaching with a methodology derived from the Nyáya-Vai*s*eshika doctrine (*cf.* Charaka, Śárírasthána, Chap. I.; Vimánasthána, Chap. VIII.; also Su*s*ruta, Śárírasthána, Chap. I.) had founded an elaborate theory of inorganic and organic compounds, which equally admitted iso-Bhautic and hetero-Bhautic combinations. Like the Vedántists, Charaka held that each of the gross Bhútas (Mahábhútas) is a peculiar ultra-chemical compound of five original subtile Bhútas. In this sense, every substance is penta-Bhautic, but for purposes of chemical analysis and synthesis, *i.e.* considered with reference to the Mahábhútas, all substances in their chemical constitution belong to one or other of the following classes : mono-Bhautic, bi-Bhautic, tri-Bhautic, tetra-Bhautic, and penta-Bhautic. Compounds of different Bhútas, again, may combine to form more complex substances, and these in their turn higher compounds still, and so on in progressive transformation, as is more specially the case with organic substances and products.

Physical Characters of the Bhútas.—The prevailing physical characters of the different Bhútas and their isomeric modes are enumerated as follows :—

Earth substances : Heavy, rough, hard, inert, dense, opaque, exciting the sense of smell.
Ap substances : Liquid, viscous, cold, soft, slippery, fluid, exciting the sense of taste.
Tejas substances : Hot, penetrative, subtle, light, dry, clear, rarefied, and luminous.
Váyu substances : Light, cold, dry, transparent, rarefied, impingent.
Ákása substances : Imponderable (or light), rarefied, elastic, capable of sound (vibrations).

गुरुखरकठिनमन्दस्थिरविशदसान्द्र-स्थूल गन्धगुणबहुलानि पार्थिवानि । द्रव-
स्त्रिग्धशीतमन्दमृदुपिच्छिलसररसगुणबहुलानि आप्यानि । उष्णतीक्ष्णसूक्ष्मल-
घुरुक्षविमदरूपगुणबहुलानि आग्नेयानि । लघुशीतरूक्षखरविमद सूक्ष्मस्पर्शगुण-
बहुलानि वायव्यानि । मृदुलघुसूक्ष्मश्लक्ष्णशब्दगुणबहुलानि आकाशात्मकानि ।—
Charaka, Śárírasthána, Chap. XXVI.; compare Suśruta,
Sútrasthána, Chap. XLI.

Charaka points out that the primary qualities or
specific physical characters of the five Bhútas are tactile
qualities, *i.e.* sensible to touch, *e.g.* hardness (or roughness) for Earth, liquidity (or yielding to pressure) for
Ap, impelling or moving force (pressure) for Váyu, heat
for Tejas, and vacuum (non-resistance, penetrability)
for Ákáśa.

खरद्रवचलोष्णत्वं भूजलानिलतेजसाम्,
आकाशस्याप्रतीघातो दृष्टं लिङ्गं यथाक्रमम् ।
लक्षणं सर्वमेवैतत् स्पर्शनेन्द्रियगोचरः ।

(Charaka, Śárírasthána, Chap. I.)

(*Cf.* the elaborate enumeration of physical characters
quoted in Vijñána-bhikshu, Yoga-Vártika, Sutra 42,
Pada I.; also Varavara's commentary on Tattva-traya,
Achit-prakaraṇa.)

The Mahábhútas—Mechanical Mixtures.—Suśruta
notes that each of the gross Bhútas (Mahábhútas) is
found mixed up with the other Bhútas—*e.g.*, the Mahábhúta Ákáśa is the receptacle (or vehicle) of air, heat-
and-light, and water vapour; the Mahábhúta Váyu, of
water vapour, light-and-heat, and even fine particles of
earth held in suspension; the Mahábhúta Tejas, of
earth particles in the shape of smoke, and also water
vapour. (अन्योऽन्यानुप्रविष्टानि सर्वाण्येतानि निर्दिशेत्—Suśruta,
Śárírasthána, Chap. I. अन्ये पुनः अन्यथा व्याचक्षते । आकाशे

पवन-दहन-तोयानि । वायौ तेजोऽम्बुनी भूरपि अणुताविशेषेण । भूमिरपि धूमादिरूपेण तेजसि । तेजोद्रव्ये पानीयमपि ।—Dalva*n*a on Su*s*ruta, *loc. cit.*)

Mono-Bhautic Earth substances :—Chara*k*a and Su*s*ruta regard the following as Earth substances : gold, the five Lohas (silver, copper, lead, iron, and tin) and their " rust," arsenic, orpiment, various mineral earths and salts, sand, precious stones. (Charaka, Sútrasthána, Chap. I. ; *cf.* also Su*s*ruta, Sútrasthána, Chap. I. पार्थिवाः सुवर्णरजतमणिमुक्तामनःशिलामृत्कपालादयः । सुवर्णस्य इह पार्थिवत्वमेवाङ्गीक्रियते गुरुत्वकाठिन्यस्यैर्य्यादिहेतुभिः । सूत्रे आदिग्रहणात् लोहमलसिकतासुधाहरितालळवणगैरिकरसाञ्जनप्रभृतीनां— Dalva*n*a on Su*s*ruta, *loc. cit.*)

The salts include common salt, saltpetre, etc. Su*s*ruta mentions the alkalis, borax, natron, Yavakshára (carbonate of potash), etc. The Audbhida salt, an inflorescence of the soil, stands for *reh* (औद्भिदं पांशुलवणं यज्जातं भूमितःस्वयम्).

Of these Earth substances some were known to be compounds, *e.g.* the chemical salts of the metals, collyrium, etc. Su*s*ruta describes the preparation of the metallic salts. The leaves of the metals were pasted over with the salts, and then roasted (अयस्कृति, Chikitsásthána, Chap. X.). These metallic salts are therefore mono-Bhautic Earth compounds. Su*s*ruta also gives the preparation of mild and caustic alkalis (Sútrasthána, Chap. XI.).

Origin of precious stones.—Some hazarded the guess that the precious stones are rocks (or earths) metamorphosed by natural process in the course of ages (Varáhamihira—केचित् भुवः स्वभावात् वैचित्र्यं प्राहुरुपलानाम् । Utpala notes—रत्नरूपत्वं प्राप्ताः कालान्तरेन ।).

Ap substances, simple and compound :—

Susruta, following Charaka, enumerates various classes of Ap substances (द्रवद्रव्य) as follows : waters, acids, milks, curds, butters, oils (vegetable as well as animal), fats, honeys, molasses, alcoholic liquors, urines, etc.

Pure Ap (Mahábhúta) is tasteless, and the six tastes are developed when the Mahábhúta Ap enters into combination, mechanical or chemical, with other Mahábhútas. Susruta notes that various kinds of Earths are dissolved in the waters of different localities, and where the particles so dissolved are predominantly earthy, the water tastes acid or salt; where predominantly watery, the resulting taste is sweet; where the Earth-particles are mixed up with Tejas, the water tastes pungent or bitter, etc. Such is the case with mechanical mixtures. In the case of bi-Bhautic or tri-Bhautic compounds Charaka mentions that substances with Mahábhúta Ap predominating in their composition taste sweet; with Mahábhútas Earth and Tejas predominating, acid; with Mahábhútas Ap and Tejas predominating, salt; with Mahábhútas Váyu and Tejas predominating, pungent; with Mahábhútas Váyu and Ákása predominating, bitter; and with Mahábhútas Váyu and Earth predominating, astringent. (Charaka, Sútrasthána, Chap. XXVI.; *cf.* Susruta, Sútrasthána, Chap. XLII.)

In fact, with the exception of Susruta's waters, which are mechanical mixtures, or rather solutions, all these Ap substances are organic products, and, as such, penta-Bhautic, *i.e.* compounded of all the five Mahábhútas, and the particular "taste" which is developed depends on the relative proportion of the Mahábhútas and the predominance of one or more of them in the penta-Bhautic compound in question.

Qualities of Compounds.—The isomeric modes of each Mahábhúta have specific colours, tastes, etc., due to their structure, *i.e.* the arrangement of their atoms, and the physico-chemical characters of compounds, whether of the same or of different Mahábhútas, result from the collocation in unequal proportion of the different forces latent in the atoms of the component substances. Charaka adds that the varied forms (textures) and colours of organic substances, whether vegetable or animal, are derived in the same way. (एवमेतेषां रसानां षट्त्वमुपपन्नं न्यूनातिरेकविशेषात् महाभूतानाम् । भूतानामिव स्थावरजङ्गमानां नानावर्णाकृतिविशेषाः ।)

Su*s*ruta ignores Charaka's distinction between Mahábhúta and subtile Bhúta, and views every substance as in reality penta-Bhautic, and it is only the relative predominance of a particular Bhúta or Bhútas in any substance that determines its class. (पृथिव्यप्तेजोवायुवाकाशानां समुदायात् द्रव्याभिनिर्वृत्तिः । उत्कर्षात्तु अभिव्यञ्जको भवति इदं पार्थिवं इदं आप्यं इदं तैजसं इदं वायव्यं इदं आकाशीयमिति । —Su*s*ruta, Sútrasthána, Chap. XLI.)

The Extant Charaka and Susruta—Succession of Medical Authorities.—The extant Charaka and Su*s*ruta, the sources of our present information regarding the progress of scientific knowledge in the medical schools of ancient India, are both redactions of original authorities. The extant Charaka is a redaction by D*ri*dhabala of the genuine Charaka Sa*m*hitá, which was itself a redaction by Charaka of the original work of Agnivesa, the disciple of Átreya Punarvasu as distinguished from Krishnátreya and Bhikshu Átreya, also well-known medical authorities. The extant Susruta is a redaction by Nágárjuna of an original work (Vriddha Susruta) by Susruta, the disciple of Dhanvantari. That Charaka preceded Susruta is almost certain. Nágárjuna was probably earlier than Dridhabala. At any rate, Dridhabala imported into Charaka much of the surgical knowledge which had till then been the traditional heritage of the Susruta school. And in the matter of the surgical treatment of certain diseases, the genuine Dridhabala is often as advanced as Susruta's redacteur himself. The latter was probably identical with the alchemist Nágárjuna (Siddha Nágárjuna), the metallurgist Nágárjuna (author of a treatise on metallurgy, Lohasástra), and the Buddhist Nágárjuna, author of the Mádhyamikasútravritti. Charaka and Susruta continued to receive additions after Dridhabala and Nágárjuna, and even after Vágbhata, but the whole of the extant Charaka is probably much earlier than the commentator Chakrapáni, and the whole of the extant Susruta earlier than Dalvana, the commentator, and Mádhava, the author of Rugvinischaya. The extracts in Vágbhata make it certain that the passages I have quoted or shall quote from the Sútrasthána and Śárírasthána of Charaka and Susruta cannot be later than the sixth century of the Christian era.

Preparation of Chemical Compounds.—The knowledge of chemical compounds and of their preparation continued to make progress in the Charaka and Suśruta schools. The great metallurgist, Patañjali, in his treatise on Metallurgy (लोहशास्त्र), gave elaborate directions for many metallurgic and chemical processes, especially the preparation of the metallic salts, alloys, and amalgams, and the extraction, purification, and assaying of metals. Probably it was Patañjali who discovered the use of the mixtures called Vidas, which contained aqua regia or other mineral acids *in potentia*. Unfortunately Patañjali's *magnum opus* appears to have been lost, but extracts from it are frequently found in mediæval works on Medicine and Rasáyana which leave no doubt as to its remarkable scientific value. The metallurgist Nágárjuna advanced the knowledge of chemical compounds by his preparations of mercury. The Harshacharita, in the seventh century, relates a fable concerning this Nágárjuna, and speaks of him as a friend and contemporary of Sátaváhana. The relative priority of Patañjali and Nágárjuna is a vexed question in the history of metallurgy. That Nágárjuna's Lohaśástra was earlier than the final redaction of Patañjali will appear from the following circumstances :—(1) Chakradatta in his summary of Nágárjuna mentions that the chemical process of testing pure iron must be repeated twice before it can be regarded as decisive, whereas Śivadása Sen's extract from Patañjali shows that the latter directed the process to be repeated seven times; (2) Patañjali in the Abhraka-vidhi (mica operation) adds mercury, which in this particular operation is wanting in Nágárjuna's recipe (*cf.* Chakradatta, and Patañjali as reported in the Yogaratnákara-samuchchaya); and (3) Nágárjuna is quoted in the earlier compilations, Patañjali in the later.

Chemical Industries.—Early in the sixth century, Varáhamihira in the V*r*ihat Samhitá gives several preparations of cements or powders called Vajra-lepa, "cements strong as the thunderbolt"; and there was ample use for these in the temple architecture of the Buddhist period, the remains of which bear testimony to the adamantine strength of these metal or rock cements. (प्रासादहर्म्यैवलभीलिङ्गप्रतिमासु कुडयकूपेषु सन्नम्रो दातव्यो वर्षसहस्रायुतस्थायी । Chapter LVI., *ibid.*) Varáhamihira also alludes to the experts in machinery (यन्त्रविद:, यन्त्रज्ञा:) and the professional experts in the composition of dyes and cosmetics (रागगन्धयुक्तिविद: Ch. XVI., also Ch. XV.). I would also refer to the interesting chapter on Perfumery (Ch. LXXVI.) where Varáhamihira gives various recipes for artificial imitations of natural flower-scents, as of the essence of Vakula, Utpala, Champaka, Atimuktaka, etc., arranges compound scents in a sort of scale according to the proportions of certain ground essences used in their preparation, and determines by the mathematical calculus of combination (लोष्टकप्रस्तार) the number of variations of the different notes in this scale. To these classes of professional experts were due three of the great Indian discoveries in the chemical arts and manufactures which enabled India to command for more than a thousand years the markets of the East as well as the West and secured to her an easy and universally recognised pre-eminence among the nations of the world in manufactures and exports : (1) the preparation of fast dyes for textile fabrics by the treatment of natural dyes like Mañjish*thá* with alum (तुवरी मंजिष्ठ रागबन्धिनी) and other chemicals (*e.g.* sulphate of iron) also cow-dung (*cf.* the "cow-dung substitute," Roscoe); (2) the extraction of the principle of indigotin from the indigo plant by a process which, however crude, is essentially an anticipation of modern chemical methods; and (3) the tempering of steel in a manner worthy of advanced metallurgy, a process to which the mediæval world owed its Damascus swords. It was this applied chemistry much more than handicraft skill which gave India her premier position in the Middle Ages and earlier (indeed from Pliny to Tavernier) in exports and manufactures; for in handicraft skill, as in design and workmanship, great as were her merits, India came to be surpassed by her disciples China and Japan.

The Vásavadattá and the Da*s*akumára Charita in the sixth century allude to the preparation of a mass of fixed or coagulated mercury (पारदपिण्डइव कालधातुवादिनः—वासवदत्ता); a chemical powder, the inhalation of which would bring on deep sleep or stupor (योगचूर्ण—दशकुमारचरित); a chemically prepared stick or wick for producing light without fire (योगवर्तिका—दशकुमारचरित); and a powder which, like anæsthetic drugs or curare, paralyses sensory and motor organs[1] (स्तम्भनचूर्णमिव इन्द्रियाणाम्—वासवदत्ता—धीन्द्रियकर्मेन्द्रियाणां—Darpa*n*a). V*r*inda (*circa* 950 A.D.) notices the preparation of sulphide of mercury (रसामृतचूर्ण),

---

[1] This last interpretation is doubtful; but in any case the familiar use of a technical term of alchemistry like Stambhana-chur*n*am (fixation-powder) shows that already in the sixth century this branch of knowledge was widely cultivated.

composed of one part of sulphur and half its weight of mercury; and also of cuprous sulphide (पर्पिटताम्र). Chakrapáni (*circa* 1050 A.D.) mentions the preparation of the black sulphide of mercury "by taking equal parts of mercury and sulphur."

The Rasárnava (*circa* 1200 A.D.) notices the colours of metallic flames, probably after Patañjali—*e.g.* copper gives blue flame; tin, pigeon-coloured; lead, pale; iron, tawny; blue vitriol, red. It may be noted that the Rasárnava regards mercury as a penta-Bhautic substance.

The Rasaratna-samuchchaya divides the mineral kingdom (Earth substances, simple and compound) into the following classes: (1) The eight Rasas: mica, pyrites, bitumen, blue vitriol, calamine, etc. (2) The eight Uparasas (useful in operations of mercury): sulphur, red ochre, green vitriol, alum, orpiment, realgar, collyrium, and medicinal earth, to which may be added the eight Sádhárana Rasas, sal-ammoniac, cowrie, cinnabar, rock vermilion, etc. (3) The gems diamond, emerald, sapphire, cat's-eye, sun-stone, moon-stone, pearl, etc. (4) The metals gold, silver, iron, copper, lead, tin, and the alloys brass and bell-metal. Other Earth substances are six salts, three alkalis, mineral earths, and several poisons.

Chemical Compositions and Decompositions—Metallurgic Processes.—In these writings[1] we frequently

---

[1] From Patañjali's and Nágárjuna's Lohasástra (*circa* 300–500 A.D. ?) downwards—(practically everything material in the enumeration that follows was discovered by the end of the sixth century A.D.).

come across instances of chemical composition and decomposition by processes, more or less crude, of calcination, distillation, sublimation, steaming, fixation, etc. (भस्मीकरण, अधःपातन, ऊर्द्ध्वपातन, स्वेदन, स्तम्भन, etc.), *e.g.* the preparation of perchloride of mercury by taking common salt and mercury (रसकर्पूर—पारदस्य श्वेतभस्मीकरणे चन्द्रिकाकारः); of sulphide of mercury (हिङ्गुल) by taking sulphur and mercury; of Sindúra from lead (सिन्दूरं नागसम्भवम्—Amarakosha, sixth century A.D.); of the medicinal compounds Svarnasindúra and Rasasindúra with mercury, sulphur, and gold, where gold may have been fancied to influence the resulting compound in some mysterious way, either as a "dynamic" or as a catalytic; also the extraction by chemical decomposition of mercury from sulphide of mercury (हिङ्गुल); of copper from sulphate of copper (तुत्थ, सस्यक) by heating this substance with one-fourth of its weight of borax (Rasaratna-samuchchaya,—*cf.* Bhávaprakása, तुत्थं तु ताम्रोपधातु किञ्चित् ताम्रेण तद्भवति); of zinc (वङ्गाभ, जसद) from calamine (रसक); of copper from pyrites (माक्षिक, विमल), etc. (though the golden pyrites were supposed to be a semi-metal of gold, containing some gold along with the essence of copper); the purification of mercury by repeated distillation from lead and tin with which it was wont to be adulterated in the market. The various metallurgic processes described are—extraction, purification, killing (formation of oxides, chlorides, and oxy-chlorides for the most part), calcination, incineration, powdering, solution, distillation, precipitation, rinsing (or washing), drying, steaming, melting, casting, filing, etc., to all which each of the known minerals was successfully subjected by the use of apparatus and reagents and the application of heat in different measures (खरपाक, मध्यमपाक, and मृदुपाक)—methods which, if often crude, especially from the absence of independent and isolated mineral acids, were yet in several instances remarkably simple and effective, and which, after all, by the use of various Vi*d*as potentially containing mineral acids (aqua regia, sulphuric acid, hydrochloric acid, etc.), virtually accomplished the practical ends kept in view. To these were added several special processes for mercury (*e.g.* fixation), bringing up the number of mercurial operations to nineteen.

It may be noted that the mixtures called Vi*d*as, which potentially contained dilute mineral acids, were regularly employed not only in killing the metals (forming their oxides and chlorides), but—what is of fundamental importance—for purposes of chemical decomposition of metallic salts, etc., and the extraction and purification of metals.

Organic Compounds.—Organic compounds are either vegetable or animal substances (स्थावर जङ्गम भूत). The molasses, the fermented liquors, the saps and juices of plants, fruit acids, vegetable ashes and alkalis, together with the tissues of plants, are vegetable compounds (औद्भिद, स्थावर भूत). Honey, milk, curd, butter, fat, bile, urine, and other excreta, together with the organs and tissues of animals, are animal substances. Charaka notices vegetable as well as animal oils. The viscous (oily) substances are classed under four heads—butters, oils, fats, and marrows (सर्पिस्तैलं वसा मज्जा स्नेहो दृष्टश्चतुर्विधः). Salt may be either mineral or vegetable salt.

Susruta divides poisons into two classes—vegetable and animal, but several poisons expressly termed mineral poisons (धातुविष) are included in the first class.

All organic substances, whether animal or vegetable, are penta-Bhautic, being compounded of greater or less proportions of the five Mahábhútas.

Taking the human body, Charaka finds that the fœtus is composed of sixteen organic substances, viz. four composing the sperm-cell which comes from the male; four composing the germ-cell which comes from the female; four added by the transformation of the nutritive material; and finally, four kinds of subtile matter, which together form the vehicle of the conscious principle. As to the four organic substances which compose the sperm-cell, or the other four which compose the germ-cell, it is not clear whether in Charaka's view they are also in their turn compounded of less complex organic substances, or whether their constituent elements are inorganic penta-Bhautic compounds.

The tissues that appear in the course of development of the fœtus are further transformations (higher compounds) of these fœtal substances. All the component substances of the body are penta-Bhautic compounds, though sometimes they are assigned to the particular Bhútas which predominate in their composition, *e.g.* bile to Tejas, lymph, chyle, blood, fat, urine, sweat, and other secretions to Ap, and skin, flesh, bones, nails, etc., to Earth. (शुक्रं वाय्वग्निभूम्यवगुणपादवत् ।—गर्भस्य चत्वारि चतुर्विधानि भूतानि मातापितृसम्भवानि आहारजानि आत्मकृतानि चैव *et seq.*—Charaka, Śárírastháṇa, Chap. II., *vide* also Charaka, Śárírastháṇa, Chap. VII., *cf.* Gaṅgádhara's

Jalpakalpataru. पिन्नं तृतीयं भूतं शरीरारम्भकतेजःप्रधानपञ्चभूतविका-रात्मकं तेजःस्वरूपं अग्निसंज्ञम् । कफश्चतुर्थं भूतमापः शरीरारम्भकसोमप्रधान-पञ्चभूतविकारविशेषः। शरीरं तु पञ्चमहाभूतविकारसमुदायात्मकम् । *Cf.* Charaka, Śárírastháná, Chap. IV., मातृजादयोऽपि अस्य महाभूतविकाराः ।)

Formation of Molecular Qualities in Chemical Compounds.—The Charaka school, which we have seen was an offshoot of the Sáṅkhya (*cf.* Charaka, Vimánastháná, Chap. VIII., यथा वादित्यः प्रकाशकः तथा सांख्यवचनं प्रकाशकमिति), supplemented the above account of inorganic and organic compounds with a characteristically Sáṅkhya explanation of the formation of molecular qualities by chemical combination. In Charaka's view, the colours, tastes, etc., of the molecules of chemical compounds result from the collocation in unequal proportion and unstable equilibrium of the different forces latent in the atoms (Paramánus) themselves. (एवमेतेषां रसानां षट्त्वमुपपन्नं न्यूनातिरेकविशेषात् महाभूतानां । भूतानामिव स्थावरजङ्गमानां नानावर्णाकृतिविशेषाः ।—Charaka.)

Chemistry of Colours.—As an interesting example of the way in which a follower of Charaka would account for the colours of chemical compounds, I may note the explanation given by the late Gaṅgádhara Kavirája Kaviratna in the Jalpakalpataru, a commentary on the Charaka-Samhitá, published at Calcutta in 1869, premising that the Kavirája's view is pure and genuine Charaka doctrine. Gaṅgádhara begins with a simple statement. The qualities of the atom, he writes, tend to produce similar qualities in the molecule. A molecular quality is therefore the result of the conjunction or opposition, as the case may be, of the atomic tendencies. When, for example, the five Bhútas combine to produce an organic compound (the human body), Tejas, Ap, and Earth tend to produce red, white, and black respectively, but in the body (compound substance) the yellow colour may happen to be produced as the result of these tendencies in that particular proportion and collocation. The point to note here is that the molecule forms a fresh collocation, *redistributes the Mass and Energy*, and sets up new forces in the system, which coming into play modify the potencies (or tendencies) in the component atoms, and thus determine the resultant. This is elaborated into a curious but complete theory of the colours of chemical compounds.

The colours (and other qualities) of a simple substance (an isomeric mode of any Bhúta) are the result of the potencies lodged in that particular collocation of Mass, Energy, and Essence. Now when two such substances unite, their colours, etc., tend to be produced, but the combination brings on a fresh distribution of Energy, Mass, and Essence, and the forces thus set free may powerfully modify or even extinguish the separate tendencies or potencies of the component simple substances. For example, when we prepare a collyrium by mixing equal parts of sulphur and mercury (the black sulphide of mercury) we find the resulting compound black. To explain this it has to be remembered that each of the substances (sulphur and mercury) contains Sattva (Essence), Rajas (Energy), and Tamas (Mass) in different proportions, and that predominant Tamas (Inertia, Mass) always produces black, predominant Sattva (Essence) white, and predominant Rajas (Energy) red. Now in the black sulphide of mercury the white of the mercury tends to produce white, and the yellow of the sulphur yellow, and if these tendencies were not obstructed the result would be a mixed colour. But, in the particular collocation in question, the Tamas of the mercury becomes intensive (तीक्ष्ण), and the black of the now intensive Tamas extinguishes the white in the uncompounded mercury, which was due to prevailing Sattva, as well as the yellow of the uncompounded sulphur, which was due to the combined operation of white-producing Sattva and red-producing Rajas. Again, when, with proper apparatus and by the application of heat, we combine mercury and sulphur to produce the red sulphide of mercury, the resulting colour is explained by the fact that in this new collocation the Rajas (Energy)—probably of the mercury, though Gaṅgádhara does not specify—becomes intensive (तीक्ष्ण), and extinguishing both the white-producing Sattva of the mercury and the yellow-producing Sattva-Rajas of the sulphur, imparts a red colour to the compound. In these cases, as also in the formation of red by mixing powdered turmeric with lime, *i.e.* whenever a new colour is produced in the compound, it is to be explained by the dominance of Tamas, Rajas, or Sattva, or their combinations, and the extinction of the uncompounded tendencies (or potencies) by the forces set free in the new collocation. But there are other cases where the colour of the compound is a mixed colour resulting from the colours of the combining substances, *e.g.*, when sulphide of mercury and calcined tin are mixed, the resulting colour is evidently a mixed one (Pátala, pink), which is easily explained by the colours of the component elements (the red of the sulphide of mercury and the white of the calcined tin); in the same way, in a mechanical aggregate, as in a piece of cloth, the colour is white where the threads are white.

तत्कार्यारम्भे पृथिव्यादिद्रव्यावस्थागुणा गन्धादयः खलु स्वस्वजातीयं गन्धविशेषादिकं आरभमाणाः यदारभ्यमाणं स्वस्वविजातीयं कार्यं स्वारम्भकं कारणञ्च अहङ्कारादिस्थं गुणांशं उभयथा कुत्रचित् हत्वा कुत्रचित् न हत्वा स्वजातीयं गुणविशेषं आरभन्ते । यथा पारदगन्धकयोः संयोगे कज्जली-भूतद्रव्ये पारदस्य शुक्लः शुक्लविशेषं आरभमाणः गन्धकस्यपीतः पीतमारभ-माणः पारदस्यतीक्ष्णेन तैक्ष्ण्यमारभमाणेन विरोधिना वध्यते । सद्वैव शौक्ल्यं सत्त्वगुणयोनिकं तमोगुणयोनिकेन तैक्ष्ण्येन विरोधिना वध्यते । गन्धकस्य-पीतत्वौ च लोहितशुक्लौ रजःसत्त्वयोनिकौ वध्येते । तयोः शुक्ललोहितवधे तैक्ष्ण्यसमानयोनिः कृष्णः अभिव्यज्यते । इति पारदगन्धकोभयात्मके कार्ये श्वेतपीतमेलनेन सम्भाव्यं कार्यं यद्वर्णं तत् तीक्ष्णगुणेन वध्यते, तत्कारणं शुक्ललोहितं हत्वा । एवं हिङ्गुले पारदगन्धकाभ्यामारभ्यमाणे यत्त्वविशेषे वह्निना पच्यमाने रजोबहुलयोनिकेन तीक्ष्णेन सत्त्वतमोयोनिकौ शुक्लकृष्णौ वध्येते । पारदस्यशुक्लगन्धकस्यपीतमेलनेन सम्भाव्यं कार्यं वर्णं च वध्यते । रजोयोनिक-लौहित्यं च अभिव्यज्यते इति । एवं हरिद्राचूर्णसंयोगेऽपि लौहित्यं अभिव्यज्यते चूर्णस्यतैक्ष्ण्येन हरिद्रास्यशुक्लकृष्णावधे । अथ अवधे यथा—हिङ्गुलवज्रभस्मसंयोगे श्वेतलोहितवर्णमेव उभयात्मकं भवति पाटलवर्णं, न च तत्र हिङ्गुलस्य लौहित्यं वज्रभस्मस्य शौक्ल्यं च केनापि वध्यते । एवं शुक्लसूत्रनिर्मितपटस्य शौक्ल्यमेव ।

(Jalpakalpataru, Sútrasthána of Charaka, pp. 198–200; edition published by Bhubanachandra Basák, Calcutta, Samvádaratnákara Press, Samvat 1925.) This is quite in a line with Charaka's explanation of the tastes of chemical compounds which has been already noticed.

Pariṇáma-váda versus Árambha-váda.—Charaka's view of the formation of a new quality or a new substance is based on the Sáṅkhya teaching as to the conservation and transformation of Energy, and brings chemical synthesis in a line with evolutionary change (परिणाम). On this view, a new substance may arise by spontaneous or isomeric change, *i.e.* by the interplay of Energies within the system of any given substance, in the absence of any action from without. New qualities like new substances are only readjustments of the old, and continual changes are going on by spontaneous disintegration and recombination. Opposed to this evolutionary view of chemical synthesis is the Nyáya-Vaiseshika doctrine of Árambha-váda, according to which no change of substance or quality, no effect, in short, can take place except by the action of one component element (substance or quality) on another. A binary molecule, for example, cannot possess any "specific quality" (विशेषगुण) of a kind not represented in each of the two component atoms. In the cosmic process no atom can exist free and uncombined with another atom, and every "specific quality" in a substance can be ultimately analysed into the union of two "specific qualities" *of the same class* in two ultimate particles which cannot be further divided. A single colour, smell, or taste in a single particle, until it can link itself on to another specific quality *of its own class* in a second particle, cannot characterise any substance formed by the union of these particles as material causes. Hence an Earth-atom cannot unite with an Ap-atom to form a new substance of which both the particles must be equally regarded as material causes. At any rate, such a compound, if effected, would be smell-less, as of the two constituent atoms only one, viz. the Earth-atom, possesses smell. A compound of Earth and Váyu would be smell-less, colourless, and tasteless, and so on. The Nyáya-Vaiseshika does not deny that there may be compounds of different Bhutas, nor does it deny the causal operation of specific qualities as efficient or energising (dynamic) causes (उपष्टम्भक, निमित्तकारण), but it refuses to place these compounds on the same footing as compounds of isomeric modes of the same Bhúta; and it accepts the "material" causality in such cases of only one of the Bhútas, regarding the others as co-efficients (निमित्तकारण).

The earlier Sáṅkhyas including the medical schools of ancient India brushed all this aside as a distinction without a difference. The Vedántists, as we shall presently see, flouted this doctrine of Arambha-váda. The Jainas, in opposing this Vaiseshika view of atomic combination, hit upon a solution of the problem of chemical affinity. Others, again, found out a *via media*. They held, as we learn from the reports of Udyotakara in the Nyáya-vártika, and of Vachaspati Misra in the Tátparyyatíká, that a molecule of the structure EA (one atom of Earth and one of Ap) would exhibit some variety of colour and taste resulting from the joint action of the atoms and of their several colours and tastes. But as in the combination EA only the Earth-atom possesses smell, and the Ap-atom is smell-less, and as moreover no quality in a compound substance can result except from the joint action of the similar (potential) qualities of at least two component elements, it follows that a molecule of the structure EA would not manifest the energy of smell potentially contained in the Earth-atom. Hence, admitting the combination EA for a smell-less compound, the upholders of this view would suppose a molecule of the type E_2A (*i.e.* two atoms of Earth and one of Ap) to explain any bi-Bhautic compound of Earth and Ap (like the plant saps and fruit juices) which exhibits smell in addition to the peculiarities of colour and taste. *Cf.* Váchaspati's comment on Udyotakara's refutation of this view :—

अयमभिसन्धिः । पृथिव्याप्परमाणू तावन्नैकं द्व्यणुकमारब्धुमुहतः तयोः रूपरसस्पर्शैवत्खेन तदारम्भसम्भवे ऽपि गन्धवत्त्वाभावप्रसङ्गात् । एवं पार्थिवाणु-समवेतस्य गन्धस्य एकत्वेन अनारम्भकत्वात् नापि पार्थिवपरमाण्वद्वयं एकश्च आप्यसीयपरसाणुः इति अणूनामारम्भकत्वे गन्धवत्त्वोपपत्तिः इति साम्प्रतं । परमाणूनां बहूनां अनारम्भकत्वात् । तथाहि त्रयः परमाणवः न कार्य्यमारभन्ते ।

Measures of Time and Space—Size of Atoms.—The Siddhánta-Śiromani gives the following measures of Time :—

30 Kshanas (क्षण) = 1 day,   30 Káshthás = 1 Kalá,
2 Ghatikás = 1 Kshana,   18 Nimeshas = 1 Káshthá,
30 Kalás = 1 Ghatiká,   30 Tatparas = 1 Nimesha,
and 100 Trutis = 1 Tatpara.

This makes a Truti of time equal to $\frac{1}{33750}$ of a second, which is nearly the measure of the Paramánu of time as given in the Vishnu Purána (*vide* Bháskara's Siddhánta-Śiromani—कालमानाध्याय).

The above measures were in use among the astronomers, but the physicists computed according to the following table given both in Udayana's Kira*n*ávali and Śrídhara's Nyáya-Kandalí :—

30 Muhúrtas = 1 day (24 hours),
30 Kalás = 1 Muhúrta, 2 Lavas = 1 Nimesha,
30 Kásh*thá*s = 1 Kalá, 2 Ksha*n*as = 1 Lava.
18 Nimeshas = 1 Kásh*thá*,

क्षण्द्वयं लवः प्रोक्तो निमेषस्तु लवद्वयम्,
अष्टादशनिमेषास्तु काष्ठा त्रिंशत्तु ताः कला ।
त्रिंशत्कला मुहूर्तैः स्यात् त्रिंशद्राच्यहणी च ते ।

(Udayana, Kira*n*ávali.)

This makes 1 Ksha*n*a of the Nyáya-Vaiseshika equal to $\frac{2}{45}$ of a second. The Nyáya assumes that the unit of physical change (or the time occupied by any single antecedent step in a causal series before the succeeding step is ushered in) is equal to a Ksha*n*a (or $\frac{2}{45}$ of a second). The astronomers were familiar with far smaller measures of time. The astronomical Tru*ti* of time measures about the thirty-four-thousandth part of a second. This is of special value in determining the exact character of Bháskara's claim to be regarded as the precursor of Newton in the discovery of the principle of the Differential Calculus, as well as in its application to astronomical problems and computations. This claim, as I proceed to show, is absolutely established; it is indeed far stronger than Archimedes' to the conception of a rudimentary process of Integration. Bháskara, in computing the "instantaneous motion" (तात्कालिकी गति) of a planet, compares its *successive* positions, and regards its motion as constant during the interval (which of course cannot be greater than a Tru*ti* of time, though it may be indefinitely less). This Tátkálika motion is no other than the differential of the planet's longitude, and Bápudeva Śástrí claims that both the conception of the instantaneous motion and *the method of determining it* plainly show that Bháskara was acquainted with the principle of the Differential Calculus. On the data before him, Mr. Spottiswoode remarks that Bápudeva Śástrí "overstates the case." Bháskara "makes no allusion to one of the most essential features of the Differential Calculus, viz. the infinitesimal magnitude of the intervals of time and space therein employed. Nor indeed is anything specifically said about the fact that the method is an approximate one." "With all these reservations," Mr. Spottiswoode continues, "it must be admitted that the formula he establishes and the method of establishing it bear a strong analogy to the corresponding process in modern mathematical astronomy" (viz., the determination of the differential of the planet's longitude—by no means the first step in transcendental analysis or in its application to astronomy). And Mr. Spottiswoode concludes by stating that mathematicians in Europe will be surprised to learn of the existence of such a process in the age of Bháskara (*circa* 1150 A.D.—born 1114 A.D.). Mr. Spottiswoode's second objection, that Bháskara does not specifically state that the method of the Calculus is only approximative, cannot be taken seriously. The conception of limit and the computation of errors came late in the history of the Calculi of Fluxions and Infinitesimals. For the rest, Bháskara introduces his computation expressly as a "correction" of Brahmagupta's rough simplification. The first objection (viz. that Bháskara makes no allusion to the infinitesimal magnitude of the intervals of space and time employed) would be more to the point if it were well founded.[1] But it is not, and Mr. Spottiswoode's error was due to the insufficiency of the data supplied to him. As a matter of fact, even Bháskara's unit, the Tru*t*i of time (or Paramá*n*u), is exceedingly small, as the very name implies, being about one thirty-four-thousandth of a second of time. And in the passage in which Bháskara describes the process, he distinguishes between Sthúla-gati and Súkshma-gati (velocity roughly measured, and measured accurately, *i.e.* by reference to indefinitely small quantities; for Súkshma, as we have seen, has always a reference to the A*n*u, the indefinitely small); indeed, he expressly mentions that the Sthúla-gati takes only Sthúla-kála (finite time) into consideration, and that the determination of the Tátkálikí-gati (Súkshma-gati) must have reference to the moment (प्रतिक्षणम्), which is an indefinitely small quantity of time, being, of course, smaller than his unit, the Tru*t*i. (*Cf.* इयं किल स्थूला गति: अथ सूक्ष्मा तात्कालिकी कथ्यते ...... यदा आसन्नस्तिथ्यनस्तदा तात्कालिक्या गत्या तिथिसाधनं कर्त्तुं युज्यते । तथा समीपचालनञ्च । यदा तु दूरतरस्तिथ्यन: दूरचालनं वा चन्द्रस्य तदा आद्यया स्थूलया कर्त्तुं युज्यते स्थूलकालत्वात् । यत्स्यन्दगति: महत्त्वात् प्रतिक्षणं समा न भवति अतस्तदर्थं अयं विशेषोऽभिहित: ;—nothing can be clearer

---

[1] It is an error to suppose that infinitesimals are indispensable to the Calculus, but I am here speaking of the earlier Calculi, and not of the modern developments which have made the Calculus independent of infinitesimals. My claim on behalf of Bháskara is limited to the historically earlier imperfect form of the Calculus.

than this conception of "momentary" motion.—Bháskara, Siddhánta-Śiromani, Ganitádhyáya, Gatisphutiprakarana; *cf.* also प्रतिक्षणं सा न समा महत्त्वतः, *ibid.*; *cf.* also Goládhyáya, Tátkálikí-karana-vásaná-prakarana, where Bháskara points out that the mode of computing adopted by the Ácháryya (Brahmagupta) is a rough simplification. The idea of resolved components of motion was familiar to the astronomers (*cf.* एवं सदाचार्येण लाघवार्थं इष्टघटीसम्बन्धिनो गतिकला सर्वे प्रक्षिप्ताः । *ibid.*). I may add *en passant* that Bháskara's formula for the computation of a table of sines also implies his use of the principle of the Differential Calculus.

Measures of Weight and Capacity.—The Amarakosha mentions measures of three kinds—weight, length, and capacity (मानं तुलाङ्गुलिप्रस्थिः).

The Krishnala (Guñjá, Raktiká, the black-and-red berry of the shrub *Abrus Precatorius*) was employed as a natural measure of weight. Eighty Krishnala berries on the average weigh 105 grains Troy, and this must be taken as the basis of our computation, though in current practice eighty Krishnalas are taken to be equivalent to 210 grains. One Krishnala was supposed to weigh as much as three medium-sized barley seeds (मध्ययव), one of the latter as much as six white mustard seeds (गौरसर्षप), one white mustard as much as three Ráji mustard seeds (राजिसर्षप), one of these seeds as much as three Likshas, and one Liksha as much as eight Rajas or Trasarenus.

We now come to conventional measures. One gold Máshá was the weight of five Krishnalas of gold, one Suvarna or Tolá weighed as much as sixteen Máshás, and one Pala as much as four Suvarnas or Tolás. A Pala of gold therefore weighs 320 Krishnalas (Manu, Chap. VIII.; Vishnu, Chap. IV.; and Yájñavalkya, Chap. I.).

A Máshá of gold therefore would weigh $6\frac{9}{16}$ grains; a Tolá, 105 grains (in current practice it weighs nearly double, as I have stated); and a Pala, 420 grains Troy.

The measures for silver were the following:— 1 silver Máshá = 2 Krishnalas, 1 Dharana = 16 silver Máshás, and 1 Pala = 10 Dharanas. A Pala of silver would therefore weigh 320 Krishnalas. In other words, the Pala was a fixed measure of weight, and was equal to about 420 grains Troy, or double this if we take the Krishnala of current practice.

A Pala, which equals 320 Krishnalas, was subdivided by 4, 16, and 5 successively for gold, and by 10, 16, and 2 successively for silver. A Suvarna (or Tolá) of gold corresponds roughly to a Dharana of silver, and a gold Máshá to a silver Máshá, but the sizes (or volumes) are not the same, and we must not therefore conclude that gold was supposed to be heavier than silver in the proportion of 5 to 2.

We find that 1296 Trasarenus equal one Krishnala. A Trasarenu, as a measure of weight, therefore, is the equivalent of $\frac{7}{6912}$ of a grain Troy, or double this according to current measures.

But the Trasarenu of physics is a different conception. It stands for the *minimum visibile*, *i.e.*, as the physicists define it, that which is *just discernible* as a glancing particle in the slanting beams of the morning (or afternoon) sun coming into a dark room through a chink or orifice of a window. This is a measure of size (or rather *stimulus limen*).

Measures of Capacity.—Here the standard was furnished by the Kudava (कुड़व), a vessel described as 3 Aṅgulis long, 4 Aṅgulis broad, and $1\frac{1}{2}$ Aṅguli deep, with a cubical capacity of $13\frac{1}{2}$ cubical Aṅgulis. 4 Kudavas = 1 Prastha, 4 Prasthas = 1 Ádhaka, 4 Adhakas = 1 Drona, and 4 Dronas = 1 Khári or Bhára.

24 Aṅgulis make 1 Hasta, cubit, which may be taken to be 18 or 19 inches. A Kudava was divided into 4 Palas, and there can be no doubt that originally water of the weight of 4 Palas was found to be actually contained in a vessel of the cubical capacity of a Kudava. If we take the ancient cubit to have been 19 inches, the Kudava would contain nearly 4 Palas of distilled water at 30° Centigrade. On a cubit of 18 inches, the Kudava would contain about $3\frac{3}{7}$ Palas.

The Kudava in current medical practice is supposed to represent a cubical vessel, each side being 4 Aṅgulis. This would give a capacity of 27 cubic inches, if we take the modern cubit of 18 inches. The Kavirajas take a Kudava to contain 8 Palas of water, and as 1 Pala = 320 Krishnalas, and 80 Krishnalas are now taken to be equal to 210 grains Troy, a vessel of a capacity of 27 cubic inches is accordingly supposed to contain about 6,720 grains Troy—which is not very wide of the mark, being about 1·3 per cent. short for distilled water at 86° Fahrenheit or 30° Centigrade.

Size of the Minimum Visibile; Size of an Atom.—The

supposed thickness of the just-discernible mote in the sunbeam (called a Paramá*n*u in Technology, Silpa-sástra, and a Trasarenu in Natural Philosophy) follows directly from Varáhamihira's table:—8 Paramá*n*us make 1 Rajas (or Ratharenu,—*cf.* the Manasara), 8 Rajas make 1 Válágra (filament of hair), 8 Válágras make 1 Likshá, 8 Likshás make 1 Yúká, 8 Yúkás make 1 Yava, 8 Yavas (the Manasara has 4) make 1 Aṅguli (superior), 24 Aṅgulis make 1 Hasta (cubit, lesser cubit, 18 inches). The thickness of the *minimum visibile* (the finest perceptible mote in the slanting sunbeam) is therefore taken to be 3.2^{-20}, or $\frac{1}{349525}$ of an inch. The volume of a spherical Trasarenu (or Paramá*n*u of the Silpa-sástra) would therefore be $\frac{4}{3}.\pi.3^3.2^{-63}$ of a cubic inch. It may be here noted that such a Trasarenu is supposed in the medical schools to contain 30 chemical atoms (Paramá*n*us of Natural Philosophy) according to one estimate, or 60 according to another. The size of an atom must then have been conceived to be less than $\pi.3.5^{-1}.2^{-62}$ of a cubic inch.[1]
(परमाणुरजोवालाग्रलिक्ष्यूकं यवोऽङ्गुलं चेति अष्टगुणानि यथोत्तरम् अङ्गुलमेकं भवति संख्या.—Varáhamihira, V*ri*hatsamhitá, Chap. LVII., Sloka 2. जालान्तरगते भानौ यदणुतरं दृश्येन रजो याति तद्द्व्यात् परमाणुं प्रथमं तद्धि प्रमाणानाम्—*ibid.*, Sloka 1.—*Cf.* Utpala, तत्परमाणुं नाम प्रमाणां जानीयात् । प्रमाणानां सङ्ख्यां तत् प्रथममाख्यं प्रमाणं परमाणुसंज्ञम् । *Cf.* also त्रसरेणुस्तु विज्ञेयः त्रिंशता परमाणुभिः)

The magnitude of a Paramá*n*u is called Párimá*n*dalya (पारिमाण्डल्य) in the Nyáya-Vaiseshika, the name suggest-

---

[1] Curiously enough, this is fairly comparable (in order of magnitude) with the three latest determinations of the size of the hydrogen atom!

ing that the Paramáṇus were conceived to be spherical in shape. The Nyáya-Vaiseshika calls a Paramáṇu a mere point with infinitesimal dimensions, *i.e.* less than any assignable fraction of any finite quantum; but in the Sáṅkhya-Pátañjala, a Paramáṇu, though indefinitely small, had still assignable dimensions, being divisible into Tanmátras, which were themselves integrations of Bhútádi. The diameter of a spherical Paramáṇu must have been conceived to be less than 3.2^{-20} of an inch (*i.e.* less than the conventional Paramáṇu with which linear measures begin), and the volume of a Paramáṇu would, therefore, in accordance with Bháskara's formula, be smaller than $\frac{3}{4}.\pi.3^3.2^{-63}$ or $\pi.3^2.2^{-61}$ of a cubic inch, where $\pi = \frac{3927}{1250}$. The Tanmátras were conceived as smaller still.

That these were conventional measures arbitrarily assumed goes without question, for of course the Hindus had no physical data for a mathematical calculation of these minute quantities. A Válágra (hair-tip, or finest filament of hair), for example, is taken to be 3.2^{-14} of an inch thick, *i.e.* less than one-five-thousandth fraction of an inch in thickness; and a fibril of the networks of Dhamaní or Náḍí (nerve) that supply the pores of the skin (papillæ? मुखानि रोमकूप-प्रतिबद्धानि, Suśruta) was supposed to be about a thousandth part of the finest hair in thickness, or $\frac{1}{125}$ of the *minimum visibile*, and, therefore, about $3.10^{-3}2^{-14}$ of an inch thick (*cf.* सूक्ष्मनाडीप्रचारतः रोम्नः सहस्रभागेनतुल्यासु प्रचरति, Pañchadaśí); but it is evident that these measures were arbitrarily fixed upon, instead of being arrived at by calculation or actual measurement. Indeed, Charaka expressly states that the number of Śirás and Dhamanís in the body (three million fifty-six thousand nine hundred) is only a conjectural estimate (अनिर्हेइयमत: परं तर्कमेव—Śárírastháná, Chap. VII.).

My account of the chemistry of the Sáṅkhya-Pátañjala, and of the affiliated Yoga and medical schools, has anticipated in several points the views of the Vedánta and the Nyáya-Vaiseshika. The chemical facts, processes, and apparatus are indeed common to all the schools. In the following account of the chemistry of the schools other than the Sáṅkhya-Pátañjala, I will confine myself to the theory of the subject, and even of this I will attempt only the briefest outline.

The Vedántic View.

The Vedántists believe Máyá to be the "material cause" (उपादानकारण) of the world. The power of Máyá is the power to realise the unreal—to impart practical Reality or mediate existence to that which does not and cannot possess absolute Reality or self-existence. Máyá is at once real and unreal, while the Brahma (Self) is absolute Reality, absolute Intelligence, and absolute Bliss. The world evolves out of Máyá (मायापरिणाम), so that Máyá in the Vedánta replaces the Prak*ri*ti of the Sáṅkhya. But Máyá, and by implication the world, originate out of Brahma, not by a process of evolution (परिणाम), but of Vivarta (self-alienation). The self-alienation of the Absolute, acting through Máyá, produces in the beginning Ákása—one, infinite, ubiquitous, imponderable, inert, and all-pervasive. The world thus begun goes on evolving, in increasing complexity. The other Súkshma Bhútas, classes of subtile matter, evolve from Ákása in an ascending linear order—Ákása giving off Váyu, Váyu giving off Tejas, Tejas giving off Ap, and Ap giving off Earth. Ákása (one, infinite, all-pervasive) has the capacity of sound. Váyu (subtile gaseous matter) emanates from the universal Ákása, and is instinct with the potential of mechanical energy (impact, pressure) (ईरण, प्रशमिन्न, वहन, व्यूहन,—वायोश्च सर्व्वचेष्टाहेतुत्वेन सर्व्वाविनाभूतत्वात् —Vidvanmanorañjiní). Tejas (subtile radiant matter) emanates from Váyu, and contains *in potentia* the energy of light and heat. Ap (subtile viscous matter) is the transformation of Tejas, and is instinct with the energy that stimulates the nerve of taste, and lastly, Earth (subtile hard matter), which is the transformation of Ap, possesses the latent energy of smell.

But the subtile rudiments of matter must be compounded in various ways to give rise to the gross constituent matter of the world. These forms of gross matter are called Mahábhútas. There are five kinds of Mahábhúta (gross matter) corresponding to the five Súkshma Bhútas (subtile matter), and the process by which a Mahábhúta is produced from the Súkshma Bhútas is called Pañchíkarana (quintuplication). All the five Súkshma Bhútas are present as ingredients, though in different proportions, in each Mahábhúta.

The Mahábhúta Earth, gross Earth-matter, is composed of four parts of subtile Earth-matter and one part each of the other forms of subtile matter. The Mahábhúta Váyu is composed of four parts of subtile gaseous matter and one part each of the other forms of subtile matter. And similarly with other Mahábhútas.

Hence if ak, v, t, ap, e, represent the five forms of subtile matter (Ákáśa, Váyu, Tejas, Ap, and Earth), and AK, V, T, AP, E, stand for the corresponding Mahábhútas, we may represent the constitution of the Mahábhútas as follows :—

$AK = ak_4 (v_1.\ t_1.\ ap_1.\ e_1)$, ak_4 being the radicle.
$V\ = v_4 (ak_1.\ t_1.\ ap_1.\ e_1)$, v_4 being the radicle.
$T\ = t_4 (ak_1.\ v_1.\ ap_1.\ e_1)$, t_4 being the radicle.
$AP = ap_4 (ak_1.\ v_1.\ t_1.\ e_1)$, ap_4 being the radicle.
$E\ = e_4 (ak_1.\ v_1.\ t_1.\ ap_1)$, e_4 being the radicle.

In forms of gross or compounded matter the potential energies (or qualities) become actualised. The Mahábhúta Ákáśa manifests sound; Váyu, sound and mechanical energy; Tejas, sound, mechanical energy, and heat-light; Ap, the energy of the taste-stimulus in addition; and finally, Earth, the energy of the smell-stimulus added to the foregoing.

The Pañchadaśí characterises the different Mahábhútas by their typical sounds : *e.g.*, Ákáśa by the echo (hollow booming sound); Váyu (air) by a sibilant sound, hissing, susurration (imitative symbol, Viśi); Tejas (fire) by a puffing (or roaring) sound (imitative symbol, Bhugubhugu); Ap (water) by a liquid sound (imitative symbol, Culu-culu, gurgle, plash-plash, glut-glut); and finally, Earth by a splitting or rattling sound, a crack or a thud (symbol, Kad-kada). (Chap. II. Bhútaviveka, Śloka 3, Pañchadaśí. *Cf.* also Jayanta, Mañjari.)

Others hold that Ákáśa (ether) never enters as a

component part, and is always one and indivisible. In this view the four Mahábhútas—Váyu, Tejas, Ap, and Earth—alone are supposed to be compounded, and by a process which may be called quaternion (*cf.* the Neo-Platonist quaternion) :—

$$V = v_3 (t_1. ap_1. e_1).$$
$$T = t_3 (v_1. ap_1. e_1).$$
$$AP = ap_3 (v_1. t_1. e_1).$$
$$E = e_3 (v_1. t_1. ap_1).$$

These compound forms, as before, are supposed to exercise their specific energies actively. Others again hold that the Mahábhútas Tejas, Ap, and Earth alone are compounded by a process named Tri*vr*it-kara*n*a (triplication). Thus $T = t_2 (ap_1. e_1)$, $AP = ap_2 (t_1. e_1)$, $E = e_2 (t_1. ap_1)$.

The Súkshma Bhútas are forms of homogeneous and continuous matter, without any atomicity of structure; the Mahábhútas are composite; but even these are regarded as continuous, and without any atomic structure. The Vedánta speaks of A*n*u (Paramá*n*u) not as an ultimate indivisible discrete constituent of matter, but as the smallest conceivable quantum or measure of matter. In the Sáṅkhya doctrine the atomic structure is ordinarily accepted. The Gu*n*as are supposed to be परिच्छिन्न and अणु, bounded and indefinitely small in size (except the Gu*n*as giving rise to Ákása and Manas, which are unlimited अपरिच्छिन्न); and hence the Tanmátras and Paramá*n*us must be conceived to have a discrete structure.

As I have already noted in my account of the

genesis of Tanmátras and Paramá*n*us, various schools of Vedántists (*e.g.* the Rámánujists and the followers of Nimbárka) combined, in the orthodox fashion of the Sm*r*itis and the Puránas, the Vedántic theosophy with the Sáṅkhya cosmology, especially as regards Prak*r*iti and the order of creation and dissolution. For example, the Vedánta-kaustubhaprabhá, fortifying itself with texts from the Vish*n*u Purá*n*a and the Subala and Gopála Upanishads, contends that, at the cosmic dissolution (Pralaya), each Mahábhúta merges into the one that preceded it in the order of creation by first disintegrating into its own proper Tanmátric form (तन्मात्रद्वारा), and that the Mahábhúta Ákása merges into the original Tanmátras, which then lapse into Bhútádi, the super-subtile rudiment-matter, proto-matter (Chap. II., Pada III., Sutra 14).

*Pari*n*áma — Evolutionary Process.* — When the Mahábhútas are once formed, the different kinds of substance are derived from them by the evolutionary process called Pari*n*áma (परिणाम, transformation). Matter is constantly undergoing change of state. The effect is only the cause in a new collocation (कारणस्यैव संस्थानमात्रं कार्य्यम्). Change is of two kind :—

(1) Change by a spontaneous process, without external influence, including isomeric change (स्वाभाविक परिणाम). The Vedántists believe in spontaneous disintegration and reintegration. Action from without, impressed force *ab extra*, is not, *pace* the Naiyáyikas, always a condition of change of state (whether of rest or of motion); nor is it necessary that more than one substance should combine to generate another substance

or variety of substance (*e.g.* the formation of curds from milk, of ice from water, etc.). All this is directed against the Nyáya doctrine (Árambhaváda).

(2) Change due to combination with other substances (द्रव्यान्तरसंयोग). Such combination may produce (*a*) a compound substance possessing like qualities with the constituents (समानजातीयोत्पत्ति), or (*b*) unlike compounds with new qualities, "heteropathic effects" (विजातीयोत्पत्ति). Any new quality thus evolved through (chemical) combination is called Saṃhata-bhúta-dharma (संहतभूतधर्मे), *e.g.* the intoxicating power of the fermented rice and molasses, which does not exist in the ingredients taken separately (मद्यबीजानां प्रत्येकं अवर्त्तमानापि समुदायशक्त्या मदशक्तिः दृश्यते). This Sambhúyakriyá (सम्भूयक्रिया, समुत्थान) corresponds to chemical combination, and the Vedántists, like the Sánkhyas, explain this only as the evolution of the latent Energy (शक्ति, अनुद्भूतशक्ति) in a new collocation (संस्थान, अवयव-सन्निवेश). But, unlike the mediæval Sánkhya, the Vedánta freely recognises the combination of heterogeneous Bhútas. Thus Earth, Ap, Tejas, and Váyu freely combine in different proportions and groupings to produce the variety of substances in the world. For example, the animal organism is a compound of all the five Bhútas (पाञ्चभौतिक). It is not merely the concomitant or efficient causes that may be heterogeneous to the material cause, as the Naiyáyikas contend, but several heterogeneous substances (or Bhútas) may unite as "material causes" to produce a new substance.

The Vedántists resolve all activity—physical, vital, as well as psychical—into modes of motion, subtile cosmic motion (परिस्पन्द, सर्व्वलोकपरिस्पन्द—Śaṅkara ; वायो: परिस्पन्दात्मकत्वात्,—प्राणस्य परिस्पन्दात्मकत्वादेव—यद्द्वैतं स्थूलं सूक्ष्मं च तत्सर्व्वं मनःस्पन्दितमात्रम्—Śaṅkara); but they give a separate substantive existence to the agents, the vital principle (प्राण), and the mind (मनः), though these are also evolutionary transformations of the Súkshma Bhútas (forms of subtle matter). What is common to the Nyáya, the Vedánta, and the Sáṅkhya is that Consciousness or Intelligence (चैतन्य) transcends Matter; but the Naiyáyikas, as pluralists, hold that vital and psychical activities are also immaterial and cannot be resolved into motion (परिस्पन्द). The Vedántists resolve these activities into subtle motion, but ascribe them to a substantive quasi-material Life Principle and Mind, the all-mirroring Intelligence (चैतन्य) alone being immaterial and transcendent; and the Sáṅkhyas accept the substantive existence of the Mind Principle (मनः) as derived co-ordinately with the Súkshma Bhútas or Tanmátras from individualised Prak*r*iti (Ahaṅkára), but resolve Life into a mere resultant activity of the bodily organs, viz. the organs of sense and movement and the psychic principle (मनः).

पञ्चीकरण :—द्विधा विधाय चैकैकं चतुर्द्धा प्रथमं पुनः ।
खखेतरद्दितीयांशैर्योजनात् पञ्च पञ्च ते ॥

यथा त्रिसर्गश्रुतौ सृष्टानां भूतानां स्फुटतरव्यवहारनामरूपस्य करणोपायतया त्रिवृत्करणं श्रुतं तद्वत् भूतपञ्चकसर्गश्रुतौ अपि तथा । तदानीं पञ्चीकरणान्तरं आकाशे शब्दोऽभिव्यज्यते स्फुटतरयेति सर्व्वत्र योजनीयं (विद्वन्मनोरञ्जिनी)— अस्ति हि शरीरे सर्व्वेषामपि भूतानां कार्य्यसंप्रतिपत्तिः स्ववकाशव्यूहनपव- नक्लेदनकाठिन्यानां सर्व्वजनानुभवसिद्धत्वात् । अतस्तत्कारणतया पञ्चानि भूतानि एकस्मिन् देहे सन्तीति स्थिते तनुपटयोरिव अवयवावयविवत्त्वमेव पञ्चभूतदेह-

योयुज्यते । न च स्पर्शशून्यत्वात् एकद्रव्यत्वात् च आकाशस्य आरम्भकत्वानुप-
पत्तिरिति वाच्यं । आरम्भवादस्य अनङ्गीकारात् । एकस्यापि दुग्धावयविनो
दध्यारम्भकत्वदर्शनात् । वस्तुतस्तु पञ्चानां भूतानां पञ्चात्मकत्वस्य दर्शितत्वात्
आरम्भवादस्य निराकृतत्वात् च । तस्मात् सिद्धं शरीरं पाञ्चभौतिकमिति ।
—Vidvanmanorañjini.

न तावत् समानजातीयमेव आरभते न भिन्नजातीयमिति नियमो वास्ति ।
समवायिकारणे एव समानजातीयत्वाभ्युपगमः न कारणान्तरविषय इति तदपि
अनैकान्तिकम् । नापि अनेकमेव आरभते नैकमिति नियमोऽस्ति । अणुमनसो-
राद्यकर्मारम्भाभ्युपगमात् । एकैको हि परमाणुश्चाद्यं स्वकर्मारभते न द्रव्यान्तरं
संहत्य इत्यभ्युपगम्यते । द्रव्यारम्भे एव अनेकारम्भकत्वनियम इति चेत् न परि-
णामाभ्युपगमात् । तदेव तु द्रव्यं विशेषवदवस्थान्तरं आपद्यमानं कार्यं नामाभ्यु-
पगम्यते । तच क्वचित् अनेकं परिणमते मृद्बीजाङ्कुरादिभावेन । क्वचिदेकं परि-
णमते क्षीरादि-दध्यादिभावेन । नेश्वरशासनं अस्ति अनेकं एव कारणं कार्यं
जनयति इति ।—Śaṅkara, Śárīraka-Bháshya, Sūtra 7,
Pada III., Adhyáya 2.

The Atomic Theory of the Buddhists.

The Buddhists recognise four essentials of matter,
viz. extension (with hardness), cohesion (with fluidity),
heat, and pressure (with motion), and four sensibles,
viz. colour, taste, smell, and touch (*vide* Dhamma-
sangani, Attha-sálini, etc.).

The later Vaibháshikas hold that the Váyu-atoms
are touch-sensibles, having impact or pressure for
their characteristic property, and by aggregation
form the element Váyu, the Tejas-atoms are colour-
and-touch-sensibles, having heat for their characteristic, and by aggregation form the Tejas Bhúta; the
Ap-atoms are taste-colour-and-touch-sensibles with a
characteristic viscosity, and form the Ap-element by

aggregation; and finally, the Earth-atoms are smell-taste-colour-and-touch-sensibles possessing a characteristic dryness or roughness (खरत्व), and by their aggregation form the Earth-element. The Bhútas thus originated combine to form aggregates, which are classed as inorganic substances, organisms, and organs. (कामेऽष्टद्रव्यकोष्णु:,—रूपरसगन्धस्पर्शा इति चत्वारि द्रव्याणि पृथिव्यप्तेजोवायु: इति चत्वारि,—also खरस्नेहोष्णेरणस्वभावानि भूतानि).

The Atomic Theory of the Jainas.

Of the nine categories of the Jainas, that of Ajíva (the not-soul or non-Ego) consists of five entities, four of which are immaterial (अमूर्त्त), viz. merit, demerit, space and time, and the fifth, material (मूर्त्त, possessing figure). The last is called Pudgala (Matter), and this alone is the vehicle of Energy, which is essentially kinetic, *i.e.* of the nature of motion. Everything in the world of not-soul (the non-Ego) is either an entity (द्रव्य) or a change of state in an entity (पर्य्याय). Pudgala (Matter) and its changes of state (पर्य्याय), whether of the nature of subtile motion (परिस्यन्द) or of evolution (परिणाम), must furnish the *physical* as opposed to the *metaphysical* basis of all our explanations of Nature. Pudgala (Matter) exists in two forms—Anu (atom) and Skandha (aggregate). The Jainas begin with an absolutely homogeneous mass of Pudgalas, which by differentiation (भेद) breaks up into several kinds of atoms qualitatively determined, and by differentiation, integration, and differentiation in the integrated (संघातात्, भेदात्, संघातभेदात्—Umásvátí, Chap. V., Sutra 26), forms aggregates (Skandhas). An A*n*u has no parts, no beginning, middle, or end. An A*n*u is not only infinitesimal, but also eternal and ultimate. A Skandha may vary from a binary aggregate (ज्यणुक) to an infinitum (अनन्ताणुक). A binary Skandha is an aggregate of two A*n*us (atoms), a tertiary Skandha is formed by the addition of an atom (A*n*u) to the binary (ज्यणुक), and so on *ad infinitum.* The ascending grades are (1) what can be numbered (संख्येय), (2) indefinitely large (असंख्येय), (3) infinity of the first order (अनन्त), (4) infinity of the second order (अनन्तानन्त), and so on.

General Properties of Matter.—The specific characters of the Pudgalas (Matter) are of two kinds, (1) those which are found in atoms as well as in aggregates, and (2) those which are found only in aggregates. Qualities of touch, taste, smell, and colour come under the first head. The original Pudgalas being homogeneous and indeterminate, all sensible qualities, including the infra-sensible qualities of atoms, are the result of evolution (परिणाम). Every atom thus evolved possesses an infra-sensible (or potential) taste, smell, and colour (one kind of each), and two infra-sensible tactile qualities, *e.g.* a certain degree of roughness or smoothness (or dryness and moistness?) and of heat or cold. Earth-atoms, Ap-atoms, etc., are but differentiations of the originally homogeneous Pudgalas. The tactile qualities (खर, स्निग्ध, उष्ण, शीत) appear first, but qualities of taste, smell, and colour are involved in the possession of tactile qualities. An aggregate (Skandha), whether binary, tertiary, or of a higher order, possesses (in addition to touch, taste, smell, and colour) the following physical characters: (1) sound, (2) atomic linking, or mutual attraction and repulsion of atoms, (3) dimension, small or great, (4) figure, (5) divisibility, (6) opacity and casting of shadows, and (7) radiant heat-and-light.

Sensible Qualities.—Tactile qualities are of the following kinds: hardness or softness, heaviness or lightness (degrees of pressure), heat or cold, and roughness or smoothness (or dryness and viscosity?). Of these the atoms (A*n*us) possess only temperature and degrees of roughness or smoothness, but all the four kinds of tactile qualities in different degrees and combinations characterise aggregates of matter from the binary molecule upwards. The Jainas appear to have thought that gravity was developed in molecules as the result of atomic linking. Simple tastes are of five kinds—bitter, pungent, astringent, acid, and sweet. Salt is supposed by some to be resolvable into sweet, while others consider it as a compound taste. Smells are either pleasant or unpleasant. Mallishena notes some elementary varieties of unpleasant smell, *e.g.* the smell of asafœtida, ordure, etc. The simple colours are five—black, blue, red, yellow, and white. Sounds may be classed as loud or faint, bass (thick) or treble (hollow), clang, or articulate speech.

The most remarkable contribution of the Jainas to the atomic theory relates to their analysis of atomic linking, or the mutual attraction (or repulsion) of atoms in the formation of molecules. The question is raised in Umásváti's Jaina Sútras (*circa* A.D. 40?)—what constitutes atomic linking? Is mere contact (or juxtaposition) of atoms sufficient to cause linking? No distinction is here made between the forces that bind together atoms of the same Bhúta and the chemical affinity of one Bhúta to another. The Jainas hold that the different classes of elementary substances (Bhútas) are all evolved from the same primordial atoms. The intra-atomic forces which lead to the formation of chemical compounds do not therefore differ in kind from those that explain the original linking of atoms to form molecules.

Mere juxtaposition (संयोग) is insufficient; *linking* of atoms or molecules must follow before a compound can be produced. The linking takes place under different conditions. Ordinarily speaking, one particle of matter (पुद्गल) must be negative and the other positive (विषमगुणयुक्त); the two particles must have two peculiar opposite qualities, roughness and smoothness (रुक्षत्व and स्निग्धत्व, or dryness and viscosity?), to make the linking possible. But no linking takes place where the qualities, though opposed, are very defective or feeble (जघन्यगुण). We have seen that, ordinarily speaking, two homogeneous particles, *i.e.* both positive or both negative, do not unite. This is the case where the opposed qualities are equal in intensity. But if the strength or intensity of the one is twice as great as that of the other, or exceeds that proportion, then even similar particles may be attracted towards each other. In every case change of state in both the particles is supposed to be the result of this linking, and the physical characters of the aggregate depend on the nature of this linking. When particles of equal intensity (negative and positive) modify each other there is mutual action; in cases of unequal intensity the higher intensity transforms the lower, it being apparently thought that an influence proceeds from the higher to the lower. All changes in the qualities of atoms depend on this linking. A crude theory, this, of chemical combination, very crude but immensely suggestive, and possibly based on the observed electrification of smooth and rough surfaces as the result of rubbing. The interpretation of रूक्ष and स्निग्ध as dry and viscous must be rejected in this connection as untenable. The Tattvárthádhigama of Umásvátí, which expounds the theory, most probably dates back to the first half of the first century A.D.

Cf. Umásvátí-Tattvárthádhigama, Chap. V. :—

अजीवकाया धर्माधर्माकाशपुद्गलाः । द्रव्याणि जीवाश्च । नित्यावस्थि-
तानि अरूपाणि । रूपिणः पुद्गलाः । आकाशादेकद्रव्याणि । निष्क्रियाणि च ।
पुद्गलजीवास्तु क्रियावन्तः । (क्रियेति गतिकर्माह) । सर्वेषां प्रदेशाः सन्ति अन्यत्र
परमाणोः । संख्येयासंख्येयाश्च पुद्गलानाम् । नाणोः । स्पर्शरसगन्धवर्णवन्तः पुद्गलाः ।
तत्र स्पर्शोऽष्टविधः कठिनो मृदुर्गुरुर्लघुः शीत उष्णः स्निग्धः रूक्ष इति । रसः
पञ्चविधस्तिक्तः कटुः कषायोऽम्लोमधुर इति । गन्धो द्विविधः सुरभिरसुरभिश्च ।
वर्णः पञ्चविधः कृष्णो नीलो लोहितः पीतः शुक्ल इति ।

शब्दस्कन्धसौक्ष्म्यस्यौल्यसंस्थानभेदतमश्छायातपोद्योतवन्तश्च । तत्र शब्दः
षड्विधः ततो वितती घनः शुषिरो घर्षो भामइति । आणवः स्कन्धाश्च । ऊर्ध्वं
च । कारणमेव तदन्त्यं सूक्ष्मो नित्यश्च भवति परमाणुः । एकरसगन्धवर्णौ द्विस्पर्शः
कार्य्यलिङ्गश्च । तत्राणवोऽबद्धाः स्कन्धास्तु बद्धा एव । स्कन्धास्तावत् संघातभेदेभ्य-
उत्पद्यन्ते । संघाताद्भेदात् संघातभेदादिति । द्वयोः परमाणवोः संघाताद्द्विप्रदेशः ।
द्विप्रदेशस्याणोश्च संघातात् त्रिप्रदेशः । एवं संख्येयानामसंख्येयानामनन्तानां
अनन्तानन्तानां च प्रदेशानां संघातात् प्रदेशाः । भेदादणुः । भेदादेव परमाणुरुत्पद्यते
न संघातादिति । अत्राह । किं संयोगमात्रादेव संघातो भवति । आहोस्विदस्ति
कश्चिद्विशेष इति । अत्रोच्यते । सति संयोगे बद्धस्य संघातो भवतीति । स्निग्ध-

रूक्षत्वाद्वन्ध्यः । न जघन्यगुणानाम् । स्निग्धरूक्षयोः पुद्गलयोः स्पृष्ट्योर्बन्धो भवतीति । जघन्यगुणस्निग्धानां जघन्यगुणरूक्षाणां च परस्परेण बन्धो न भवतीति । उक्तं भवता जघन्यगुणवज्जानां स्निग्धानां रूक्षेण रूक्षाणां च स्निग्धेन सह बन्धो भवतीति । अथ तुल्यगुणयोः किमत्यन्तप्रतिषेध इति । अत्रोच्यते । न । गुणसाम्ये सदृशानां । गुणसाम्ये सति सदृशानां बन्धो न भवति । तद्यथा तुल्यगुणस्निग्धस्य तुल्यगुणस्निग्धेन तुल्यगुणरूक्षस्य तुल्यगुणरूक्षेण इति । अत्राह सदृशग्रहणं किमपेक्षते इति । अत्रोच्यते । गुणवैषम्ये सदृशानां बन्धो भवति इति । अत्राह किमविशेषेण गुणवैषम्ये सदृशानां बन्धो भवतीति । अत्रोच्यते । द्व्यधिकादिगुणानां तु द्व्यधिकादिगुणानां सदृशानां बन्धो भवति । द्विगुणाद्यधिकस्निग्धेन द्विगुणाद्यधिकस्निग्धस्य स्निग्धेन । रूक्षस्यापि द्विगुणाद्यधिकरूक्षस्य रूक्षेण । एकादिगुणाधिकयोस्तु सदृशयोर्बन्धो न भवति । अत्राह परमाणुषु स्कन्धेषु च ये स्पर्शादयो गुणास्ते किं व्यवस्थिताः तेषु आहोस्विदव्यवस्थिता इति । अत्रोच्यते । अव्यवस्थितायुतः । परिणामात् । अत्राह द्वयोरपि वर्धमानयोर्गुणवत्त्वे सति कथं परिणामो भवति इति । उच्यते । बन्धे समाधिकौ पारिणामिकौ । बन्धे सति समगुणस्य समगुणः परिणामका भवति । अधिकगुणो हीनस्येति ।

The Nyáya-Vaiseshika Chemical Theory: a Brief Summary.

I must content myself here with a brief and rapid sketch of the chemistry of the Nyáya-Vaiseshika, which I shall elaborate in connection with the mechanics and physics of the ancient Hindus in a separate paper.

The relation of the specific characters of molecules (and higher aggregates) to the original atomic qualities is reduced in the Nyáya-Vaiseshika to the following canons: (a) कार्य्यगुणं कारणगुणपूर्व्वकम् । (b) समानजातीयसंयोगः द्रव्यारम्भकः न विजातीयसंयोगः (here द्रव्य is used in a narrow technical sense, so as to exclude the quasi-compound substances); (c) अपाकजरूपरसगन्धस्पर्शपरिमाणैकत्वैकपृथक्त्वगुरुत्वद्रवत्व-स्नेहवेगाः कारणगुणपूर्व्वकाः । (d) रूपरसगन्धानुष्णस्पर्शशब्द-परिमाणैकत्वैक-

पृथक्बेहा: समानजात्यारम्भका: । No separate explanation is necessary, as the canons are embodied in the following exposition.

Theory of Atomic Combination.—Atoms are eternal, ultimate, indivisible, and infinitesimal.

The four kinds of Atoms are Earth, Ap, Tejas, and Váyu atoms, possessed of characteristic mass, numerical unit, weight, fluidity (or its opposite), viscosity (or its opposite), velocity (or quantity of impressed motion— Vega) ; also characteristic potential colour, taste, smell, or touch, not produced by the chemical operation of heat (अपाकजरूपरसगन्धस्पर्शपरिमाणैकत्वैकपृथक्त्वगुरुत्वद्रवत्वस्नेहवेगा:). Akása has no atomic structure (निरवयव), and is absolutely inert (निष्क्रिय), being posited only as the substratum of sound, which is supposed to travel wave-like in the manifesting medium or vehicle of Váyu (air). Only the other four Bhútas unite (or disunite) in atomic or molecular forms. The orthodox view is that the presence of Earth-atoms is necessary whenever chemical transformation under the operation of heat (पाकजोत्पत्ति) takes place.

Atoms cannot exist in an uncombined state in creation (Śiváditya, Sapta-padárthí, *vide* commentary), where, however, it is noted that still atmospheric air is believed to be monatomic in structure, *i.e.* to consist of masses of atoms in a loose uncombined state (स्तिमितवायुस्तु परमाणुसमूह एव अनारब्धद्रव्य:).

The atoms may combine in one or other of the following ways :—

I. One Earth-atom, by an original tendency, unites with another to form a binary molecule (द्व्यणुक). In

H 2

the same way binary molecules of the other Bhútas are formed. The atoms are possessed of an inherent Parispanda (rotary or vibratory motion), and when they unite in pairs, *so long as there is no chemical operation under the action of heat-corpuscles*, the original qualities of the atoms produce homogeneous qualities in the binary molecules.

The question as to the existence of a triad, a tetrad, a pentad, etc., of atoms is one of the moot points of the Nyáya-Vaiseshika. The orthodox view is that the primordial infinitesimal particles (atoms) start with an incessant vibratory motion (अनवरतपरिस्पन्दमानापरिमितपवना-दिपरमाणव:, Raghunátha Síromani ; गतिशीलत्वात् पतत्र्यपदेशा: पतन्तीति, Udayana, Kusumáñjali) and an inherent impulse that drives them to unite in pairs—a sort of "monovalency," as it were, exhausted with the formation of a binary molecule. The binary molecules now combine by threes, fours, fives, etc., to form larger aggregates as well as the variety of elementary substances, the particular collocation in any case being not only determined by physical causes, but also serving to satisfy the ends of the moral law in creation (अदृष्ट, कर्म). (ह्यणुकैर्बहुभिरारभ्यते इत्यपि नियमो, न द्वाभ्यां । बहुत्वनियम: । कदाचित् त्रिभिरारभ्यते इति त्र्यणुकमित्युच्यते, कदाचिच्चतुर्भिरारभ्यते कदाचित् पञ्चभिरिति यथेष्टं कल्पना । अदृष्टवशात् तथा तथा तेषां व्यूहो यथा यथा तदारब्धेषु अपरजातयो व्यज्यन्ते । अदृष्टकारिता सर्व्वभावानां सृष्टि: ।—Srídhara, Nyáya-Kandalí, पृथिवीनिरूपणम् । *Cf.* Váchaspati's report, Bhámatí, Chap. II., Pada II., Sutra 2. यदा चतुरणुकमारभते चतुर्णां ह्यणुकानामारम्भकत्वात्।) Prasastapáda appears to have originated this view (परमाणुद्ध्यणुकेषु बहुत्वसंख्या—तैरारभ्ये त्र्यणुका-दिलक्षणे—Prasastapáda, परिमाणनिरूपणम्) ; but that another view was also maintained in the Vaiseshika school is evident from the brief summary of Kanáda's system given in Utpala's commentary on the Vrihatsamhitá, and this indeed also follows from Srídhara's admissions in the Kandalí. On this view, also, atoms have an inherent tendency to unite; but some unite in pairs, others in triads, others in tetrads, etc. This may happen in two ways—either by the atoms falling into groups of threes, fours, etc., direct, or by the successive addition of one atom to each preceding aggregate.

A triad (Tryanuka), then, holds together three atoms (Anus), not three binary molecules (Dvyanukas), as on the orthodox hypothesis. Similarly with tetrads, pentads, etc. (चतुर्विधाः परमाणवः क्षितिजलाग्निवायूनाम् । द्वाभ्यां परमाणुभ्यां द्व्यणुकमारभ्यते त्रिभिः परमाणुभिस्त्र्यणुकमारभ्यते इति क्रमेण स्थूलकार्य्यद्रव्यस्योत्पत्तिः ।—Utpala, Chap. I., Sloka 7; *cf.* also Srídhara's admission, अथवा यदि परमाणवो द्व्यणुकमारभ्य तत्सहिता-स्त्र्यणुकमारभन्ते व्यणुकसहितास्तु द्रव्यान्तरम् तथापि कुता विश्वस्य अग्रहणम्). Sankara seems to speak of two binary molecules in the Vaiseshika as forming a tetrad (यदापि द्वे द्व्यणुके चतुरणुकमारभेत —Saríraka-Bháshya, Chap. II., Pada XX., Sutra 2, where the Bhámati gives a forced interpretation).

In Prasastapáda's view, these binary molecules are grouped by threes, fours, fives, etc. (व्यणुक, चतुरणुक) to form different isomeric modifications. The variety of Earth substances is due to differences in the arrangements of the molecules (*e.g.* their greater or less density, and, above all, their grouping or collocation, व्यूह, अवयवसन्निवेश), which account for the specific characters (अपरजाति) manifested by these isomeric substances. सा (पृथिवी) च स्थैर्य्याद्यवयवसन्निवेशविशिष्ट

अपरजातिबहुत्वोपेता । — Praśastapáda, पृथिवीनिरूपणम् । स्थैर्यं निविड़त्वम् । आदिशब्दात् प्रश्लिष्टत्वादिपरिग्रहः । परमाणवादिषु अपरजात्य-भावेऽपि अदृष्टवशात् तथा तथा तेषां व्यूहः यथा यथा तदारम्भेषु अपरजातयो व्यज्यन्ते ।—Srídhara, Kandalí, *ibid.*

स्थैर्यं स्थिरता चिरकालावस्थायित्वमिति यावत् । आदिग्रहणाद्दृष्टमकत्वं जलादिव्यूहविरोधित्वञ्च । अवयवसन्निवेशाः तत्तत्सामान्यविशेषाभिव्यञ्चकसंस्था-नविशेषाः । न हि एतद्द्रव्यान्तरे सम्भवति । जलादीनां यत्किञ्चित्स्पर्शवद्-वेगवद्द्रव्योपनिपातमात्रेणैव भङ्गुरत्वात् ।—Udayana, Kiranávali, *ibid.*

These original differences in molecular grouping, leading to distinctions of genera and species, however mechanically or physically explained, come also under the operation of moral and metaphysical causes (अदृष्ट, कर्म), *i.e.* of ideal ends in the moral government of the Universe, which are superimposed upon the physical order, but which do not come within the scope of Natural Philosophy. An elementary substance thus produced by primary atomic combination may, however, suffer qualitative change under the influence of heat (पाकजोत्पत्ति). The process is as follows :—(1) The impact of heat-corpuscles decomposes the binary (tertiary, or quaternary) molecules into homogeneous atoms possessing only the generic characters of the Bhúta concerned; (2) the impacts of heat-particles continue, and transform the characters of the atoms, determining them all in the same way; (3) the heat-particles continue to impinge, and reunite the atoms so transformed to form binary (or other) molecules, in different orders or arrangements, which account for the specific characters or qualities finally produced. The Vaiseshika holds that there is decomposition into homogeneous atoms, transformation of atomic qualities, and finally

re-combination, all under the influence of heat (पिलुपाक).
The Nyáya, on the other hand, thinks that the molecules
and larger aggregates assume the new characters under
the influence of heat without decomposition into homogeneous atoms or change of atomic characters (पिठरपाक).

तेषामनुमानेन विनाशः परिकल्प्यते । सर्व्वावयवेषु अन्तर्वहिष्च पाकपूर्व्वक-
पूर्व्वरूपादिविलक्षणगुणोपलब्धेरन्तःप्रवेशः कृशानोरनुमीयते तेन वेगवता वह्नि-
द्रव्येण नोदनात् अभिघातात् वा नूनं घटाद्यारम्भकेषु अवयवेषु क्रिया जायते
क्रियातो विभागः विभागात् द्रव्यारम्भकसंयोगविनाशः । तद्विनाशात् द्रव्य-
विनाशः । पक्काश्च श्यामादिगुणानवजहतः रक्तादिगुणान्तरयोगमनुभवनः—
अदृष्टप्रेर्य्यमाणाः परस्परं संयुज्य अणुकादिप्रक्रमेण तादृशमेव घटादिकार्य्यमारभन्ते ।
एवं तपनातपदृश्यमानेषु आम्रादिफलेषु एष एव न्यायः । शरीरे अपि उदर्य्येण
तेजसा पच्यमानेषु अन्नपानादिषु रसमलधातुभावेन परिणाममुपगच्छत्सु प्रायेण
प्रतिक्षणमुत्पादविनाशौ संभवत इति । (Jayanta, Nyáyamañjarí,
भूतचैतन्य-पूर्व्वपक्ष.) This is the Vaiseshika view, but Jayanta
himself inclines to the opposite view: प्रकृतिसुषिरतयैव
कार्य्यद्रव्यस्य घटादेः आरम्भात् अनलतेजःकणानुप्रवेशकृतपाकोपपत्तेः अलं
विनाशकल्पनया । पिठरपाकपक्ष एव पेषलः । ibid. The Nyáya
view: ये वीजावयवास्ते पूर्व्वव्यूहपरित्यागेन व्यूहान्तरमापद्यन्ते व्यूहान्तरापत्तौ
च पृथिवीधातुरब्धातुना संगृहीत आन्तरेण तेजसा पच्यमानो रसद्रव्यं निर्वर्त्तयति
स रसः पूर्व्वावयवसहितोऽङ्कुरादिभावमापद्यते । परमाणवस्थानि वीजानि
भवन्तीत्येतत् न प्रतिपद्यामहे । यस्माच्छाल्यादिवीजमुच्छूनावस्थामादिं कृत्वा
यावदुपान्त्यं शालिवीजकार्य्यं तावत् कदाचित् परमाणवस्थं भवति । यदि
तु स्यात् कदाचित् नोपलभ्येत ।—Udyotakara, Chap. III.,
Áhnika 1, Sutra 4.

II. *Chemical Combination* (सम्भूयक्रिया, संहतक्रिया).—
Chemical combination takes place either between two or
more substances which are isomeric modifications of the
same Bhúta, or between substances which are modes of
different Bhútas.

A. *Mono-Bhautic Compounds.*—The simplest compounds are mono-Bhautic compounds, *i.e.* compounds of different substances which are isomeric modes of the same Bhúta.

(*a*) Mono-Bhautic compounds of the first order. Under the impact or impulse (अभिघात or नोदन) of heat-corpuscles, the substances in chemical contact (आरम्भक संयोग) break up into their atoms. These atoms are homogeneous, possessing only the original physical and chemical characters of the Bhúta concerned. As the specific differences between isomeric substances arise from the arrangement or collocation of the atoms, the substances lose their distinctive marks on decomposition into the latter. (न च परमाणुषु अपरजातिभेदो विद्यते न च यववीजशालिवीजपरमाणूनां कश्चिद्विशेषः ।— Udyotakara, Chap. III., Áhnika 1, Sutra 4. न च शुक्रशोणितपरमाणूनां कश्चिद्विशेषः पार्थिवत्वाविशेषात् ।—Srídhara, Nyáya-Kandalí, पृथिवीनिरूपणम् ।) Under the continued impact (or, it may be, impulse) of heat-particles (वेगवता वह्निद्रव्येण नादनात् अभिघातात् वा—Jayanta), these atoms take on new characters. It is heat, and heat alone, that can cause this transformation of the colours, tastes, smells, etc., in these original Bhúta-atoms. What particular colours, tastes, smells, or physical characters will be produced in the atoms depends (1) on the colours, etc., of the constituent substances in contact; (2) the intensity or degree of the heat (खर, मृदु, or मध्यम पाक); and (3) the species of Tejas-corpuscles that impinge on the atoms, or the nature of the impact (विलक्षणतेजःसंयोग). (न ब्रूमोऽग्निसंयोगात् एकस्मात् रूपादय इति अपि तु पूर्व्वरूपादिविशेषापेक्षात् । यद्द्रव्यं पच्यते अग्निसंयोगेन तस्य ये पूर्व्वरूपादयस्तेषां यः खगतो विशेषस्तमपेक्षमाणः अग्निसंयोगः उत्तरान् रूपादीन् विशिष्टानारभते । *Vide* also Udyotakara, III., 2, Sutra 14. *Cf.* also Váchaspati, I., 1, Sutra 4. अस्माकमभेदे अपि उपादानस्य पिठरस्य औष्ण्यापराख्यस्य च वहिःसंयोगस्य पूर्व्वरूपादिप्रध्वंसानां कारणानां भेदात् भिन्नजातीया जायन्ते गन्धरूपरसस्पर्शा इति सिद्धान्तः ।)

Now when the atoms have all been determined in the same way, they begin to re-combine again under the impact (or impulse) of the heat-particles in binary molecules (or tertiary, etc.), and these in higher aggregates. It seems to be generally held that at the final step one or more atoms of one constituent substance unite with one or more atoms of the other constituent substance or substances to form a molecule of the compound; but the question is not of much significance for mono-Bhautic compounds of the first order, as in these cases the atoms have before this all lost their distinctive characters and become homogeneously transformed. The compound so produced will possess the new characters of the transformed atoms, so far as taste, colour, smell, etc., are concerned, but as the molecular arrangement or structure (व्यूह, अवयवसन्निवेश) may vary, different compound substances may result from the same components.

(b) Mono-Bhautic compounds of higher orders. Again, mono-Bhautic compounds of the first order may chemically combine to form higher compounds, and as the ultimate Bhúta substratum is the same, the process of decomposition and re-composition will be essentially the same as before. The only doubtful point is whether in this case the component compound substances are broken up only into their constituent molecules, or into the original homogeneous Bhúta-atoms. Some of the later Vaiseshika scholiasts hold that the latter happens in every case of chemical composition, however complex, but the earlier Vaiseshika conceived that in the case of compounds of compounds the decomposition does not proceed so far as the original Bhúta-atoms, but that it is the specifically determined atoms constituting the molecules of the component compounds that are transformed under the impact of the heat-corpuscles; and then one such transformed atom (one or more according to another version) from the molecule of one component unites with one similarly transformed atom (one or more according to the other version) from the molecule of the other component. Praśastapáda, the great Vaiseshika doctor, holds this view. When, for example, in the fertilised ovum, the germ and the sperm substances, which, in the Vaiseshika view, are both isomeric modes of Earth (with accompaniments of other Bhútas), unite, both are broken up into homogeneous Earth-atoms, and it is these that chemically combine under the animal heat (and biomotor Enery, वायु) to form the germ-plasm (कलल). But, next, when the germ-plasm develops, deriving its nutrition from the chyle (blood) of the mother, the animal heat breaks up the molecules of the germ-plasm into its constituent atoms (कललारम्भकपरमाणवः), *i.e.* into atoms specifically determined, which by their grouping formed the germ-plasm, and then these germ-plasm atoms as radicles chemically combine with the atoms of the food-constituents, and thus produce cells and tissues. (समुत्पन्नपाकजैः कललारम्भकपरमाणुभिः अदृष्टवशात् उपजातक्रियैः आहारपरमाणुभिः सह समभूय शरीरान्तरमारभ्यते इत्येषा कल्पना । पितुः शुक्रे मातुः शोणिते तयोः सन्निपातानन्तरं

जठरानलसम्बन्धात् शुक्रशोणितारम्भकेषु परमाणुषु पूर्व्व-रूपादिविनाशे सति समानगुणान्तरोत्पत्तौ ह्रयणुकादि-प्रक्रमेण कललशरीरोत्पत्तिः । . . . तत्र मातुराहाररसः भान्त्या संक्रामति अदृष्टवशात् तत्र पुनर्जठरानलसम्बन्धात् कललारम्भकपरमाणुषु क्रियाविभागादिन्यायेन कललशरीरे नष्टे समुत्पन्नपाकजैः कललारम्भकपरमाणुभिः अदृष्टवशात् उपजातक्रियः आहारपरमाणुभिः सह सम्भूय शरीरान्तर-मारभ्यते इत्येषा कल्पना । —Śrídhara, Kandalí, पृथिवीनिरूपणम् ।) In this hypothesis (कल्पना) it is assumed that the atoms are similarly transformed, *i.e.* become endowed with the colour, taste, smell, etc., of the product (the cell or tissue) the moment before the chemical combination takes place. Similarly, when milk is transformed into curd, one view is that the transformation takes place (under internal heat) in the constituent atoms of the milk-molecules, atoms specifically determined as milk, and not in the original atoms of the Bhúta (or Bhútas) entering into the composition of milk. (*Cf.* एवं महादुग्धारम्भकैः परमाणुभिरेव दध्यारभ्यते । एकमहिन्नेव दध्यारम्भकैरेव परमाणुभिर्नवनीतारम्भः इति दिक् । Nyáyabodhiní, on Annam Bhaṭṭa's Tarka-saṅgraha. *Cf.* Dinakarí—ह्रयणुकरूपदुग्धध्वंस-जन्यत्वेऽपि तस्य (दध्नः) ।) In these cases the atomic contact is called constituent contact (आरम्भकसंयोग), and all the atoms are equally regarded as material causes (उपादान-कारण or समवायिकारण) of the compound.

B. *Hetero-Bhautic " Quasi-compounds."*—The Nyáya-Vaiseshika maintains that in the case of bi-Bhautic (or poly-Bhautic) compounds, which are only quasi-compounds, there is another kind of contact between the heterogeneous atoms of the different Bhútas, which may be called dynamic contact, and is distinguished in its operations as Upash*t*ambha, Vish*t*ambha, or Avash*t*ambha (उपष्टम्भ, विष्टम्भ, or अवष्टम्भ). In some cases it so happens that the atoms of different isomeric modes of the same Bhúta do not chemically combine under the mere application of heat; they require to be surrounded (and "excited," "energized") by atoms of different Bhútas. For example, in the case of the oils and fats, as well as of plant saps and fruit juices, the Earth-atoms must be dissolved in water (Ap), and it is only when the water-atoms (Ap-atoms) congregate round the former that dynamic intra-atomic forces are set up, and the Earth-atoms (with the water-atoms in dynamic contact) now take on peculiar infra-sensible characters (colours, tastes, smells) under the impact of the heat-corpuscles, and then, under further impact, fall into groupings or collocations (of a very peculiar nature, to be presently explained) which determine the nature of the composite substance thus produced. Here it is the water-atoms that are dynamic (उपष्टम्भक), and excite the Earth-atoms, and these substances, oils and fats (तैलवर्ग and घृतवर्ग), as well as acids (अम्लवर्ग) are, because of the Earth-radicles, regarded as Earth compounds (or Earth substances). (पाकज-तथाविधगन्धरसरूपादिमद्रि: परमाणुभिर्द्वयणुकादिक्रमेण घृता-दिद्रव्यमारभ्यते । तत्र च उपष्टम्भकतया निमित्ततामापन्ना: पानी-यावयवाः । तेषां संयुक्तसमवायेन स्नेहस्तत्रोपलभ्यते । तैलक्षीरादिषु पार्थिवत्वसिद्धिः । तैलस्य भौमानलेन्धनत्वात् घृतवत् ।—Udayana.) In the above instances, Ap (water) acts as dynamic (Upash*t*ambhaka, उपष्टम्भक), but Tejas and Váyu can also act in the same way on Earth-particles. Conversely, Earth-particles may act dynamically on the atoms of the other Bhútas. For example, in the case of mercury and the metals which are conceived in the Nyáya-Vaiseshika to be igneous bodies (in fact, they are supposed to be formed under the subterranean heat, आकरज), the Tejas-corpuscles are believed to form the radicles, and the Earth-particles are dynamic (उपष्टम्भक). (सुवर्णादि निरन्तरं ध्यायमानमपि न पूर्वरूपं जहाति । तेनैव त्र्यणुन्तरेण प्रतिवद्धत्वात् उपष्टम्भकोऽपि पार्थिवभागः सदृशरूप श्वानुवर्त्तते, यत्तु पुठपाकादिना रक्तसारता दृश्यते तन्मिश्रीभूताभिभावकतत्तद्द्रव्योपगमात् । एतेन पारदादि व्याख्यातम् ।—Udayana, Kira*n*ávalí, तेजोनिरूपणम् । *Cf.* also योऽपि तैजसमिच्छति सुवर्णं तेनाप्यत्र पार्थिवोभाग उपष्टम्भक एष्टव्यः ।)

It may be here noted that Gangesa, the author of the Tattvachintáma*n*i, conjectures that even gold can be evaporated or made to disappear by the application of intense heat: अथ द्रुतद्रुततरादेः क्रमशः प्रतीतेः प्रबलानलसंयोगेन सुवर्णनाशात् तद्द्रवता नश्यति । But Mathuránátha notes here: भस्मप्राक्कालोच्छेदसमये । (सन्निकर्षवादरहस्य).

But while every Bhúta can act dynamically

as उपष्टम्भक, "energizer," "exciter," it is the Earth Bhúta alone which is capable of exercising (1) the power of arrest or inhibition of molecular motion, or the motion of particles due to gravity as in fluids (Vish*t*ambha, विष्टम्भ) ; or (2) the power of counteracting the tendency in a given set of atoms to fall into a peculiar order or group (व्यूहविरोधित्वम्). (न च पार्थिववत् अम्भो द्रव्यान्तरं गच्छदिष्टम्भाति पूर्वव्यूहं वा विरुणद्धि ।—Udayana, Kira*n*ávalí, पृथिवी- निरूपणम्। विष्टम्भकत्वं स्वाभाविकगुरुत्वाश्रयद्रव्यान्तरगतिप्रतिबन्ध- कत्वम्। व्यूहविरोधित्वं च स्वाभाविकगुरुत्ववत्पतनप्रतिबन्धकत्वम्।
—Vardhamána, Kira*n*ávalíprakása, *ibid.*)

Oils, Fats, Milks.—Bi-Bhautic quasi-compounds, with Ap as energizer : Oleaginous substances (आज्यतैलादयः स्नेहाः) are divided by Udayana into (1) oils derived from vegetables, (2) butters derived from milk, and (3) fats derived from animals. The medical schools, as we have seen, recognise animal oils as distinguished from vegetable oils. Vegetable fats (*e.g.* विडङ्गघृत) are also mentioned. Váchaspati and Udayana contend that among oils, fats, milks, etc., differences in flavour and odour imply differences in kind (जाति) and in molecular structure, since it is only a variation in such structure that constitutes a variation in natural kind (अवयव- सन्निवेशः—तत्तत्सामान्यविशेषाभिव्यञ्जकसंस्थानविशेषाः—Udayana, Kira*n*ávalí). Mustard-oil, for example, has not the flavour and smell characteristic of sesamum-oil (Taila), and is classed with the latter only by reason of similarity of specific qualities and structure. Judged by the flavour test, Ámikshá (the casein substance formed by mixing milk curd with hot boiled milk) is to be classed with milk substances. So also Takra, whey; but Vájina, the thin fluid that is left after the Ámikshá (casein substance) is separated, cannot be classed as milk. It may be added that the milks and curds, as well as oils and fats derived from different species of vegetables or animals, are supposed to differ in their ultimate structural arrangement, and therefore in kind; but Vallabha thinks that the ghees (clarified butters) prepared from different kinds of milk are of the same kind; in other words, the milks and curds are "polymeric," the ghees (clarified butters) "isomeric," using these terms, as before, in a loose general sense. (.... तैलघृतवसानां बीजक्षीरमांसयोनित्वात् । अतएव नारिकेलस्नेहस्यापि तैलत्वं रसादिसारूप्यादपि तु घृतव्यपदेशश्च ।—Udayana, Kiranávalí, पृथिवीनिरूपणम् । Vallabha notes that ghees do not differ in kind as milks (and curds) do: अतो नाहिमगव्यादिदुग्धेषु दधित्ववत् घृतादिषु जातिभेदश्चास्तामिति चेन्न ।—Vallabha, Lílávatí. Compare Váchaspati, II., 2, 65: आज्यतैलादीनां जातिस्तु गन्धेन वा रसेन वा व्यज्यते । अतएव न सार्षपादीनां तैलत्वमस्ति । तद्व्यञ्जकयोगेन्धरसयोरभावात् । भाक्तस्तु तैलशब्दयोगः । क्षीरजातिरपि रसव्यङ्ग्येव । अतएवामिक्षायाः क्षीरत्वम् । न तु वाजिनस्य तद्व्यञ्जकस्य रसभेदस्य वाजिने अभावात् आमिक्षायां च भावात् ।)

III. *Mixtures like Solutions, etc.*—A solution (of an Earth substance in Ap or water) is a physical mixture of a peculiar kind, from which evaporation (or precipitation) ordinarily sets the water free. Udyotakara notices gruels, baths, and lyes (alkaline solutions) as mixtures of this class (एतेन पाककाञ्चिकविवेकावक्षारादयः प्रत्युक्ता :—Udyotakara). A soup is also a physical mixture. When meat is boiled in water there is the application of heat with chemical changes in the meat, but the combination of meat particles and water particles in the soup is only physical combination and not a chemical one. It is, of course, not a true compound, neither is it a quasi-compound like milk (in which the water particles are "energizers" of the Earth particles). Milk, for example, retains its milky substance when it coagulates or becomes solid (this, of course, is also the case with mono-Bhautic substances whether elementary or compound, *e.g.* water, which becomes ice), but the substance we call a soup or solution ceases to be a soup or solution the moment it solidifies. (यूषो हि नाम उत्पन्नपाकजानां द्रव्याणां कालविशेषानुग्रहे सति द्रव्यान्तरसंपृक्तानां पाकजोत्पत्तौ यः संयोगः स यूष इति । एतेन पाककाच्चिकविवेकावक्षारादयः प्रयुक्ताः ।—Udyotakara, Vártika, Chap. I., Áhnika 1, Sutra 14. *Vide* also Váchaspati's comment: उत्पन्नपाकजानां तैले सर्पिषि वा पिष्टमांसविराडावयवानां द्रव्यान्तरेण तोयेन संयुक्तानां पाकजोत्पत्तौ सत्यां न चासौ सहसा इत्युक्ते कालविशेषानुग्रहे सतीति । स च संयोगभेदएव तोयमांसयोर्नेतु अवयवी विजातीययोरनारम्भकत्वात् । नापि यूषज्ञातीयं तोयसंयोगि द्रव्यं क्षीरजातीय- मिवेति युक्तम् । तोयविरहे काठिन्येऽपि क्षीरबुद्धिव्यपदेशयोस्तादवस्थ्यात् । इह तु काठिन्ये न यूषबुद्धिव्यपदेशो इति सम्बन्धभेद एव तोयमांसयोर्यूष इति न्याय्यम् । स च अनुभवसिद्धः संयोगिव्यतिरिक्तः ।—Váchaspati, Tátparyyatíká, *ibid.* For earthy salts in sea-water, *vide* Kiranávalí : यत् पुनरम्बुधिसिन्धुभेदेन क्षारादिरपि रसः पाथसे उपलभ्यते स दशमूलकमायस्येव पार्थिवद्रव्योपाधिकः । कथमन्यथा तस्यैव घनपीतमुक्तस्य रसो मधुर एव ।—Udayana, Kiranávalí, जलनि- रूपणम् ।)

Chemical Action and Heat.—The operation of heat is of course universally implied in chemical combinations. Where the application of external heat is

I

wanting, Vátsyáyana, the great doctor of the Nyáya, points to the operation of internal heat (*e.g.* पृथिवीधातुः अबधातुना संगृहीतः आन्तरेण तेजसा पच्यमानः रसद्रव्यं निर्वर्तयति ।— Vátsyáyana-Bháshya, Chap. IV., Áhnika 1, Sutra 47). In the case of combustion we have seen Vijñána-bhikshu explain the heat as latent in the Earth substance, the fuel, from which it breaks forth. Udayana points out that the solar heat is the source of all the stores of heat required for chemical change in the world. The change of colours in grasses, for example, is due to Tejas in the form of latent (invisible) heat, not in the form of Agni; and the cold in winter cannot take away this store derived from the sun. (तृणादिविकारो हि यदि रूपादिपरावृत्तिमात्रहेतुः स नूनमौष्ण्यापेक्षेण तेजसा कर्तव्यः । तादृश च पाके अनिमित्तं हिममिति । न किंचिदनिष्टमापद्यते । न हि सौरस्य तेजसः त्रैलोक्यपाकहेतोर्हिमादपगमः क्षमते । अथ विकारो भस्मादिरूपो विवक्षितः सोऽसिद्ध एव हिमहेतुषु तृणादिषु क्व विरोधो बाधो वा । अथ रूपादिपरावृत्तिमात्रेणैव अग्निः साध्यते तदशक्यम् । तस्य दर्शनस्पर्शन-ग्राह्यस्य योग्यानुपलम्भबाधितत्वात् अतादृशस्य तेजोमात्रस्य निवृत्तेरशक्यत्वात् अनिष्टत्वात् च ।—Udayana, Kiranávalí, सृष्टिसंहारविधिनिरूपणम् ।) Similarly it is under this solar heat that the unripe mango ripens, *i.e.* changes colour, taste, smell, etc., showing that there is chemical transformation or subtle decomposition and recomposition going on; and this is also the case with the rusting of the metals, which is a combustion due to the solar heat (सूर्यपाक) even as the conversion of food into chyle and of chyle into blood are instances of chemical action due to the internal animal heat (जठरानल or औदर्यं तेजः). But the kind of contact with heat-corpuscles, in other words, the kind of chemical action (पाक) which transforms colours, is supposed to differ from that which transforms flavour (विलक्षणतेज:संयोग and पाक), and this last from that which produces a change of smell, or tactile quality. (पाको नाम विजातीयतेज:संयोग: । स च नानाजातीय: । रूपजनको विजातीयतेज:-संयोगस्तदपेक्षया रसजनको विजातीय: । एवं स्पर्शादौ अपि तथा । एवंप्रकारेण भिन्नभिन्नजातीया: पाका: कार्यवैलक्षण्येन कल्पनीया: । तथाहि तृणपुञ्ज-निक्षिप्ताम्बादौ उष्णलक्षणविजातीयतेज:संयोगात् पूर्वहरितरूपनाश रूपान्तरस्य पीतादेरुत्पत्ति: पूर्वरसस्य अम्लस्यैवानुभवात् । क्वचित् पूर्वहरितरूपस्त्वेऽपि रसपरावृत्तिदृश्यते विजातीयतेज:संयोगरूपपाकवशात् पूर्वतनाम्लरसनाशे मधुर-रसस्यानुभवात् । तस्मात्रूपजनकापेक्षया रसजनको विलक्षण एवं गन्धजनको विलक्षण एवाङ्गीकार्य: रूपरसयोरपरावृत्तौ अपि पूर्वगन्धनाशे विजातीयपा-कवशात् सुरभिगन्धोपलम्भे । एवं स्पर्शजनकोऽपि पाकवशात् कठिनस्पर्शनाशे मृदुस्पर्शानुभवात् । अतएव पार्थिवपरमाणूनामेकजातीयत्वेऽपि पाकमहिम्ना विजातीयद्रव्यान्तरानुभव: । यथा गोभुक्ततृणादीनां आपरमाखन्तं भङ्गे तृणा-रम्भकपरमाणुषु विजातीयतेज:संयोगवशात् पूर्वरूपादिचतुष्टयनाशे तदनन्तरं दुग्धे यादृशं रूपादिकं वर्त्तते तादृशरूपरसगन्धस्पर्शजनकात्तेज:संयोगा जायन्ते । तदुत्तरं तादृशरूपादय उत्पद्यन्ते । तादृशरूपादिविशिष्टपरमाणुभिर्दुग्धद्व्यणुकमा-रभ्यते । तत: त्र्यणुकादिक्रमेण महादुग्धारम्भइति ।—Nyáyabodhiní on Annam Bha*tt*a's Tarkasangraha.) Heat- and light-rays are supposed to consist of indefinitely small particles which dart forth or radiate in all directions rectilineally with a sort of conical dispersion and with inconceivable velocity. They may either (1) penetrate through inter-atomic (or inter-molecular) spaces as in cases of conduction of heat, which when applied under the pot boils the water or fries the paddy, where there is no chemical action in the pot, no decomposition and recomposition of its atoms, no change in the molecular collocation; or, as with light-rays in cases of trans-lucency or transparency (स्वच्छता), penetrate through the inter-atomic spaces with Parispanda of the nature of deflection or refraction (तिर्य्यंग्गमन, Udyotakara), in the same way as when fluids penetrate through porous bodies (तत्र परिस्पन्दः तिर्य्यंग्गमनं परिस्रवः पात इति—Udyotakara, commenting on Vátsyáyana's परिस्पन्दपरिस्रवौ, Sutra 47, Áhnika 1, Chap. III.); or (2) impinge on the atoms, and rebound back—which explains reflection (मूर्च्छन, किरणविघट्टन —Varáhamihira, रश्मिपरावर्त्तन—Vátsyáyana), or otherwise be obstructed by the atoms in their path, which would explain degrees of opacity, the casting of shadows, etc., all these operations being also physical, and unattended by decomposition and recomposition or alteration of molecular grouping; or (3) lastly, strike the atoms in a peculiar way, so as to break up their grouping, transform the physico-chemical characters of the atoms, and again recombine them, all by means of continual impact with inconceivable velocity, an operation which explains all cases of chemical combination. (अचिन्त्यो हि तेजसो लावघातिशयेन वेगातिशयः यत् प्राचीनाचलचूड़ावलम्बिनि एव भगवति मयूखमालिनि भवनोदरेषु आलोकइत्यभिमानो लौकिकानाम् ।—Udayana, Kiranávalí, तेजोनिरूपणम्, taken from Váchaspáti, Tátparyyatíká, प्रत्यक्षलक्षणसूत्रम् । Cf. also चाक्षुर्षं तेजः वेगवता सविचेन तेजसा न प्रतिहन्यते ।—Váchaspati. वर्त्तिदेशे पिहितमपि तेजः प्रसर्पेत् प्रासादोदरं व्याप्नोति । तत् कस्य हेतोः पृष्यत्वात् । स्वभावतः प्रसरदपि न स्वपरिमाणानुविधायिनं प्रत्ययमाधत्ते किं तु विषयभेदानुविधायिनम् । —ibid. Cf. स्फटिकाद्यन्तरितोपलब्धिरपि प्रसादस्वभावतया स्फटिकादीनां तेजोगतेरप्रतिबन्धकतया प्रदीपप्रभावादेवोपपन्ना ।—Udayana, तेजोनिरूपणम्, in reply to the objection: यदि हि प्राप्य गृह्णीयात् प्रतिघातिना स्फटिकद्रव्येण विष्टम्भाद्प्राप्तं प्रसर्पन्नूष्णादिकं नाददीत तस्मादप्राप्यकारि ततो न तैजसम् ।—Udayana, ibid. Definition of खच्छता—द्व्यानारासम्पृक्तद्रव्यसमवायः स्वच्छता । दृष्टश्चाप्रतिघातः काचाभ्रपटलस्फटिकान्तरितोपलव्धः । ..... स्यात्यादिषु च पाचकस्य तेजसाऽप्रतिघातात् ।—Udyotakara, Chap. III., Áhnika 1, Sutra 38. आदित्यरश्मे: स्फटिकान्तरितेऽपि दाह्येऽविघातात्।—Sutra 47, where Udyotakara notes : कोऽयमविघात:—यस्य द्रव्यस्यावयवा न व्यूह्यन्ते तस्य अन्तरावयवै: अव्यूह्यमानस्य योऽभिसंबन्ध: सोऽविघात इति। Váchaspati explains यस्य द्रव्यस्य भर्जनेनकपालादे: अवयवा न व्यूह्यन्ते पूर्वोत्पन्नद्रव्यारम्भकसंयोगनाशेन द्व्यणुजनकसंयोगोत्पादनं व्यूहनं तत्र क्रियन्ते तस्य द्रव्यस्य भर्जनेनकपालादे-रव्यूह्यमानस्य अन्तरावयवैर्योऽभिसम्बन्धो वह्ने: सोऽप्रतियात:। *Cf.* Vátsyáyana on Sutra 47, Áhnika 1, Chap. III. On the other hand, in chemical combination, अन्त:प्रवेश: कृशानोरनुमीयते। तेन वेगवता वह्निद्रव्येण नोदनात् अभिघातात् वा अवयवेषु क्रिया, क्रियातो विभाग:, विभागात् आरम्भकसंयोगविनाश: etc.—Jayanta, Mañjarí, भूतचैतन्यपूर्वैपक्ष। For opacity, shadows, etc., *vide* छाया तु तेज:परमाणोरावरणात् भूच्छिमता परमाणुना तेज:परमाणुराव्रियते। यत्र च अस्य आवरणं तत्र छायेति। विरलतेज:सम्बन्धीनि द्रव्यगुणकर्म्माणि छाया इत्यभिधीयते। सर्ब्बतो व्यावृत्ततेज:सम्बन्धीनि तु तानि तम:संज्ञकानि।— Udyotakara, Chap. IV., Áhnika 2, Sutra 25. For reflection and its laws, I quote passages in my Paper on Hindu Physics, to which the student of the history of Optics is referred.)

Arrangement of Atoms in Space.—The Nyáya conceives atomic magnitudes as Párimándalya, a term which indicates a spherical shape. (नित्यं परिमण्डलम्— परिमण्डलमेव पारिमाण्डल्यम्— Sankaramisra). To conceive position in space, Váchaspati takes three axes, one proceeding from the point of sunrise in the horizon to that of sunset, on any particular day (roughly speaking, from the east to the west); a second bisecting this line at right angles on the horizontal plane (roughly speaking, from the north to the south); and the third proceeding from the point of their section up to the meridian position of the sun on that day (roughly speaking, up and down). The position of any point in space, relatively to another point, may now be given by measuring distances along these three directions, *i.e.* by arranging in a numerical series the intervening points of contact, the less magnitude or distance being that which comes earlier in this series, and the greater that which comes later. The position of any single atom in space with reference to another may be indicated in this way with reference to the three axes. But this gives only a geometrical analysis of the conception of three-dimensioned Space, though it must be admitted in all fairness that by dint of clear thinking it anticipates in a rudimentary manner the foundations of solid (co-ordinate) geometry. (एकस्वेऽपि दिशः आदित्योदयदेश-प्रत्यासन्नदेशसंयुक्तो यः स इतरस्मात्विप्रकृष्टप्रदेशसंयोगात् परमाणोः पूर्वः एवमादित्यास्तमयदेशप्रत्यासन्नदेशसंयुक्तो यः स इतरस्मात्विप्रकृष्टदेशसंयोगात् परमाणोः पश्चिमः तौ च पूर्वपश्चिमौ परमाणू अपेक्ष्य यः सूर्योदयास्तमयदेश-विप्रकृष्टदेशसंयोगः स मध्यवर्त्ती । एवमेतयोर्यौ तिर्य्यगदेशसम्बन्धिनौ मध्यस्य स्राजेवेन व्यवस्थितौ पार्श्ववर्त्तिनौ तौ दक्षिणोत्तरौ परमाणू । एवं मध्यन्दिन-वर्त्तिसूर्य्यसन्निकर्षेविप्रकर्षौ अपेक्ष्य उपर्य्यधोभावो द्रष्टव्यः । संयुक्तसंयोगात्यत्व-भूयस्त्वे च सन्निकर्षेविप्रकर्षौ पूर्व्वसंख्यावच्छिन्नत्वं च अल्पत्वं परसंख्यावच्छिन्नत्वं च भूयस्त्वम्।—Váchaspati, Tátparyyatíká, Chap. IV., Áhnika 2, Sutra 25.)

The original physical arrangement of atoms is also given. Each (spherical) atom is in contact with six other atoms. एवं दिशोऽपि एकस्या अपि संयोगा एव भागाः सोऽयं परमाणोः षट्केन युगपद्योगो मूर्त्तत्वमात्रप्रयुक्तः न सावयवत्वप्रयुक्तः ।—*ibid*. *Cf.* also the objection in the Buddhist Káriká, षट्केन युगपद्योगे परमाणोः षड्ंशता । यस्मां समानदेशत्वे पिण्डः स्यादणुमात्रकः ॥ This is the typical primordial arrangement, and variations in the collocation of atoms and molecules (व्यूह, अवयवसन्निवेश),

as we have seen, were conceived to account for the variety of isomeric modes of the same Bhúta, as well as of mono-Bhautic and poly-Bhautic compounds.

The molecular arrangement in the case of bi-Bhautic compounds is very peculiar. Two substances, say Earth and Ap (water), form a quasi-compound first, and each substance breaks up into atoms; one atom of Earth comes into contact with one of Ap. But the two do not form a binary molecule. Instead, this contact of heterogeneous atoms leads to a curious result. The atom of Earth combines with a neighbouring atom of its own class, and forms a binary molecule. Simultaneously the atom of Ap combines with another Ap-atom, and forms a binary molecule. Now the first binary molecule links on to the atom of Ap, and similarly the second binary molecule links on to the atom of Earth. The moment after, the two binary molecules take on the physico-chemical characters of Earth and Ap respectively, and simultaneously with the assumption of these physico-chemical characters, the binary molecules enter into complex contact (संयोगजसंयोग). In all this process work is done only in the first instant, in the contact of an atom of Earth with one of Ap; the resulting contacts, of atom with binary molecule and of the binary molecules with each other, involve no further expenditure of Energy. Thus we get a particle holding two binary molecules (of Earth and Ap respectively) in complex contact, and such particles continue to be formed. In this way the particles of the two substances arrange themselves, and the peculiarity of this molecular arrangement explains the resulting mixed or compound qualities of this class of quasi-compounds. (संयोगजस्तु (संयोग:) उत्पन्नमात्रस्य चिरोत्पन्नस्य वा निष्क्रियस्य कारणसंयोगिकारण: कारणा-कारणसंयोगपूर्वकः कार्य्याकार्य्यगतः संयोगः । ... एकस्माच्च द्वयोरुत्पत्तिः । कथम् । यदा पार्थिवाप्ययोरणुः संयोगे सति अन्येन पार्थिवेन पार्थिवस्य अन्येन आप्येन च आप्यस्य युगपत्संयोगो भवतस्तदा ताभ्यां संयोगाभ्यां पार्थिवाप्येद्व्यणुके युगपदारभ्येते । ततो यस्मिन् काले द्व्यणुकयोः कारणगुणपूर्वक्रमेण रूपाद्युत्पत्तिः तस्मिन्नेव काले इतरेतरकारणाकारणगतात् संयोगात् इतरेतरकार्य्याकार्य्यगतौ संयोगौ युगपदुत्पद्यते । किं कारणम् । कारणसंयोगिना हि अकारणेन कार्य्यं अवश्यं संयुज्यते इति न्यायः । अतः पार्थिवं द्व्यणुकं कारणसंयोगिना आप्येन अणुना सम्बध्यते । आप्यमपि द्व्यणुकं कारणसंयोगिना पार्थिवेनेति—Prasastapáda-Bháshya, गुणग्रन्थे संयोगनिरूपणम् ।)

The whole process may be graphically represented as follows :—

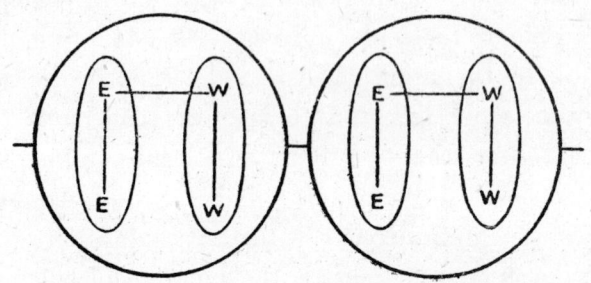

MOLECULES OF A BI-BHAUTIC QUASI-COMPOUND :
GRAPHIC FORMULA OF COMPLEX CONTACT.

E = an atom of Earth.   W = an atom of water (Ap).
$\begin{matrix}E\\|\\W\end{matrix}$ = { a binary molecule of Earth. $\begin{matrix}W\\|\\W\end{matrix}$ = { a binary molecule of water (Ap).

I will conclude this account of ancient (and mediæval) Hindu chemistry with a note on the conception of molecular (atomic) motion, Parispanda, and the different varieties of such motion which were conceived to account for the physical phenomena of sound, light, and heat. Any attempt to differentiate rigidly between Mechanics and Physics on the one hand and Chemistry on the other at this primitive stage would be an idle affectation. My Paper on Hindu Mechanics and Physics will give a detailed exposition in a separate treatise.

PARISPANDA :—RESOLUTION OF ALL PHYSICAL ACTION INTO MOTION.

Parispanda sometimes stands for motion molar as well as molecular, but more often for the subtle motion of atoms or molecules. The radical meaning of the term is whirling or rotary motion, a circling motion, but it may also include simple harmonic motion (*e.g.* vibration). All action, operation, work (क्रिया, व्यापार) is ultimately traced to this form of subtle motion lodged in the atoms or in the matter-stuff. The Vedánta, for example, speaks of a cosmic vibratory motion (सर्व्वलोकपरिस्पन्दनम्—Sankara). Ákása, in the Vedánta, as we have seen, is the first stadium in the evolution of Matter, which gives off Váyu, which gives off Tejas, and so on; but Ákása (ether) itself passes through two stages before the emanation of the Súkshma-bhúta Váyu : (1) the motionless ubiquitous primordial matter-stuff (answering to the Sánkhya Bhútádi) called Puránam Kham (पुरार्ण खं) ; and (2) a subtile integration, the pure un-quintuplicated Súkshma Bhúta called Váyuram Kham (वायुरं खं), answering to the Sánkhya Tanmátra stage. It is this subtile Ákása, in its Tanmátric integration, *i.e.* in the derivative form, which is subject to an incessant Parispanda. The gaseous stage of matter (the Vedántic Váyu) is indeed

matter in a state of Parispandic motion (वायोः परिस्पन्दा-
त्मकत्वात्—Saṅkara). So also the biomotor and sensori-
motor principles apart from the directive intelligence of
the Self (प्राणस्य परिस्पन्दात्मकत्वादेव—यदृद्वैतम् स्थूलं सूक्ष्मञ्च तत्सर्व्वं
मनःस्पन्दितमात्रम्—Saṅkara). The Sāṅkhya also conceives
this Parispanda to characterise every process and
phenomenon of cosmic evolution (व्यक्तं सक्रियं परिस्पन्दवत्—
Vāchaspati, Kaumudī). Bhūtas, organisms, mental
organs, as modes of Prakṛiti (considered apart from the
Intelligence of Purusha) are all subject to this Pari-
spanda (बुद्ध्यादयो देहं त्यजन्ते देहान्तरं उपाददते इति तेषां परिस्पन्दः ।
शरीरपृथिव्यादीनां च परिस्पन्दः प्रसिद्ध एव ।—Vāchaspati on Kārikā 10). On the other hand, Prakṛiti as the Avyakta,
the a-cosmic, the un-manifest ground, with resolution
only of like to like (सदृशपरिणाम), is devoid of all Parispandic motion (यद्यपि सव्यक्तस्यापि परिणामलक्षणा क्रिया, तथापि
परिस्पन्दो नास्ति ।—*ibid.* on Kārikā 10). The Nyāya-Vaiseshika finds Parispanda in all forms of matter, except
Ākāsa, which in that system is non-atomic and incapable of any change or activity (निष्क्रिय). But all
atoms, from those of Vāyu downwards, are in incessant
motion. The world at bottom is an infinitude of continually whirling (or vibratory) particles (अनवरतपरिस्पन्द-
मानापरिमितपवनादिपरमाणवः—Raghunātha ; compare also
Udayana-Kusumāñjali, Stavaka V.—परमाणवः हि गतिशी-
लत्वात् पतनव्यपदेशाः पतन्तीति ।). All physical action consists
in motion. The Nyāya-Vaiseshika rejects force, power,
operation (शक्ति) except as modes of motion. Jayanta,
indeed, states : We do not acknowledge any mysterious
power or operation which the senses do not and cannot
report to us. But this denial of Force (शक्ति) and of

unperceived and unperceivable operation (अतीन्द्रियव्यापार) is put forward as a philosophical (epistemological and metaphysical) proposition to justify the Nyáya analysis of the causal *nexus* into mere invariable and unconditional antecedence among phenomena without productive power or efficiency (अन्यथासिद्धिशून्यस्य नियतपूर्ववर्त्तिता—Bhásha-Parichchheda). It is not, of course, intended to question the existence of Parispanda, which is of the nature of motion, and which, though subtile and therefore infra-sensible (सूक्ष्म and अनुद्भूतरूप, not अतीन्द्रिय), is the ultimate form of all physical activity. (परिस्पन्द एव भौतिको व्यापारः करोत्यर्थः । अतीन्द्रियस्तु व्यापारः नास्तीति ब्रूमहे । ... तस्मात् कारकचक्रेण चलता जन्यते फलम् । न पुनश्चलनादन्यो व्यापार उपलभ्यते ।—Jayanta, Nyáyamañjari, Áhnika 1.) The effect (no less than the action) is, in all cases of material causation, the resultant of the combined motions of the various (material and efficient) causes involved (*e.g.* in the case of पाक, समुदितदेवदत्तादिसकलकारकनिकरपरिस्पन्द एव विशिष्टफलावच्छिन्नः पाक इत्युच्यते । ... अथ व्यापार एवैषः सर्व्वैः संभूय साध्यते । किं फलेनापराङ्‌ वः तद्धि संभूय साध्यताम् ।—Jayanta, Nyáyamañjari, Áhnika 1.)

But, in the Nyáya-Vaiseshika, though all action of matter on matter is thus resolved into motion, conscious activity is sharply distinguished from all forms of motion, as against the Sáṅkhya-Vedánta, which, as we have seen, considered everything other than Intelligence, the Purusha or the transcendental Self, to arise in the course of cosmic evolution, and therefore to be subject to Parispandic motion. (क्रियाविशेष एवायं व्यापारो ज्ञातुरान्तरः । स्पन्दात्मकवहिर्भूतक्रियालक्षणविलक्षणः ।—Quoted in Jayanta's Nyáyamañjari, Áhnika 4.)

ADDENDA.

Empirical Recipes from Varáhamihira (*circa* 550 A.D.) relating to Chemical Technology.

A. Searing of hard rocks to enable them to be cut (or pulverised) (शिलादारण).

Sprinkle on the rock taken red-hot from the fire of Palasa and Tinduka wood (Butea Frondosa and Diospyros Embryopteris) :—(*a*) diluted milk, or (*b*) a solution of wood ashes (the ashes of the *Mokshaka* mixed with those of reeds), or (*c*) a decoction of (the fruit of) the jujube (Zizyphus Jujuba) kept standing for seven nights in a mixture of whey, vinegar, and spirits, in which Kulattha (Dolichos Uniflorus or Biflorus) has been steeped, or (*d*) a solution of the ashes of the Neema bark and leaves (Azadirachta Indica), the sesame-pod, the resinous fruit of the Diospyros Embryopteris, and the Guduchi (Tinospora Cordifolia), with cow's urine. Repeat the process seven times (in the last case six times).—(Varáhamihira, V*ri*hat Samhitá, Chap. XXXIII., Ślokas 112–117.)

B. Hardening of steel (शस्त्रपान).

(1) Plunge the steel red-hot into a solution of plantain ashes in whey, kept standing for twenty-four hours; then sharpen on the lathe.

(2) Make a paste with the juice of the Arka (Calotropis Gigantea), the gelatine from the horn of the sheep, and the dung of the pigeon and the mouse;

apply it to the steel after rubbing the latter well with (sesame) oil. Plunge the steel thus treated into fire; and when it is red-hot, sprinkle on it water, or the milk of the horse (or the camel or the goat), or ghee (clarified butter), or blood, or fat or bile. Then sharpen on the lathe.—(Varáhamihira, खड्गलक्षणम्, Chap. XLIX., Ślokas 23-26.)

C. Preparation of cements (for rocks, metals, etc.) (वज्रलेप).

Varáhamihira gives the following recipes among others:—

(1) First, prepare a levigated powder with lac, the resinous exudation of the Pinus Devadara, the Balsamodendron Mukal, the Feronia Elephantum, the kernel of the fruit of the Ægle Marmelos (the *bel*), the Diospyros Embryopteris, the Neem (Azadirachta Indica), the Mhow (Bassia Latifolia), the Indian madder (Rubia Manjistha), the Phyllanthus Emblica, and the resin of the Sala tree (Shorea Robusta); then make a decoction of this in 256 Palas of water reduced by boiling to 32 Palas, and apply the decoction hot.

(2) The horns of cows, buffaloes, and goats, asses' hair, buffaloes' skin, with *gavya* (cow's urine, etc.), the Neem (Azadirachta Indica), and the Feronia Elephantum, similarly treated.

(3) A mixture of eight parts of lead, two of "bell-metal," and one of brass, melted and poured hot (Maya's cement).

The first, it will be seen, has lac, gum, and turpentine as principal ingredients; the second makes use of gelatine; and the third is a metallic cement.

D. Nourishment of Plants (from Varáhamihira, Chap. LIV., on वृक्षायुर्बेद).

The most suitable ground to plant in is soft soil that has been sown with the Sesamum Indicum, and dug up or trodden over with the sesame in flower. Grafts should be smeared with cow-dung. For transplanting, the plants should be smeared with ghee (clarified butter), sesame oil, the honey of the Kshudra variety of the bee, the oil of the Usira (Andropogon Laniger or Andropogon Citrarum), the Vidanga (Embelia Ribes), milk, and cow-dung. Trees should be planted at intervals of 20 or 16 cubits.

As a sort of general prophylactic, mud kneaded with ghee (clarified butter) and Vidanga (Embelia Ribes) should be applied to the roots, after which milk diluted with water should be poured. As a remedy against barrenness a hot decoction should be made of Kulattha (Dolichos Uniflorus or Biflorus), Masha (Phaseolus Roxburghii), Mudga (Phaseolus Mungo), Tila (Sesamum Indicum), and Yava (barley), which, when cooled, should be poured round the roots.

To promote inflorescence and fructification, a mixture of one Ádhaka (64 Palas) of sesame, two Ádhakas (128 Palas) of the excreta of goat or sheep, one Prastha (16 Palas) of barley powder, one Tula (100 Palas) of beef, thrown into one Drona (256 Palas) of water, and standing over for seven nights, should be poured round the roots of the plant. The measures given are for one plant.

To ensure inflorescence, etc., the seed before being sown should be treated as follows:—The seeds should be taken up in the palm greased with ghee (clarified butter) and thrown into milk; on the day following the seeds should be taken out of the milk with greased fingers and the mass separated into single seeds. This process is to be repeated on ten successive days. Then the seeds are to be carefully rubbed with cow-dung, and afterwards steamed in a vessel containing the flesh of hogs or deer. Then the seeds are to be sown with the flesh, with the fat of hogs added, in a soil previously prepared by being sown with sesame and dug up or trodden down.

To ensure the formation of Ballarís (*i.e.* sprouting and the growth of luxuriant stems and foliage), the seeds should be properly soaked in an infusion of powdered paddy, *Masha* (bean), sesame, and barley, mixed with decomposing flesh, and then steamed with Haridrá (turmeric). This process will succeed even with the Tintidí (Tamarindus Indica). For the Kapittha (Feronia Elephantum), the seeds should be soaked for about two minutes (*lit.* such length of time as it would take one to make a hundred rhythmic claps with the palms—तालशब्द) in a decoction of eight roots (Ásphota, Ámalaki, Dhava, Vásika, Vetasa, Suryyavalli, Syáma, and Atimukta, *i.e.* the jasmine, the myrobalan, the Grislea Tomentosa, the Justicia Ganderussa, the Calamus Rotang, the Gymandropsis Pentaphylla, the Echites Frutescens, and the Dalbergia Oujeinensis) boiled in milk. The seeds should then be dried in the sun. This process should be repeated for thirty days. A circular hole should be dug in the ground, a cubit in diameter and two cubits deep, and this should be filled with the milky decoction. When the hole dries up, it should be burnt with fire, and then pasted over with ashes mixed with ghee and honey. Three inches of soil should now be thrown in, then the powder of bean, sesame, and barley, then again three inches of soil. Finally, washings of fish should be sprinkled, and the mud should be beaten and reduced to a thick consistency, then the seed previously prepared should be placed in the hole under three inches of soil, and fish-washings poured. This will lead to luxuriant ramification and foliage, which will excite wonder. The Agnipurána adds that the mango is specially benefited by cold fish-washings (मत्स्योदकेन शीतेन आम्राणां सेकः इष्यते—वृक्षायुर्वेदे, Agnipurána). It will be seen that these elaborate recipes are empirical contrivances for supplying the requisite nitrogen compounds, phosphates, etc., these being potentially contained in the mixtures and infusions prescribed.

CHAPTER II.

HINDU IDEAS ON MECHANICS (KINETICS).

Section 1.

ANALYSIS OF MOTION.

In his Bhâṣya[1] on the Vaiśeṣika[1] Aphorisms, written probably in the third or fourth century of the Christian era, if not earlier, Praśastapâda begins the Section on Motion (कर्म्मग्रन्थ) with the definition of *karma* (motion, *lit.* work) as the unconditional cause of conjunction and disjunction, *i.e.* of change of place in a particle (संयोगविभागनिरपेक्षकारणं). He regards *karma* (motion) as instantaneous (क्षणिक) in its simplest form, distinguishing it from *vega* (impressed motion, momentum), which is a persistent tendency, Sanskâra, and implies a series of motions. Accordingly in one and the same particle there can be only one motion (*karma*) at any given moment, since its change of place at that moment is one and definite (एकदा एकस्मिन् द्रव्ये एकमेव कर्म्म वर्त्तते । प्रशस्तपादभाष्य, कर्म्म पदार्थनिरूपणं). The supposition of two (instantaneous) motions in the same particle is superfluous. They may be so opposed as to neutralise each other, in which case the particle would be at rest. If they are not so opposed, and motion (*i.e.* an instantaneous change of place) follows, then, since this change of place is a definite change, one

---

[1] The system of transliteration adopted in Chapters II.–VI. differs from that adopted in Chapter I. and Chapter VII.

K

motion would be sufficient to account for it, and the hypothesis of two motions would be meaningless (अथ अविरुद्धकर्म्मद्वयसमावेशः तदा एकस्मादेव उपपन्नः द्वितीयकल्पनावैयर्थ्यम् —Praśastapâda). One and the same motion can effect only one particle, as the changes of place of different particles must be different (एकं कर्म्म न अनेकत्र वर्त्तते—*Ibid.*).

Now motion is always marked by a certain direction (दिग्विशिष्टकार्य्यारम्भकत्वमस्य विशेषः).

(i) The successive motions of a particle may be in the same direction (rectilinear), *e.g.* (*a*) upward or downward vertical motion, as in throwing upwards or downwards in the case of objects moved by volition directly or indirectly (उत्क्षेपणं, अपक्षेपणं), or (*b*) other forms of rectilinear motion, contraction, dilation (आकुञ्चनं, प्रसारणं); or

(ii) the directions of the successive motions may be different, as in curvilinear motion (यदनियतदिक्प्रदेश- संयोगविभागकारणं तद्गमनं), *e.g.* भ्रमण (rotatory motion), स्पन्दन (vibratory motion), etc. All these are varieties of Gamana (गमन, curvilinear motion). उत्क्षेपणादिशब्दैः अनवरुद्धानां भ्रमणपतनस्यन्दनादीनां अवरोधार्थं गमनग्रहणं कृतम्—*Ibid.*; *cf.* Śankara Miśra, गमनत्वं च जातिविशेषः भ्रमणरेचनस्यन्दनोद्धर्व- ज्वलननमनोन्नमनादिष्वपि. In another sense, all kinds of motion in material (inanimate) objects, whether rectilinear or curvilinear, are called Gamana (गमन).

(एतत् पञ्चविधमपि कर्म्म शरीरावयवेषु च तत् सम्बद्धेषु तत् प्रत्ययं असत्- प्रत्ययं च । यत् अन्यत् अप्रत्ययमेव तेषु अन्येषु च तत् गमनमिति Praśasta- pâda, कर्म्मग्रन्थ) ।

Single particles, then, may have a serial motion. When particles (अवयवाः) combine to form a body (अवयवी), they may move continuously in a straight line, in which case the body is said to move in that direction (अवयविक्रियाया यावदवयवक्रियानियतत्वात्, the action of a composite whole is determined by the action of the constituent parts taken together). But different particles may move in different directions, or again, the particles may have a curvilinear motion, and in such cases it appears as if different motions are impressed on the body, *e.g.* the falling leaf driven by the wind may have a rotatory or vibratory motion (भ्रमण, स्यन्दन) and a vertical downward motion (पतन) at the same time. Here each particle of the leaf taken separately has only one motion or change of place at the same moment, but from the point of view of the observer दृष्टा, the particles have a rotatory or vibratory motion in one relation, and the leaf as a whole has a downward motion in another relation. The motion at any instant is really one, but for convenience of analysis we consider the rotatory change of place as separate from the change of place in the downward direction. एकस्मिन् कर्मणि युगपत् दृष्टृणां भ्रमणपतनप्रवेशनप्रत्यया: कथं भवन्ति । अत्र ब्रुम अवयवावयविनो दिग्विशिष्ट-संयोगविभागानां भेदात्—*Ibid.*

Section 2.

MOTION CONSIDERED IN RELATION TO ITS CAUSES

Various kinds of motion are observed:—

I. Movements which are not caused by contact with matter :—

(1) Movements caused by volition (प्रयत्न), *e.g.* the movement of the hand.

(2) Movement as of a falling body. This is caused

by gravity (गुरुत्व), which in the astronomical treatises of Âryabhata, Brahmagupta, and Bhâskara is ascribed to the attraction (आकर्षण, pulling force) exercised by the earth on a material body. The force of gravity may be counteracted by volition (विधारकप्रयत्न), as in holding up the hand, or by contact, as when a body rests on a support, or by Vega (वेग), impressed motion, as in the flying arrow which is kept from falling by the motion impressed on it.

(3) Motion of fluids, as the downward flow in a stream (स्यन्दन). This is due to fluidity (द्रवत्व), which is a characteristic property of certain kinds of atoms, in some cases original, in others produced by the contact of these atoms with the atomic particles of heat (*e.g.* in the fire). But Śankara Miśra points out that this property, fluidity, is only a concomitant condition (असमवायिकारण); the efficient cause (निमित्तकारण) is even in this case gravity (गुरुत्व) in the particles of the fluid. यत्तूरसंसरणं स्यन्दनं तत् द्रवत्वात् असमवायिकारणात् उत्पद्यते, गुरुत्वात् निमित्तकारणात् असमवायिकारणेषु (Śankara Miśra, Upaskâra, on Sûtra 4, Âhnika 2, Chap. V., of the Vaiśesika Sûtras).

(4) Certain motions, not due to material contact, of which the mechanical causes are unknown, and which may be ascribed to the universal final cause, Adrista (अदृष्ट), *e.g.* the first motion in atoms at the beginning of Creation, the upward motion of fiery particles or atoms, and the oblique motion of gaseous particles, *vâyu* (वायु), the movement of iron towards the magnet, capillary motion (अभिसर्पण) as of liquid particles from the root to the stem of a plant. The upward motions

(आरोहण) of water-particles in evaporation and in boiling do not require the hypothesis of Adriṣṭa, as these are caused by the pressure of heat-corpuscles (तेजः परमाणु) and the contact with air-particles (नोदनापीडनात् संयुक्तसंयोगाच्च—Vaiśeṣika Sûtra, Chap. V., Âhnika 2).

MEANING OF ADRIṢṬA (अदृष्ट).

Adriṣṭa (*lit.* unseen) stands for "unknown cause" or "unexplained Nature" in the earlier Vaiśeṣika writers. Several classes of cases falling under Adriṣṭa are distinguished, *e.g.*—

(1) The operation of merit and demerit (धर्म and अधर्म), a transcendental cause, which has to be posited in explaining the conjunctions and disjunctions of souls with their organic vehicles (bodies), which cannot be ascribed to natural causes, but presuppose the law of Karma, or the operation of moral causation, as superimposed on the natural order.

(2) Various kinds of motion in the different classes of elements, *e.g.* their natural modes of operation, such as the dispersion of *vâyu* (air, gas), the upward motion of fire, the attraction of the needle by the magnet, etc., motions which serve the ends of Creation and of created beings (उपकारकं अपकारकं). Such natural properties must be ascribed to Adriṣṭa, final causality (उपकारापकारसमर्थं अदृष्टकारितं), provided the *cause cannot be ascertained by observation or inference.*

1. लघ्वृत्तिभ्याम् धर्माधर्माभ्याम् कर्मोत्पद्यते—*Ibid.* अपसर्पणकर्म उपसर्पणकर्म, etc.

2. एवमन्यदपि महाभूतेषु यत्प्रत्यक्षानुमानाभ्यामनुपलभ्यमानकारणं उपकारापकारसमर्थं च भवति तदपि अदृष्टकारितं—*Ibid.*

Jayanta in the Nyâya-Manjarî notes that Adriṣṭa is resorted to in explanation of observed phenomena only when these cannot be derived in any way from the operation of known causes—यदि अदृष्टमन्तरेण दृष्टं न सिद्ध्यति काममदृष्टं कल्प्यताम् अन्यथा अपितु तदुपपत्तौ किं तदुपकल्पनेन । दृष्टसिद्धयेहि अदृष्टं कल्प्यत्वे नतु दृष्टविघाताय । न्यायमञ्जरी—Âhnika 1.

Similarly, Jayanta notes that, when anything is put down as natural (स्वाभाविक), we may mean either that it has no cause or no uniform cause, or no known cause. Of these the first two alternatives must always be dismissed; and "natural" can only mean something of which the cause has not yet been ascertained (स्वाभाविकं नाम किमुच्यते किमहेतुकं अविज्ञातहेतुकं अनियतहेतुकं वा । न तावद्धेतुकं कार्यं सम्भवति .... नापि अनियतहेतुकं कार्यं किञ्चिदस्ति - न्यायमञ्जरी - चार्वाकमतनिरास ।)

This sound interpretation of Adriṣṭa was afterwards obscured. In modern writers of the Nyâya-Vaiśeṣika school, physical and mechanical ideas have suffered a set-back, and even the formation of the hail-stone is ascribed to the operation of moral causes (धर्माधर्म्मे).

II. We come now to motions produced by contact (संयोग). Such motions may be classed as follows, according to the nature of the contact originating them:—

(1) Motion due to direct contact with a body exercising continued pressure (नोदन), *e.g.* the motion of an object pushed or pulled by the hand, the motion of the mud under heavy stones, the motion of the arrow due to the pressure exercised by the bow-string, the motion of the bow-string due to the pressure of the elastic bow as it recovers its original shape, the motion of clouds, of volumes of dust, of balloons, sailing vessels and other

vehicles under the impelling force (pressure, नोदन, प्रेरण) of the wind, etc. वायुर्मेघादिप्रेरणधारणादिसमर्थः Praśastapâda, वायुनिरूपण-मेघादीयादिपदेन यानपोतादिपरिग्रहक्षेमामपि वायुना प्रेर्य्यमाणत्वात् । Srîdhara मेघादीति आदिग्रहणात् वैहायसानां विमानादीनां (balloons in the sky) भौमादीनां च पानपात्रपांशुपटलादीनां जलानलयोश्च परिग्रहः (Udayana, Kiraṇâvalî, वायुनिरूपणम्).

N.B.—Udayana makes a similar reference to balloons filled with gas or smoke (धूमापूरितचर्मपुटकं) in discussing the opinion that air has weight (Kiraṇâvalî, वायुनिरूपणम्). These passages show that balloons were known in Udayana's time (970 A.D.—*vide* उदयन, Lakṣaṇâvalî).

(2) Motion due to direct contact for an instant with a body that strikes and produces an impact (अभिघात), *e.g.* in the cases of a stone falling against a hard object (पाषाणादिषु निष्ठुरेवस्तुनि अभिपतितेषु—Srîdhara), the potter's rod striking the wheel, the mortar struck against the pestle. Instantaneous disjunction is necessary to impact. If there is continued contact, the result is pressure (नोदन). In some cases there may be disjunction (*i.e.* a rebound) after continued pressure (यत्र अभिघातकं द्रव्यं भूप्रदेशं अभिहत्य किञ्चिदधो नोत्वा उत्पतति—श्रीधर—न्यायकन्दली).

(3) Motion due to direct contact with an elastic body which exercises a moving force by means of its elasticity (स्थितिस्थापकत्व) in the act of restitution of the original form (यथास्थितं स्थापयति), *e.g.* the motion of the bow-string due to the force exercised by the piece of bamboo (the bent bow). This force of restitution in an elastic body is a kind of *sanskâra*, *i.e.* persistent tendency (धनुःशाखाशृङ्गदन्तास्थिसूत्रवस्त्रादिषु भुग्नसम्वर्तितेषु स्थितिस्थापकत्वकार्यं संलक्ष्यते—प्रशस्तपादभाष्य, bows, twigs, tooth-bones, horn, thread, cloth, etc., are noted as elastic).

(4) Motion due to contact with a body which is itself in contact with another which possesses Vega (impressed motion or momentum) (वेगवद्द्रव्यसंयुक्तसंयोग). This is the fact of the transmission of pressure or moving force, and the consequent production or communication of motion, as, for example, in the pulling of an object by means of a string, the pushing of the potter's wheel by the potter's rod, etc.

Section 3.

CAUSE OF MOTION, OR FORCE.

Force is of the following kinds :—

1. Continued pressure (नोदन).
2. Impact (अभिघात).
3. Persistent tendency (संस्कार), of which there are two kinds : (a) Vega (वेग, impressed motion, momentum), the persistent tendency to motion in a moving body, and (b) the tendency to restitution of shape in an elastic body (स्थितिस्थापकसंस्कार).

N.B.—The psychical *sanskâra* (भावना) is here omitted.

4. Transmitted force, as in pulling by a string, pushing by a rod, etc.
5. Gravity.
6. Fluidity.
7. Volition.
8. Adriṣṭa, comprising various unknown agencies.

In every case of motion produced by contact, Vega is a contributory cause, as the body originating the motion must possess Vega (impressed motion, momentum).

The Concept of Vega (वेगाख्यसंस्कार).

A motion (*karma*) being conceived as a change of place in a particle is held to be incapable of producing another motion; but the pressure, impact, or other force which produces the first motion produces through that motion a *sanskâra* or persistent tendency to motion (Vega), which is the cause of continued motion in a straight line, *i.e.* in the direction of the first motion (नियतदिक्क्रिया प्रबन्धहेतुः यद्दिगाभिमुख्येन क्रियावेगो जन्यते तद्दिगभिमुखतयैव क्रियासन्तानस्य हेतुरिति—श्रीधर, न्याय-कन्दली, संस्कार-निरूपणम्).

The Vaiśeṣikas accept one *sanskâra* (impressed motion, momentum) lasting till the cessation of the motion. Udyotakara and other writers of the Nyâya school suppose a series of *sanskâras*, each generating the one that succeeds it. (संस्कारेण उत्तरोत्तरकर्म्मसन्तानो जायते खजन्योत्तरसंयोगेन कर्म्मणि नष्टे संस्कारेण कर्म्मान्तरजननात् एक एव संस्कारः कर्म्मसन्तानजनकः नतु कर्म्मसन्तानवत् संस्कारसन्तानोऽपि अभ्युपगन्तुमुचितः—शङ्करमिश्र।) It will be seen that the Nyâya view is adequate to explain acceleration, which it logically implies. The force of *sanskâra* (शक्ति) diminishes by doing work (कार्य्यकरणात्) against a counteracting force, and when the *sanskâra* is in this way entirely destroyed, the moving body comes to rest (संस्कारो यावत्पतनमनुवर्त्तते । यथा यथा चास्य कार्य्यंकरणात् शक्तिः क्षीयते तथा तथा कार्य्यमन्दतरतमादि-भेदभिन्नमुपजायते—श्रीधर—न्याय-कन्दली-कर्म्मग्रन्थ). Vega, it will be seen, corresponds to inertia in some respects, and to momentum (impressed motion) in others. This is the nearest approach to Newton's First Law of Motion in the Vaiśeṣika theory of motion.

Vega (impressed motion), or this tendency to move on in a straight line, is counteracted by contact with tangible objects (स्पर्शवद्द्रव्यसंयोग), *e.g.* by impact or friction, including friction with the still atmosphere (स्तिमितवायु), as in the case of the arrow.

Vega (momentum) produces work in opposition to the resisting force, and thereby becomes weaker and weaker (मन्दतर मन्दतम) until it comes to an end (तत्र वेगो मूर्तिमत्सु पञ्चसु द्रव्येषु निमित्तविशेषापेक्षात् कर्म्मणा जायते, नियत-दिक्-क्रिया-प्रबन्धहेतुः स्पर्शवद्द्रव्यसंयोग-विशेषविरोधी Praśastapāda, संस्कार-निरूपणम्—मन्दस्तु वेगः स्पर्शवद्द्रव्यसंयोगमात्रेण विनश्यति यथा अतिदूरगतस्य इषोः स्तिमितवायु-प्रतिवद्धस्य—श्रीधर, संस्कारनिरूपणम्).

Causes of Pressure (नोदन) and of Impact (अभिघात).

Pressure is produced by contact acting in conjunction with Vega (impressed motion), elasticity, gravity, fluidity or volition, *e.g.* the Vega of the wind produces pressure (नोदन) on the grass, that of a current of water on the reed, that of the bow-string on the arrow. Gravity with contact produces pressure, as when the earth sinks under a heavy load.

Impact is produced by contact with a body possessing Vega (impressed motion) where the contact is instantly followed by disjunction (or rebounding). If the contact continues, the result is pressure (नोदन). (तत्र नोदन गुरुत्व-द्रवत्व-वेग-प्रयत्नान् समस्त-व्यस्तान् अपेक्षामानः यः संयोग-विशेषः नोदनं अविभाग-हेतुः एकस्य कर्म्मणः कारणं तस्मात् चतुर्षु अपि महाभूतेषु कर्म्म भवति ...... वेगापेक्षो यः संयोग-विशेषः विभागहेतुः एकस्य कर्म्मणः कारणं स अभिघात तस्मादपि चतुर्षु-महाभूतेषु कर्म्म भवति—प्रशस्तपाद-भाष्य ।)

It is expressly noted that the four elements, earth,

water, air, and fire, are all subject to the forces of pressure and impact. Pressure and impact may be of different degrees (तीव्रमन्दादिभेद). So also Vega (impressed motion, momentum).

Illustrations of Combination of Forces.

(1) Pressure acting concurrently with impressed motion or Vega, as when the moving hand possessing Vega throws the quoit or a projectile. (पाणिमुक्तेषु गमनविधिः) (ततः संस्कारनोदनाभ्यां तावत् कर्माणि भवन्ति यावत् हस्ततोमर-विभाग इति—प्रशस्तपादभाष्य ।)

Similarly, in the case of the bow-string impelling the arrow, or the potter's wheel impelled by the rod, the first motion is due to pressure (नोदन), and results in a *sanskâra* (persistent tendency to motion, impressed motion or momentum), but the subsequent motions are produced by the pressure acting concurrently with the *sanskâra* (impressed motion). (तस्मात् संस्कारात् नोदन-सहायात् तावत् कर्माणि भवन्ति यावत् इषुन्या-विभागः—प्रशस्त-पाद, कर्मग्रन्थ—प्रथमं चक्रावयविनि दण्डसंयोगात् कर्म उत्पद्यते उत्तरोत्तराणि कर्माणि अभिघातात् कर्मजात् संस्कारात् च भवन्ति दण्डविगमे तु चक्रं तदवयवेषु च संस्कारादेव केवलात् । श्रीधर, न्याय-कन्दली, कर्मग्रन्थ ।)

(2) Impact (अभिघात) with impressed motion (संस्कार), as when the mortar thrown by the hand rebounds after striking the pestle (संस्कारापेक्षात् अभिघातात् मुसले उत्पतन-कर्म—प्रशस्तपाद भाष्य).

(3) Pressure (नोदन) acting concurrently with impact (अभिघात), as when the mud sinks when we strike against the ground with the feet. Here, if the feet be not in contact with the mud, but only with the surrounding ground, there is transmitted force (संयुक्तसंयोग).

(पदादिभिर्नुद्यमानायामभिहन्यमानायाम् वा पंकाख्यायां पृथिव्यां यत् संयो-गोनोदनाभिघातयोरन्यतरापेक्षो उभयापेक्षो वा स संयुक्तसंयोग: । तस्मादपि पृथिव्यादिषु कर्म्म भवति ।—Praśastapâda.)

(4) Gravity concurrently with *sanskâra* or persistent tendency, as in the case of a falling body in the second and following instants. Also the case of a stone thrown against the mud, where gravity (the weight of the stone) combines with the Vega of the stone to produce motion in the mud (Praśastapâda). (आद्यं कर्म्म गुरुत्वात् भवति । तेन कर्म्मेणा संस्कार: क्रियते तदनन्तरं उत्तरकर्म्माणि गुरुत्वसंस्काराभ्यां जायते द्वयोरपि प्रत्येकं अन्यत्र सामर्थ्यावधारणात्—श्रीधर, न्याय-कन्दली, कर्म्मेग्रन्थे सप्तप्रतय-कर्म्मनिरूपणम् ।) This case will be further noticed below.

Udyotakara, the commentator on the Nyâya-Bhâsya, states that a heavier body falls to the ground with greater Vega (and velocity) than one that is lighter. Udyotakara also holds, and Śrîdhara agrees with him, that the gravity (गुरुत्व) of a body (अवयवी) as a whole composed of particles (अवयवा:) is not the same as the sum of the gravities of the particles. There is a difference in amount which is, however, so small as to be imperceptible. The concept of mass in the New Mechanics of Lorenz may lend some countenance to this curious metaphysical speculation. (Śrîdhara, गुणग्रन्थ, गुरुत्वनिरूपणम् ।)

(5) Volition acting concurrently with gravity, as in lifting up the hand. This is accompanied by transmission when an object, *e.g.* the quoit, is lifted by the hand.

Sanskâra (impressed motion, momentum), with or without pressure (नोदन) or impact (अभिघात), may be transmitted (दण्डसंयुक्तस्य अवयवस्य उत्तरोत्तरकर्म्माणि संस्कारात् नोदनाच्च अपरेषां संस्कारात् संयुक्तसंयोगाच्च ।—Śrîdhara).

Composition of Gravity with Vega (Momentum).

When a body is let go and falls to the ground, the force acting on it is gravity (गुरुत्व), which the astronomers ascribe to the attraction of the earth. Motion is produced in the first instance by gravity alone, and this leads to a *sanskâra* (impressed motion) in the same direction. But the force of gravity continues to operate, so that, in the moments following the first, the motion is due to gravity as well as *sanskâra*. The resultant motion is one, but both the causes must be conceived as contributing to the resultant. The reason for supposing this combined action is that both gravity and *sanskâra* (impressed motion or momentum) are seen elsewhere to produce motion separately.

In the case of the falling body, therefore, there is the composition of the two, gravity and Vega, acting in the same direction (उभयसमावेशः) from the second instant onwards. It is as if two motions coalesced and resulted in one.

Here a good foundation is laid for the explanation of the accelerated motion of falling bodies, but Galileo's discovery was not anticipated, as Galileo's observations and measurements of motion were wanting. (आद्यं कर्म्मे गुरुत्वात् भवति तेन कर्म्मेणा संस्कारः क्रियते तदनन्तरं उत्तरकर्म्माणि गुरुत्व-संस्काराभ्याम् जायन्ते द्वयोरपि प्रत्येकं अन्यत्र सामर्थ्यावधारणात्—श्रीधर, कर्म्मग्रंथ—तत् आद्यं गुरुत्वात् द्वितीयादीनि तु गुरुत्वसंस्काराभ्याम्.—प्रशस्तपाद, कर्म्मग्रन्थ ।)

But in the case of the flying arrow or other projectile, the impulsive force which produces Vega counteracts the force of gravity; in the end, this Vega is lost through friction with air, and then gravity (गुरुत्व) brings the arrow to the ground. The meaning of this "counter-action" is not clear. Is it intended that the action of gravity is suspended as long as the Vega continues? We have seen that, in the case of a body let fall, Praśastapâda expressly states that gravity (गुरुत्व) and *sanskâra* (Vega, momentum) both act in the second and following instants. Praśastapâda seems to have thought that some *sanskâras* (*e.g.* the Vega of an arrow or other projectile) suspend the action of gravity (गुरुत्वं संयोगप्रयत्न संस्कारविरोधि, Praśastapâda, गुणग्रन्थ । वेगेन प्रतिबन्धात् अपतनं बहिःक्षिप्तस्य शरशलाकादेः निवृत्ते नोदने कर्म्माणि उत्तरोत्तराणि इषु-संस्कारादेवापतनादिति Praśastapâda, कर्म्मग्रन्थ). Other *sanskâras* (*e.g.* in the case of a falling body) coalesce with gravity to produce a single resultant motion. The later commentators (from Śrîdhara downwards) certainly interpret the Vaiśeṣika Sûtras in this sense.

Motion of a Particle in the Case of a Composition of Forces.

Any number of motions or Vegas may be impressed on a particle, but so long as these are in a uniform direction (नियतदिग्विशिष्ट) the resultant motion or Vega is in a straight line, and may be conceived as one (द्वितीयकल्पना-वैयर्थ्यम्, Praśastapâda, कर्म्मग्रन्थ). It is only when we come to Gamana (curvilinear motion) and its causes that the question of composition assumes a real significance. In all such cases, each separate particle has only one Vega (impressed motion) in a definite direction (नियतदिगाभिमुख्य) at any given instant, but the composition of the successive motions and Vegas in the same particle produces the curvilinear motion (गमन), *e.g.* the rotation of each constituent particle of the potter's wheel. The motion of the body (अवयवी, *e.g.* the wheel) results from the combined motions of the particles (अवयवाः). If pressure or impact produces motion in an opposite direction to the Vega already impressed on the body, the original direction would be changed, as is seen in the case of rebounding (उत्पतन) after impact (अभिघात). The mortar rebounding after striking the pestle is a typical instance of such change of direction in Vega or motion. The impressed force, *e.g.* impact (अभिघात), produces a changed motion in a different direction. One view is that the original Vega (momentum) is destroyed before a new motion and a new Vega are produced by the impact. Others hold that the impact does not destroy the original Vega (momentum), but conjointly with it produces the changed motion and, through such motion, a changed Vega in a new direction. (उलूखलमुसलयोरभिघाताख्यः संयोगो-मुसलगतवेगमपेक्षमाणः मुसले उत्पतनकर्म करोति यद्यपि प्राक्तनसंस्कारो विनष्टः तथापि मुसलोलूखलयोः संयोगः पटुकर्मोत्पादकः तस्य संस्कारारम्भ-साचिव्यसमर्थो भवति अथवा प्राक्तन एव पटु संस्कारः अभिघातात् अविनश्यन् अवस्थित इति *et seq.*, Praśastapâda, कर्मैयन्थ ।)

Typical Cases of Curvilinear Motion (Gamana).

Vortical Motion.—This is due to the contact of two bodies moving in opposite directions with a like or equal Vega, *e.g.* two currents of air or water meeting from opposite directions. The change of direction is seen in the fact that water which flows downwards, or air which moves obliquely, may receive an upward motion as the result of such collision. (अथ किमिदं संमूर्च्छनं नाम । समानजवयोः (तुल्यवेगयोः) वाय्वोर्विरुद्ध-दिक्क्रिययोः सन्निपातः Praśastapâda, वायुनिरूपणं). The scholiast Udayana adds: वाय्वोरितिप्रकृतत्वेन स्पर्शवतोरिति तु विवक्षितम् । अपां यथा द्रव्यान्तर-संमूर्च्छनात् ऊर्ध्वगमनं परस्पराभिहतनदीपयः — उदयन, द्रव्यकिरणावली. Sridhara notes : तिर्यग्गतिस्वभाव-द्रव्यौर्ध्वगतित्वात् परस्पराभिहत-ऊर्ध्वतरङ्गौर्ध्वगमनवत् असमानवेगयोः संमूर्च्छनं न भवति एकेन अपरस्य विजयात् —Sridhara.)

Vibratory Motion (कम्पन, स्पन्दन).

This will be analysed in the chapter on Acoustics.

Rotatary Motion (भ्रमण).

Each particle of the rotating body, *e.g.* the potter's wheel (चक्र), has, at any given instant, a motion in a definite direction. The rotatory motion of the body results from the separate motions of the particles and their persistent tendencies (संस्काराः), joined with the fact of the rigid conjunction of the particles. When the rod strikes one part of the wheel, the motion in the part struck is in the first instant produced by impact (अभिघात); while the other parts move through the transmission of force due to the rigid cohesion of parts. The subsequent motions in the part struck are due to continued pressure (नोदन) and the persistent tendency (संस्कार) set up by the first motion; while the subsequent motions in the other parts are explained by their own persistent tendencies and the transmission due to rigid cohesion. When the rod is disjoined from the wheel the rotatory motion continues, being due merely to the persistent tendencies in the constituent parts and the resultant persistent tendency in the whole.

Other varieties of curvilinear motion in bodies are to be similarly explained (*i.e.* by the composition of Vegas) (तथा चक्रादिषु अवयवानाम् पार्श्वतः प्रतिनियतदिग्देशसंयोगविभा- गोत्पत्तौ यदवयविनः संस्कारादनियतदिग्देशसंयोगविभागनिमित्तं कर्म्म तद्- भ्रमणमिति । एवमादयो गमनविशेषाः—Praśastapâda,—कर्म्मग्रन्थ । एवं वेगात् दृढसंयोगचक्रावयवे आद्यं कर्म्म दृढसंयोगात् । अवयवान्तरेषु च संयुक्तसंयोगात् दृढसंयुक्तस्य अवयवस्य उत्तरोत्तरकर्म्माणि संस्कारात् नोदनात् च । अपरेषां संस्कारात् संयुक्तसंयोगात् च दृढविगमेतु चक्रे तदवयवेषु च संस्कारादेव केवलात् एवमादयो गमनविशेषाः—Śrîdhara).

Section 4.

MOTION OF FLUIDS.

Current motion (स्यन्दन, downward flow in a stream), upward motion (आरोहण, *e.g.* evaporation, boiling, etc.), and capillary motion (अभिसर्पण, as in plants and porous vessels) are three varieties of fluid motion which require explanation. To this may be added vortical motion (संमूर्च्छन), and स्यन्दन, wave motion, which will be noticed in the chapter on Acoustics.

1. Current Motion (स्यन्दन).

This is conditioned by fluidity in particles, but Śankara Miśra notes that in the downward flow of water, gravity in the fluid-particles is the efficient cause (गुरुत्वात् निमित्तकारणात् असमवायिकारणेषु—Śankara Miśra, उपस्कार). When the water is enclosed on all sides, as in a vessel, the downward flow (स्यन्दन) is counteracted. Here the fluidity does not produce motion, because, in the case of the particles in contact with the enclosing

L

body, there is the resistance (प्रतिबन्ध) of the latter, which is transmitted to the other particles, and this counteracts the fluidity. (श्रोतोभूतानामपां स्थलान्निस्साभिसर्पणं यत् तत् द्रवत्वात् स्यन्दनं कथं समन्तात् रोधः संयोगेन अवयविद्रवत्वम् प्रतिबद्धं उत्तरोत्तरावयवद्रवत्वानि संयुक्तसंयोगैः प्रतिबद्धानि—Praśastapāda, कर्म्मग्रन्थ ।)

2. Upward Motion (आरोहण, *e.g.* evaporation).

In evaporation the fluid-particles are rarefied, and remain in a fine state of suspension; the rarefaction is due to the impulse (नोदन) or impact (अभिघात) of the heat-particles in the sun's rays, and the upward movement is due to their contact with the air under this impulse or impact. Śankara Miśra notes that in boiling there is a similar upward movement of water-particles under the impact of heat-rays. (नाड्यो वायुसंयोगात् आरोहणं नोदनापीडनात् संयुक्तसंयोगात् च। Sûtras 5 and 6, Âhnika 2, Chap. 5, Vaiśeṣika Aphorism. यथा स्थाल्यिस्था आपः क्वथ्यमानाः वायुनुन्नवह्नि-रश्मय ऊर्द्ध्वं नयन्ति—Śankara Miśra, उपस्कार ।)

N.B.—These two Sûtras of Kanâda have been interpreted by the late Gangâdhara Kaviratna in his commentary to refer to the upward conduction of water in pipes by the pressure of air.

The mention of the transmitted pressure (संयुक्तसंयोग) of the air seems to lend some countenance to Gangâdhara's view, and the word Nâḍi (नाड्यः) offers no difficulty, being taken in its usual sense, "pipe" (नालिका, Nalikâ), while the current interpretation does violence to the common acceptation of the word.

3. Capillary Motion (अभिसर्पण).

Two instances are given—the ascent of the sap in plants from the root to the stem (अभितः सर्पणं मूले निषिक्ता-

नामपां वृक्षे—Śankara Miśra), and the penetrative diffusion of liquids in porous vessels, *e.g.* of the oil or ghee in an earthen jar (कुम्भादौ अन्तर्निहितानां तैलघृतादीनां स्यन्दनं अपनच). Heat-particles have a like penetrative power (दृष्टश्चानिरोधो भज्जनकपालादौ तेजसः पच्यमानद्रव्यपाकसिद्धेः कलशे च निषिक्तानां अपां शीतस्पर्शीग्रहणादनिरोधः—Jayanta, न्यायमञ्जरी, Âhnika 8, इन्द्रियाणां प्राप्यकारित्वम्).

This is ascribed to *adriṣṭa*, as the cause cannot be ascertained by either perception or inference (including hypothesis) (प्रत्यक्षानुमानाभ्यां अनुपलभ्यमानकारणम्—Śrîdhara).

SECTION 5.
INTERESTING EXAMPLES OF MOTION ASCRIBED TO ADRIṢṬA (UNKNOWN CAUSE, UNEXPLAINED NATURE, FINAL CAUSE).

The first motions in primordial atoms at the beginning of Creation are attributed to *adriṣṭa*. Among movements in masses of matter so caused are noted the motion of the globe of the earth and similar other bodies (महाभूतानां भूगोलकादीनां प्रक्षोभनं चलनम्—Praśastapâda with Śrîdhara's commentary, कर्मग्रन्थ). Most probably this means earthquakes, tides, etc. Âryabhata and his school would no doubt bring under this head the diurnal motion of the earth. It is interesting to note in this connection that Bhâskara refutes the Buddhist hypothesis of the earth falling perpetually *in vacuo* by arguing that the earth must remain balanced in space as there is nothing outside to attract it.

The movement of the needle (iron in general, as Śankara Miśra notes) towards the magnet is another example of unexplained motion in matter. Cleaning and right-placing of the magnet (संमार्जनम्, ऋजुस्थापनम्) are necessary (सूचीनां लौहशलाकानां, अयस्कान्ताभिमुखगमनम्, सूचीत्युपलक्षणम् अयस्कानाकृष्टलोहमाचमभिप्रेतम्—Śankara Miśra).

Similarly, amber attracts grass, straw, etc. (तृणकान्तम्-ख्याकृष्टानां तृणानां गमने—Śankara Miśra, on Sûtra 15, Âhnika 1, Chap. V.).

Involuntary movements of the hand under the influence of the hypnotist's *mantras* (incantations) are also attributed to *adriṣṭa*.

Section 6.

MEASUREMENT OF MOTION.—UNITS OF SPACE AND TIME.

The solar day was taken as a natural measure or division of time. In the Nyâya-Vaiśeṣika school the day of twenty-four hours (solar) is stated to contain $30 \times 30 \times 30 \times 18 \times 2 \times 2$ units of time (*kṣaṇas*). The Nyâya unit of time therefore measures $\frac{2}{45}$ of a second. The smallest measure of time mentioned by the astronomers is the Truti, which is $\frac{1}{33750}$ of a second.

The natural measure of length was the cubit (Hasta), of which there were two fixed standards, the greater and the lesser cubit. The smallest measure of length mentioned in the Śilpa-śâstra (Technology) is the Paramânu, which is about $\frac{1}{349525}$ of an inch. This is the same as the Trasareṇu of the Nyâya-Vaiśeṣika school, which stands for the thickness of the *minimum visibile* (the finest mote perceptible in the sunbeam as it comes slanting into a dark room through a chink).

Average velocity (स्थूलगति—Bhâskara) was measured in accordance with the formula $v = \frac{s}{t}$, but no unit of velocity appears to have been fixed upon. There was no idea of acceleration, and of course no measurement of force. Mahavîrâchâryya gives formulæ for computing the space travelled over in cases of Sankalita-gati (velocity with regular increment at stated intervals), but this does not amount to acceleration, as the intervals are not indefinitely small. Where the velocity is uniform, the interval of time may be of any amount (स्थूलकाल), but where the velocity is variable (प्रतिक्षणं न समागति:—Bhâskara), an indefinitely small quantity of time (सूक्ष्मकाल) must be taken; in other words, the positions of the particle in two successive *instants* must be considered, and the velocity must be supposed to be uniform during this interval (conceived as indefinitely small, सूक्ष्म). It was in this way that Bhâskara determined the instantaneous motion of a planet (तात्कालिकी गति).

Component of Velocity.

The astronomers measured the motion of a heavenly body in different directions (longitude, right ascension, etc.), and calculated separately the components of motion (गतिकला:) in these directions, and they adopted the device of transferring such component velocities from one body to another in the computation of relative motion (*e.g.* एवं सति आचार्येण लाघवार्थं इष्टघटीसम्बन्धिनो गतिकला अर्के प्रक्षिप्ता:—Bhâskara, Siddhânta-Śiromaṇi, Gaṇitâdhyâya, Ghatîsphutî-prakaraṇa).

Section 7.
NOTION OF THREE AXES.

Motion, we have seen, was defined as the change of position of a particle in space. To conceive position in space, Vâchaspati takes three axes, and the position in space of one particle relatively to another may be indicated by distances measured along these three axes. This remarkable analysis (*circa* 842 A.D. : वस्वङ्गवसुवत्सरे, Vâchaspati, Nyâyasûchînibandha) anticipates in a rudimentary manner the foundations of solid (co-ordinate) geometry, eight centuries before Descartes (*vide* p. 118, *supra*).

The Principle of the Differential Calculus applied to the Computation of Motion (Variable Motion).

Bhâskara (1150 A.D.), in computing what he calls the "instantaneous" motion (तात्कालिकी गति) of a planet, compares its successive positions in two successive instants, and regards the motion as constant during the interval, which he conceives to be indefinitely small (सूक्ष्मकाल). This is equivalent to the determination of the differential of the planet's longitude, and the process bears "a strong analogy" (to quote the words of Mr. Spottiswoode, the Astronomer Royal) "to the corresponding process in modern mathematical astronomy." I have elsewhere shown that Bhâskara's process was not merely analogous to, but virtually identical with, that of the Differential Calculus, Mr. Spottiswoode's cautious reservation having been due to his want of acquaintance with the original and the insufficiency of the materials placed before him (*vide* pp. 78-79 *supra*).

Section 8.

RELATIVE MOTION.

The phenomenon is noticed among the hallucinations of sense (नाव्यारूढाइव गच्छतः पर्वतादीनि विजानन्ति भ्रमेण भ्रमतश्च तान् —Kumârila, Śloka-Vârtika, p. 520). Astronomers like Âryabhata and Lalla, who believed in the diurnal revolution of the earth from the west to the east, explained the apparent revolution of the starry heavens in the opposite direction by the principle of relative motion.

Section 9.

SERIAL MOTION.

Several Santânas (series) of motions are incidentally noticed, *e.g.* vibration (स्पन्दन, कम्पसन्तान), wave motion (वीचितरङ्ग), current motion (स्पन्दन).

In an interesting passage, Charaka notes three instances of serial motion, viz. those of water, sound, and light (जलसन्तान, शब्दसन्तान and अर्चिःसन्तान), to which he compares the course (सन्तान) of chyle (or chyle-blood) in the Dhamanîs (veins) and other ducts of the body.

Dalvana thinks that downward, oblique, and upward currents of chyle are respectively intended by the three illustrations; but Chakrapâṇi points out that the Santâna (wave) of sound travels in all directions (the same is of course true also of light), and that differences in speed (and not in direction) are here meant. In other words, a Santâna of sound travels more rapidly than that of water, and less rapidly than one of light (अर्चिःसन्तान), and Charaka's meaning is that the metabolic course may complete its circuit with greater or less speed. Whether, in this passage, the three Santânas are viewed as waves or currents, is not specified; but the difference between a wave (वीचि) and a current (स्यन्दन) was well known.

A current of water (स्यन्दन, downward flow) consists of particles moving in an uninterrupted series under the action of gravity and fluidity (गुरुत्व and द्रवत्व, Śankara Miśra). A wave (वीचितरङ्ग), on the other hand, is constituted by the transmission of vibratory motion (स्यन्दन) in the water-particles (*e.g.* Jayanta, पतदूघनप-योविन्दुसन्दोहस्यन्दनक्रमात्—Nyâya-Manjarî, Âhnika 2).

A ray of light, on the other hand, was supposed to imply the rectilinear propagation of indefinitely minute corpuscles in all directions, with inconceivable velocity, and a sort of conical dispersion (अचिन्त्यौहि वेगातिशयः तेज: प्रसर्पति पृथग्यत्नात्—Udyotakara, Vâchaspati).

CHAPTER III.

HINDU IDEAS ON ACOUSTICS.

SECTION 1.

ANALYSIS OF SOUND.

The Mimâmsakas.—In their analysis of Sound, the Mimâmsakas distinguish between three elements: (1) Nâda, a quality of Vâyu (air), which is the physical basis of audible sound; (2) Dhvani, sound as heard, audible sound; and (3) in the case of significant sound, Sphota, "transcendental" or "intelligible" sound, representing the Platonic ideas or *logoi*, which are eternal (नित्य,) ubiquitous (व्यापक), and noumenal (निराधार, *lit.*, without substrate or ground—Kumârila). The Sphotas are manifested by the Dhvanis (audible sounds), of course only in the case of words (शब्द, संज्ञा). Upavarṣa, the teacher of Panini, rejected the Sphotas in favour of the Varnas, which were conceived to be "phonetic moulds" with natural significance.

As regards sound in its physical aspect and the mode of its propagation, some of the Mimâmsakas content themselves with saying that Vâyu (air) has a special quality (Nâda) which causes audible sound (नादो वायुगुणः वायुर्वा यदि कल्प्येत—Kumârila, Śloka-Vârtika; वायुरेव ताल्वादिस्थानसंयोगात् शब्दगुणको निष्पद्यते, शब्दस्यापि वायुगुणत्वं वेदितव्यम्— Pârtha-Sârathi Miśra, Nyâyaratnâkara).

Others, including the teachers of the Śikṣā (Vedic chanting), hold that the physical basis of sound is a series of air movements (वायुसन्तान, *cf.* Udyotakara's and Vâchaspati's reports); in other words, the air-particles themselves flow in a current in all directions, being obstructed in their path by the impact of tangible objects (*i.e.* material bodies), and the movement ceases, as in the arrow, when the moving force is thus exhausted (*e.g.* स गच्छन्सर्वतोदिक्षु उद्दामवेगाहितक्रियः शरवत् वेगशान्त्येव न दूरं गन्तुमर्हति ... शिक्षाविदस्तु पवनात्मकमेव शब्दमाचक्षते —Jayanta, Nyâya-Manjarî). But the orthodox Mimâmsâ view is that of the Mimâmsâ doctor, Śabara Svâmi, who holds that Nâda (the physical basis of sound) is a wave-motion of air, being the transmission of conjunctions and disjunctions in the minute particles of air, the wave originating in the first impact, and being continued by the successive impacts of the minute particles (*e.g.* संयोगविभागानैरन्तर्येण क्रियमाणाः शब्दमभिव्यञ्जन्तो नादशब्दवाच्याः (17-1-1) अभिघातेन हि प्रेरिता वायवः स्तिमितानि वायवन्तराणि प्रतिघ्नन्तः सर्वतो दिक्षु संयोगविभागान् उत्पादयन्ति यावद्वेगं अभिप्रतिष्ठन्ते । ते च वायोरप्रत्यक्षत्वात् संयोगविभागा नोपलभ्यन्ते । अनुपरतेषु एव तेषु शब्द उपलभ्यते । नोपरतेषु अतएव च अनुवातं दूरात् उपलभ्यते शब्दः—Śabara-Bhâṣya, Sûtra 13, Pâda 1, Adhyâya 1). In this view, the particles of air (वायवयवाः) are subject to a vibratory motion (a sort of *parispanda*) in the production of sound (परिस्पन्दवल्लक्षण —Jayanta, Nyâya-Manjarî). The Vâkyapadiya describes articulate sounds (*varnas*), and indeed all sounds (*sabdas*), as only forms of air set in motion, with rare-faction and condensation (प्रचय), and capable of variations of velocity and configuration (लब्धक्रियः प्रयत्नेन वक्रुरिच्छानु-

वह्निना स्थानेभ्यभिहतो वायुः शब्दत्वं प्रतिपद्यते । तस्य कारणसामर्थ्यात् वेगप्रचयधर्मिण: संनिपातात् विभज्यन्ते सारवत्योऽपि मूर्त्तय: । Vâkya-padîya, Kânda 1, Śloka 109).

Nyâya-Vaiśeṣika.—The early Nyâya writers hold that the sound-wave (शब्दसन्तान) has its substrate in Âkâśa (ether) and not Vâyu (air). Later writers (*e.g.* Vâchaspati in the Tattvavindu) add that sound itself as a phenomenon is not to be conceived as a mode of motion (*parispanda*), for Âkâśa, the substrate, is, in the Nyâya view, incapable of motion (न तावत् परिस्पन्दस्य मूर्त्तत्वनुविधायिनो द्रव्ये विभुनि विभुगुणे वा शब्दे मूर्त्तभावेनासंभवात्— Tattvavindu). At the same time the propagation of sound must be conceived on the analogy of waves in water (वीचितरङ्गन्याय). Udyotakara in the Vârtika, Vâchaspati in the Tâtparyyatîkâ, and Jayanta in the Nyâya-Manjarî controvert the three views current in the Mimâmsâ school—(1) that Nâda, the physical basis of audible sound, is a specific quality of Vâyu (air), (2) that sound, in its physical aspect, is constituted by a series of air movements of the nature of a current (वायुसन्तान), and (3) that it is not air-currents but air-waves, series of conjunctions and disjunctions of the air-particles or molecules (वार्ववयवा:, वायुपरमाणव:), that constitute the Nâda, the sound physical, to which, in the case of significant sounds, the Mimâmsakas assign the function of manifesting the Sphota, "transcendental" or "intelligible" sound (*logos*, the word). *Vide* Udyotakara Vârtika, Adhyâya 2, Âhnika 2, Sûtra 14; also Tâtparyyatîkâ, माभूत् वायुसन्तानो मा च भूतत्तद्गुणो नाद: शब्दस्य व्यञ्जक: वायवीयास्तु संयोगविभागव्यञ्जका भवन्ति इत्यत्राह, etc., *loc. cit.* Against these views the early Nyâya doctors maintain that sound is a specific quality of Âkâśa (ether) and not of Vâyu (air). At the same time they admit that the impact which originates the sound phenomenon (अव्याप्यवृत्ति अयावद्द्रव्यभावि विशेषगुण) in Âkâśa does so by setting up a vibration in the molecules of the object struck (*e.g.* a bell), and that these vibrating molecules impinge against the air-molecules in contact (वायुपरमाणवः, आध्यात्मिकवायुः). In other words, though Âkâśa is the substrate (आश्रय), the efficient cause of sound (निमित्तकारण) is to be found in the mechanical impact (अभिघात) of vibrating molecules of sonorous bodies against contiguous molecules of air. As to the propagation of sound, the early Nyâya-Vaiśeṣika writers content themselves with stating that the first sound thus produced in the substrate Âkâśa by the impact of the vibrating molecules (*e.g.* of a bell) against the contiguous molecules of air, produces a second sound in the contiguous Âkâśa, and the second sound a third, and so on, in the same way as waves are generated in water, until the last sound sets up a vibration in the ear-drum (कर्णशष्कुलि). Of course, this propagation of sound-wave in Âkâśa (ether) is effected by means of the air-wave as its vehicle. This is the Nyâya-Vaiśeṣika hypothesis (कल्पना) of an independent sound-wave (शब्द-सन्तान). Âkâśa (ether) is motionless, but the air-wave would not be transmitted if the air-molecules were not interconnected by Âkâśa. Praśastapâda, the Vaiśeṣika doctor, for example, describes the first sound as giving off a second, the second a third, and so on, expanding in Âkâśa, in the same way as waves are supposed to propagate themselves in the ocean.

शब्दोऽम्बरगुणः संयोगविभागशब्दजः . . . . स्थानवायुसंयोगापेक्षमानात्
स्थानाकाशसंयोगात् वर्णोत्पत्तिः । अवघट्टलक्ष्योऽपि भेरीदण्डसंयोगापेक्षात्
भेर्याकाशसंयोगात् उत्पद्यते । वेणुपर्वविभागात् वेण्वाकाशविभागाच्च शब्दाच्च
शब्दाच्च संयोगविभागनिष्पन्नात् वीचिसन्तानवत् शब्दसन्तान इत्येकं सन्तानेन
श्रोत्रप्रदेशमागतस्य ग्रहणम्। Praśastapâda, यथा जलवीच्या तदव्यवहिते
देशे वीच्यन्तरमुपजायते ततोऽन्यत् ततोऽप्यन्यदित्यनेन क्रमेण वीचिसन्तानो
भवति तथा क्रमेण शब्दसन्तानो भवति । नन्वेषा कल्पना कुतः सिद्धेतीयाह
etc. (Śrîdhara, *ibid.*). On this hypothesis the locus of
the sound at any moment forms a circle in Âkâśa, and
the propagation is carried on in the air by means of
ever-expanding circles, as in the case of waves in water.
But this analogy is rejected by some (*e.g.* Udyotakara),
who hold that the first sound gives off not one sound
in a circle, but an indefinite number of sounds in all
directions, and each of these again gives off another,
and so on, so that sound may be said to expand by
successive concentric spherical layers, even as the
Kadambakoraka (the so-called bud of the *Nauclea
Kadamba*) expands by successive concentric spherical
layers of filaments which shoot forth from one another.
On the first of these two hypotheses, the air-wave
implied in the transmission of sound is of the nature of
what we call transverse waves ; on the second, of the
nature apparently of longitudinal waves. In any case, it
is clear that the orthodox Mimâmsa view of Śabara Svâmi,
that the air-wave constituting physical sound means
a series of mere conjunctions and disjunctions of air-
particles with rarefaction and condensation (*e.g.*, सर्वतोदिक्षान्-
संयोगविभागानैरन्तर्येण, Śabara, प्रचय, Vâkyapadîya), implies
longitudinal waves, वीचितरङ्गन्यायेन तदुत्पत्तिस्तु कीर्तिता कदम्बकोरक
न्यायादुत्पत्तिः कस्यचिन्मते (Viśvanâtha, Bhâshâ Parichheda,

Śloka 165); परिश्रेषान्तु सन्तानसिद्धिः । तन्नाद्यः शब्दः संयोग-विभाग-हेतुकः । तस्मात् शब्दान्तराणि कदम्बगोलकन्यायेन सर्वदिक्षाणि । तेभ्यः प्रत्येकमेकैकः शब्दः मन्दतरतमादिभावेनाश्रयाप्रतिबन्धमनुविधीयमानः प्रादुरस्ति । ततोऽन्यस्यातिमान्द्यात् शब्दान्तरोत्पत्तिः—शक्तिविघातो येन केनचित् प्रतिबन्धात् भवति (Udyotakara, II., 2, 14). As the momentum of the impact series (which constitutes the efficient cause of the sound-wave) grows feebler and feebler in the course of transmission through the air-particles, the sound at last dies away. Gangeśa, in the Chintâmaṇi, holds that the propagation is not from molecule to molecule, but travels in ever-expanding circles as in water-waves, perhaps in spherical layers by compression of masses of air; and these air-waves, the vehicles of sound, are exceedingly swift. This explains the velocity of sound. शब्देन च अव्यवहितपरमाणुदेशोत्पादक्रमेण न शब्दारम्भो येन मेघजादि शब्दानां भूलोकप्राप्तिर्युगान्तरेऽपि न स्यात् । किन्तु मेघाद्यभिहतं सर्वतोगामि-महावायोर्महति देशे संयोग-निमित्तमासाद्य आद्यशब्देन सर्व दिग्वतशब्दः एक एव जन्यते उत्तरोत्तरेणापि अधिकाधिकदेशतः सर्वत्र एकैक एव शब्दः वीचितरङ्गवदुपपद्यते वायोश्च नयनवत् महावेगतया शीघ्रगामित्वेन अग्रिमशब्दारम्भात् आद्यशब्दानन्तरं अचिरेणैव शब्दोपलम्भः । वायोरेव च मन्दतरतमादिक्रमेण मन्दादिशब्दोत्पत्तिः यथा आद्य शब्देन कदम्बगोलकवत् दशदिशि दशशब्दा आरभ्यन्ते तैश्च दशशब्द सन्ताना इति (Gangeśa, Tattva Chintâmaṇi).

But how does the first sound produce the second, the second the third, and so on? At every step the efficient cause, the impact of some vibrating molecule against a contiguous molecule of air, must be posited, and this is equally applicable to a sound produced by a sound (शब्दजशब्द) as to one produced by conjunction and disjunction (संयोगज or विभागज). In other words, the sound-wave (शब्दसन्तान) in Âkâśa necessarily implies an air-wave. The Mimâmsaka view, then, that explains the propagation of sound by the transmission of the original oscillatory motion through the successive layers of air by means of successive impacts or pressures producing conjunction and disjunction of air-molecules (वायवीयाः संयोगविभागाः—Śabarabhâṣya), or rarefaction and condensation (प्रचय—Vâkyapadîya), is also implied in the Nyâya-Vaiśeṣika doctrine of the sound-wave (शब्दसन्तान), the difference being that in the latter the air-wave, which is conceived as a mode of serial motion (गति-सन्तान), is only the vehicle or medium of propagation of a so-called sound-wave in Âkâśa, which is not itself a mode of motion. This is what we find expressly and elaborately formulated in the later Nyâya-Vaiśeṣika (*vide* Gangeśa, Chintâmaṇi, *supra*).

Section 2.

ANALYSIS OF VIBRATORY MOTION, *e.g.* OF A BELL (IN AIR).

The molecules of a bell vibrate when the bell is struck. The question is—what is the nature of this vibratory movement? Vâtsyâyana and Udyotakara answer that, when the hand strikes the bell, some of the molecules are displaced (from their stable position—*i.e.* there is *karma* in the molecules), and thus a Sanskâra (here a kinetic Sanskâra, momentum) is generated (संस्कार, कम्पसन्तानसंस्कार—Vâtsyâyana and Vâchaspati), and the molecules swing forward under the action of this Sanskâra until they strike the contiguous molecules of air. This now is a case of mutual impact, which divides the momentum between the colliding masses, and the bell-molecules begin to swing backward, the motion continuing under the action of the diminished Sànskâra until they come in collision again with other air-molecules; and then the process is repeated, and the bell-molecules begin to swing forward and backward until the original energy which is parted with in some measure at each impact becomes so feeble as to be unable to produce any kinetic disturbance (कर्मे). Similarly, the air-molecules themselves are set vibrating by means of these impacts, and the transmission of the motion would form the wave of air, which the later Nyâya-Vaiśesika expressly posit as the vehicle of the sound-wave. But Udyotakara never conceived vibration *in vacuo*, nor does it appear if he meant to include the second species of Sanskâra (elasticity, Sthitisthâpaka-sanskâra) as converted from its potential state (अतीन्द्रियता) into kinetic energy, and thus contributing to the momentum (*vega*). He uses the generic term Sanskâra, which comprehends elasticity as well as momentum due to impressed force. His commentator, Vâchaspati, does not go into details, and does not analyse the momentum. Later writers, however, expressly state that elasticity (Sthitisthâpaka-sanskâra) is one of the causes of vibration, and that elasticity resides not only in the element of earth, but also in air, water, and *tejas* (*cf.* Viśvanâtha).

घण्टायामभिहन्यमानायां तारस्तारतरो मन्दी मन्दतर इति श्रुतिभेदान्वाना-शब्दसन्तानोहि अविच्छेदेन श्रूयते (Vâtsyâyana, II., 2, 3, 6) पाणिसंश्लेष-मपेक्षमाणात्कर्म्मण: पाणि-घण्टासंश्लेषात् पाणिगतवेगापेक्षात् घण्टायां कर्म्म तत्कर्म्मे पाण्यभिघातमपेक्षमाणं विभागसमकालं संस्कारं करोति । सा चलन्याध्यात्मिकं वायुमुपगृह्णाति सा च वायुनाभिहता पुन: कर्म्मे करोति ।

ततः कर्म्मणः संस्कारः संस्कारेण पुनः कर्म्मे पुनर्वायूपग्रह इत्येवमादिन्यायेन संस्कार उत्पद्यते । तत्र अन्यस्यातिमान्द्यात्पटहायां महाभूतक्षोभशक्तेरभावः ततो वायुपग्रहोच्छेदः ततःसंस्कारक्षय इति (1) Udyotakara Vârtika, Adhyâya 2, Âhnika 2, Sûtra 36. (यटातद्वयवसंयुक्ता वायुपरमाणव एव आध्यात्मिको वायुः—Vâchaspati, Tâtparyyatîkâ, loc. cit., also संस्कारं वेगाख्यं करोति). But cf. Visvanâtha, संस्कारभेदो वेगोऽथ स्थितिस्थापकभावने । मूर्तमात्रेतु वेगः स्यात् कर्म्मजो वेगजः क्वचित् । स्थितिस्थापकसंस्कारः क्षितौ केचिच्चतुर्ष्वपि । अतोन्द्रियोऽसौविज्ञेयः क्वचित् स्पन्देऽपि कारणम्—Bhâshâ-parichchheda, Slokas 157–159.

As the air-wave forms the vehicle of the sound-wave, if it does not constitute the sound-wave itself, the favourable or retarding influence of currents of wind is easily explained. The presence or absence of water (and other intervening objects) offering greater or less resistance to the transmission of the wave-motion also easily accounts for the greater or less distance to which the sound is carried.

Section 3.
ECHO.

प्रतिध्वनि (Echo) was supposed to be a reflection of sound. Some consider it to be an after-sound, a sound generated by sound. Others suppose it to be due to the reflection of sound in the same way as an image in water or in a mirror (प्रतिबिम्ब) is due to the reflection of light. There is an element of hallucination in either case (बुद्धिपरिणामविशेषः)—the image in water is not a real image, neither is the echo the real sound it is taken to be. (रूपवच्चं च न सामान्यतः प्रतिबिम्बप्रयोजकं शब्दस्यापि प्रतिध्वनिरूपप्रतिबिम्ब

दर्शनात् । न च शब्दजन्यशब्दान्तरमेव प्रतिध्वनिरिति वाच्यं स्फटिकलौहित्या-
तेरपि जपासन्निकर्षजन्यतापस्या प्रतिबिम्बमिव्यात्सिद्धान्तक्षतेरिति । प्रतिबिम्बश्च
बुद्धेरेव परिणामविशेषो बिम्बाकारो जलादिगत इति मन्तव्यम् ।—Vijnâna-
bhikṣu, Pravachana-Bhâṣya, Chap. I., Sutra 87.)

Section 4.
PITCH, INTENSITY, AND TIMBRE.

Sounds differ from one another by their pitch
(तारमन्दादिभेद), by their intensity (तीव्रमन्दादिभेद), and by
their quality or timbre (असाधारण धर्मे). When a bell is
struck, an indefinite number of notes (श्रुतिभेद, tones and
overtones) are emitted, of varying pitches; and the
notes die away, becoming less and less intense. Now,
we know that the molecules swing to and fro, and that
the Sanskâra (momentum, *vega*) of the vibrations
(कम्पसन्तानसंस्कार) grows feebler and feebler. The differences in pitch (tones and overtones) as well as in intensity must be due to variations in the Sanskâras of the
vibrations. The distinguishable pitches (called Srutis,
श्रुतिभेद) as well as the degrees of intensity (तीव्रमन्दादि)
must be ascribed to variations in the *vega* (momentum), and, by implication, the frequency, etc., of the
vibrations.

Cf. Vâtsyâyana, II., 2, 36—घटास्यं सन्तानवृत्तिसंस्कारभूतं
पटुमन्दमिति वर्तते तस्यानुवृत्या शब्दसन्तानानुवृत्तिः पटुमन्दभावाच्च
तीव्रमन्दता शब्दस्य तत्कृतश्च श्रुतिभेदः *Vide* also Udyotakara's
analysis of vibration based on Vâtsyâyana: घटायाम्-
भिहन्यमानायां तारतारतरो मन्दोमन्दतर इति श्रुतिभेदान्नानाशब्दसन्तानो हि
अविच्छेदेन श्रुयते । सन्तानवृत्तित्वात् मन्दतरमन्दतमादिभिरूपानुविधायिनं
शब्दमुत्पादयन्ति तच्च कारणं संस्कारः—Udyotakara, Vârtika,

Adhyâya 2, Âhnika 2, Sûtra 36. सन्तानवृद्धिना कारणेन
श्रुतिभेदोत्पत्ति:—Vâchaspati, Tâtparyyatîkâ, *loc. cit.*

Sounds also differ from one another in volume or massiveness in the case of coalescence (समानजातीयोपचय). A sound both loud and massive is called महान् (large)— एवं शब्दसन्तान एव तार: महान् इत्युच्यते तत्राप्यस्ति समानजातीयोपचय: अस्ति व स्फुटतरत्वम् महानपि स्फुटतर: । अयमपि तथा इति महानित्युच्यते—Vâchaspati, II., 2, 36.

Śabara, the Mimâmsâ doctor, explains massiveness (महत्त्व) as due to नादवृद्धि, the coalescence of different air-waves, which by their simultaneous impact affect a comparatively large tract of the ear-drum (यच्चैतत् बहुभिर्नेरीमाध्मानाद्भि: शब्दमुच्चारयद्भिर्महान् शब्द उपलभ्यते । न वर्द्धते शब्द: । मृदुरेकेन बहुभिश्रोच्चार्य्यमाणे तान्येव अक्षराणि कर्णशष्कुलीमण्डलस्य सर्वां नेमिं व्याप्नुवद्भि: संयोगविभागनैरन्तर्य्येण अनेकशो ग्रहणात् महान् इव अवयववानिव उपलभ्यते । संयोगविभागनैरन्तर्य्येण क्रियमाणा: शब्दमभिव्यञ्जन्तो नादशब्दवाच्या: । तेन नादस्यैषा वृद्धि: न शब्दस्य—Śabara on Jaimini, Sûtra 17, Adhyâya 1, Pâda 1). The Mimâmsakas, who resolve sounds into air-waves, attribute all differences, whether of pitch, intensity, or massiveness, to differences in the series of conjunctions and disjunctions of air-particles that form the waves (*vide* Vâchaspati's report, शब्दानां तु संयोगविभागयोनीनां युक्तहृद्भेदेन रूपभेद: ; *cf.* also the later Nyâya-Vaiśeṣika, which accepts air-waves as vehicles of sound-waves: वायोरेव मन्दतरतमादिक्रमेण मन्दादि-शब्दोत्पत्ति:—Gangeśa, Tattva Chintâmaṇi). It may be noted that the terms तीव्र and मन्द are occasionally used in a general sense, and applied to express higher and lower degrees of pitch as well as of intensity.

There are also differences of quality (शब्दस्य असाधारणधर्म्मः). The same sound *ga* (ग), of the same pitch and intensity, uttered by men and parrots, can be distinguished; so also the sounds, even the same notes of the scale, given out by a wind instrument like the *venu* and a stringed instrument like the *vina*. Similarly, there are sexual and even individual differences of voice (अस्ति हि शुकसारिकामनुष्यवक्त्रप्रभवेषु कुक्कारादिषु स्फुटतरः रूपभेदप्रत्ययः पुंसाम् । एवं स्त्रीपुंसप्रभवेषु स्त्रीपुंसभेदप्रभवेषु च—Vâchaspati, Tâtparyyatîkâ, II., 2, 14. वीणा वाद्यते वेणुः पूर्य्यते वीणावेणुशब्दयोर्-साधारणो धर्मः:—Udyotakara, II., 1, 15. वेणुवीणामृदङ्गादिप्रभवेषु भेदप्रत्ययः शुकसारिकामनुष्यकखोष्ट्यादिभेदप्रत्ययः—Gangeśa and Mathurânâtha). The sounds emitted by impact of the different Bhûtas (echo from Âkâśa, hissing from the wind, puffing from fire, bubbling from water, and splitting or cracking from earth) are characteristic examples of such differences of timbre (*vide* Panchadaśî, Bhûtaviveka, Śloka 3).

The Vâkya-padîya (Kânda I, Śloka 109), as we have seen, ascribes all differences (whether of pitch, volume, or timbre) to the characteristic forms of the air-waves, which differ from one another by their configuration (सन्निपातात् विभज्यन्ते मूर्त्तयः:), and are capable of variations of velocity (momentum, *vega*) as well as of rarefaction and condensation (कारणसामर्थ्यात्) प्रचयधर्मिणः:

There are passing references to the obscuration (अभिभव) of sounds in Vâtsyâyana, Udyotakara and Vâchaspati, but the subject is treated more from a psychological than from a physical point of view. (तीव्रभेरीशब्दः मन्दतन्त्रीशब्दमभिभवति न मन्दः । नानाभूतेषु शब्दसन्तानेषु सत्सु श्रोत्र-प्रणासन्निभावेन कस्यचित् शब्दस्य तीव्रेण मन्दस्य अभिभवो युक्तः —Vâtsyâyana, II., 2, 14; *vide* Udyotakara and Vâchaspati, *loc. cit.* Here तीव्र = loud, and मन्द = low.)

Section 5.

MUSICAL SOUNDS.

Śrutis and Svaras.—We have already seen that the distinguishable pitches are called Śrutis, and they are proportioned to the *vega* (momentum) of the *kampasantana* (vibration). Now the ratio of a note to its octave (in respect of pitch) is given as 1 : 2 ; we may therefore conclude that the *vega* of the vibration in the latter case was considered to be twice as great as in the former. An indefinite number of Śrutis could be interposed between a note and its octave (आनन्त्यं हि श्रुतीनां च सूचयन्ति विपश्चित: यथा ध्वनिविशेषाणाममानं गगनोदरे । संगीतरत्नाकर । *cf*. संगीतपारिजात । केशाग्रव्यवधानेन बह्व्योऽपि श्रुतय: स्मृता:—संगीतपारिजात, Śloka 40). Twenty-two such are named and recognised for musical purposes. But a Śruti as such cannot constitute a musical tone (Svara). A Śruti is a simple (unmixed) and fundamental tone of a certain pitch, whereas an ordinary musical tone (Svara) is really composed of a fundamental tone (Śruti) and certain partial tones (harmonics, Anurananas, अनुरणन्). The musical tones (Svaras), vocal or instrumental, are therefore of the nature of what we call clangs, because, either accompanying or following the Śrutis or simple fundamental tones (हृस्वादिमात्र), are always found certain partial tones (अनुरणन). व्यवहारे त्वसौ त्रेधा हृदि मन्द्रोऽभिधीयते । कण्ठे मध्यो मूर्ध्नितारो द्विगुणश्चोत्तरोत्तर: (संगीतरत्नाकर) हृदिमन्द्रोगलेमध्यो मूर्ध्नि तार इति क्रमात् । द्विगुणः पूर्वपूर्वस्मात्—Dâmodara, Sangîta-darpaṇa, Chap. I., Śloka 49. श्रवनन्तरभावी य: स्निग्धोऽनुरणा-नात्मक: । स स्वर: उच्यते—Sangîta-ratnâkara. स स्वरो य: श्रुतिस्थाने खनन् हृदयरञ्जक: (संगीतदामोदर) द्वाविंशतिविधो मन्द्रोध्वनि: सञ्जायते

हृदि । स एव द्विगुणो मध्यः कण्ठस्थाने यथाक्रमम् । स एव मस्तके तारःस्यान्मध्यात् द्विगुणक्रमात्—Sangîta Samaya Sâra, 1. नादाच्च श्रुतयो जातास्ततः षड्जादयः स्वराः । प्रथमश्रवणाच्छब्दः श्रूयते हृस्वमात्रकः सा श्रुतिः सम्परिज्ञेया स्वरावयवलक्षणा । स्वरूपमान्त्रश्रवणाब्बादोऽनुरणनं विना । श्रुतिरित्युच्यते—Dâmodara, Sangîta-darpaṇa, Chap. I., Śloka 51. The relation between a Śruti and a Svara is variously conceived as (1) परिणाम modal change; (2) व्यञ्जन manifestation; (3) तादात्म्यं जातिव्यक्तेरिव the relation of genus and species; (4) विवर्त्तेन (मुखं यद्वद् दर्पणेषु विवर्तितं) reflection; (5) कार्य्यकारणभाव, the relation of cause and effect; *cf.* संगीतपारिजात by Ahobala, श्रुतयस्तु स्वरा भिन्नाः आवरणत्वेन हेतुना । अहिकुण्डलवत् तत्र भेदोक्तिः शास्त्रसम्मता ।—संगीत-पारिजात, Śloka 38.

SECTION 6.

THE NOTES OF THE DIATONIC SCALE: DETERMINATION OF THEIR RELATIVE PITCH.

The pitch of a note is inversely proportional to the length of the wire (तन्त्रीतनुस्वरो ज्ञेयः तद्दैर्घ्यव्यस्तमानतः—शेषलीलावती, quoted by Mr. Devala in his "Hindu Musical Scale").

The pitch of the fundamental note to that of its octave is as 1 : 2 (मध्यस्थानस्थः षड्जः द्विगुणसमः—रागविबोध, quoted by Mr. Devala).

The pitch of the fourth note (F) to that of the fundamental (C) is as 4 : 3 (उभयोः षड्जयोर्मध्ये मध्यमं स्वरमाचरेत्—संगीतपारिजात, quoted by Mr. Devala).

The vibrations of the fifth note (G) to those of the fundamental (C) are as 3 : 2 (त्रिभागात्मकवीणायां पञ्चमः स्यात्-दयिग्रे ।—संगीतपारिजात, quoted by Mr. Devala).

Concord (सम्वादित्व) is either perfect or imperfect. The

ratio of perfect concord is 3 : 2 ; that of imperfect concord, 4 : 3 (स-प-स-म मुख्याः संवादिनः स्वराः एकसंश्रयाः प्रायः —रागविबोध, quoted by Mr. Devala); *e.g.* if D be the Vâdî, A would be a Samvâdî ; if E be the Vâdî, B would be a Samvâdî : in each case a perfect concord. The pitch of D is determined from that of G, and the pitch of A from that of D, in each case, by the rule of perfect concord.

Determination of the pitches of E and B (after Mr. Devala). This may be done in either of the following ways :—

(1) E may be determined from A, and B from E, by the rule of perfect concord. This would give $303\frac{3}{4}$ as the value of the pitch of E, and $455\frac{5}{8}$ as that of the pitch of B, if the pitch of C be taken as 240 ; *or*

(2) E may be determined from C by reduction of the fifth harmonic by two octaves, a sort of imperfect concord; and then B may be determined from E by the rule of perfect concord. This would give 300 for E, and 450 for B, if C be taken as 240.

Mr. Devala, in his investigations with the " Sonochord," finds that Hindu musicians (and Sanskrit writers on music) adopted the latter values for E and B, as they tested their notes by harmonics (मेहगतस्वयम्भूस्वर- पंक्तिप्रामाण्येन—रागविबोध, quoted by Mr. Devala). The Hindus therefore followed just intonation.

Section 7.
MUSICAL INTERVALS.

Musical tones are related to one another in four ways as Vâdîs, Samvâdîs, Vivâdîs, and Anuvâdîs. The mediæval compilations explain these in reference to melody, and harmony is altogether unknown, but the terms might be used to indicate relations of harmony as well. The Vâdî might in that case answer to the key-note (or tonic), and the Samvâdîs to the two consonances, the fifth (2 : 3), and the fourth (3 : 4).

The rule given for the determination of a Samvâdî is 12 or 8 Śrutis intervening, the intervals being, therefore, 13 and 9 Śrutis respectively (giving the ratios $\frac{2}{3}$ and $\frac{1}{3}$).

C being the Vâdî, G and F are stated to be the Samvâdîs.

In the same way, it is stated that if D be the Vâdî, A would be a Samvâdî. If E be the Vâdî, B is given as a Samvâdî.

On the other hand, a two-Śruti interval (*i.e.* a difference of a semitone) gives a Vivâdî, which would thus answer to a dissonance. This is given as a general rule (द्विश्रुत्यन्तरौस्वरौविवादिनौ Matanga). Other cases are also noticed, *e.g.* E is a Vivâdî to D, and B to A, and *vice versa* (ratio of 9 : 10).

The notes that do not come under these heads are Anuvâdîs (*e.g.* the sixth); *cf.* Bharata, Nâtya-Śâstra, Chap. XXVIII., Ślokas 23–24.

Also Sangîta-ratnâkara :—

चतुर्विधा स्वरा वादी सम्वादी विवादचपि अनुवादीति । वादीतु प्रयोगे बहुलस्वरः अतयो द्वादशाङ्गौ वा ययोरन्तरगोचराः मिथः सम्वादिनौ तौ स्तो निगावन्यविवादिनौ । रिधयोरेव वा स्यातां तौ तयोर्वारिधावपि । शेषाणा-मनुवादित्वम् । (स्वराध्याय).

CHAPTER IV.

HINDU IDEAS ABOUT PLANTS AND PLANT-LIFE.

Section 1.

CLASSIFICATION OF PLANTS.

Charaka :—Plants according to Charaka are divisible into (1) *Vanaspatis*, trees bearing fruit without flowers; (2) *Vânaspatyas*, trees bearing flowers as well as fruits; (3) *Auṣadhis*, herbs that wither after fructification; and (4) *Vîrudhs*, other herbs with spreading stems.

Chakrapâṇi notes in his commentary on Charaka: The *Vîrudhs* comprise two classes, (1) *Latâs*, creepers; (2) *Gulmas*, herbs with succulent (or cactaceous) stems and shrubs. The *Auṣadhis* are sub-divided into (1) annuals or perennials, bearing fruit, and (2) plants that wither away after maturing and without fructification, *e.g.* grasses like the *Dûrvâ* (Cynodon dactylon).

Suśruta :—Suśruta's division is identical with Charaka's. Dalvana, the commentator, gives some details. The *Plakṣa* (Ficus infectoria) and the *Udumvara* (Ficus glomerata) are given as instances of trees bearing fruits without flowers (*Vanaspatis*). It appears that plants with naked and incomplete flowers (achlamydeous plants) were considered as flowerless, as also trees whose flowers, like those of the fig, are placed on the internal walls of a common receptacle. Of the *Brikṣas*, flower- and fruit-bearing trees, the mango-tree, the *Jambu*-tree (Eugenia jambolana), etc., are given as examples. The *Virudhs* are of two classes, (1) creepers with stems spreading on the ground (प्रतानवत्यः), and (2) herbs with succulent (or cactaceous) stems (गुल्मिन्यः or स्तम्बिन्यः वर्तुललतासन्ततिविशिष्टः). *Auṣadhis* are those that wither away after fructification, *e.g.* wheat, barley, etc. (फलपाकनिष्ठा गोधूमादयः). Some divide *Auṣadhis* into two classes, (1) those that wither after bearing fruit, *e.g.* paddy, linseed, pulses, etc., and (2) plants that wither after maturity, and bear neither flowers nor fruits, *e.g.* the mushroom, etc.

Praśastapâda :—Praśastapâda, the Vaiśeṣika doctor, classifies plants as follows :—(1) *Triṇas*, grasses; (2) *Auṣadhis*, herbs that wither after fructification; (3) *Latâs*, spreading and creeping herbs; (4) *Avatânas*, arboraceous plants and shrubs; (5) *Brikṣas*, trees bearing flowers and fruits; and (6) *Vanaspatis*, trees bearing fruits without flowers.

Śrîdhara in the *Kandalî* gives *Ulapa* as an example of a grass, wheat as an example of *Auṣadhi* (annual), the *Ketakî* (Pandanus odoratissimus) and the *Vîjapura* (Citrus medica) as examples of *Avatânas* (Vitapas, arboraceous plants), the *Kovidâra* (Bauhinia) as an example of flower- and fruit-bearing tree, and the *Udumvara* (Ficus glomerata) as an example of a *Vanaspati* (flowerless fruit-bearing tree).

Udayana in the *Kiraṇâvalî* notes the *Kuṣmânda* (a species of Cucurbita) as an instance of a creeper (*Latâ*), and the palms तालादयः as modifications of the grasses (*Triṇas*).

Amara :—Amara, the lexicographer, in the *Vanauṣa-dhivarga* and the *Vaiśyavarga* (enumeration of wild plants and of food-grains) gives some interesting particulars. (1) The trees (the flowering *Brikṣas* and the flowerless *Vanaspatis*) are fruit-bearing, and possess woody stems काष्ठदारु or trunks (प्रकाराड—प्रकाराड: स्कन्ध: स्यान्मूलात् शाखाविस्तर:). Next come (2) arboraceous plants and shrubs (क्षुप, ह्रस्वशाखाशिफः क्षुपः) bearing flowers as well as fruits. (3) The *Latâs* are next noticed, flowering plants with herbaceous stems, some of them creeping on the ground (प्रतानिनी), others succulent (गुल्मिनी), others twining or voluble (मूलाच्चाग्रंगता लता, वृक्षगामिनी लता— Amara, *cf.* Mukuta, तरुमूलात् प्रभृति वृक्षाग्रपर्यन्तं गता गुडूच्यादि लतापि अवरोहः :—others call this शिफा). *Cf.* Suśruta—लताः प्रतानवत्यः गुल्मिन्यश्च. (4) Next come the *Auṣadhis* (in the narrower sense), herbaceous plants bearing fruit with or without flowers, and dying or withering away after fructification. Some instances of *Kandaśûka* (tubers, rhizomes, corms) are noticed, *e.g.* the *Palându* (the onion, पलाराडुस्तु सुकन्दकः), the *Laśuna* (garlic, महाकन्द), etc. But the graminaceae enumerated in the *Vaiśyavarga* are the chief instances of the *Auṣadhis*—plants that die after fructification. These are cultivated *Auṣadhis*, but their affinities with the next class, the grasses (*Triṇas*), are also noted (*e.g.* धान्यं व्रीहि सस्यकरी। सस्यैर्गुच्छस्तृणादीनाम्। तृणधान्यानि नीवाराः। नाड़ीनालं च काराडोऽस्य). Next are enumerated (5) the *Triṇas*, grasses, of which the characteristic is the formation of *gulmas* (culms of grasses with annular knots from which leaves spring—स्तम्बो गुल्मे तृणादीनामकाराडस्तु्मगुच्छयोः). It is worthy of note that, in the enumeration of the grasses, the bamboo is considered as a sort of giant grass

(तृणध्वज, grass flag, तृणेषु ध्वज इव). The reeds (नलादयः) are also placed among the grasses (नलादयस्तृणं गर्भुच्चग्राशाकप्रमुखमपि । प्रमुखशब्दात् नीवाराद्याः). (6) Finally, the Palmaceæ (including the cocoanut, date, areca, and other palms) are classed as Tree-grasses, probably because, like the grasses, they are endogens characterised by spikes and parallel veins. तृणद्रुम: । (तृणराजाह्वयस्ताल: नारकेलस्तु लाङ्गली etc., एते च हिंतालसहितास्त्रय: खर्जुर: केतकी ताली खर्जुरा च तृणद्रुमाः,—cf. also the *Râjanighantu*).

I may add that Amara places parasitical plants among the *Latâs* (वन्दा वृक्षादनी । वृक्षरुहा । जीवन्तिकेत्यपि). They climb trees and feed upon them. These are to be distinguished from climbing plants, like the *Guḍuchî* (Tinospora cordifolia), which have separate roots of their own. They are also to be distinguished from the adventitious roots descending from the branches of trees, like the Ficus religiosa, which are usually termed *avarohâs* (अवरोहाः). The name *śiphâ* is ordinarily applied to the rootlets and suckers by which the tendrils of various creepers are attached to the soil. (शाखाशिफा अवरोहः स्यात् । वटादे: शाखायाः अवलम्बिनी शिफा । मूलाच्चाग्रं गता लता । मूलादूर्ध्वं गता लता स्यात्—Amara with Bhânuji Dikṣita's commentary. But the Mukuṭa notes :—तरुमूलात् प्रभृति वृक्षाग्रपर्य्यन्तंगता गुडुच्यादि लताऽपि अवरोहः ।) The *Guḍuchî* is also called वत्सादनी, छिन्नरुहा ।

The Hindu Materia Medica mentions *Âkâśavallî*, *lit.* sky-creeper, a name which seems to have been originally intended for some orchids ; also *Plava* (*lit.* floating), weeds that float in stagnant ponds, and *Śaivâla*, mosses and lichens (*e.g.* दूर्वाकसेरुप्रभशैवालं जलेन क्षिपेत् पीतं शुक्रमेहहरं— *Chakrapâṇi - Samgraha*, also *Bhâva*-

Prakâsá). These are not classified, but like the mushrooms must come under the *Pâkaniṣṭha auṣadhis*, Auṣadhis that die after maturing, without bringing forth flowers or fruits.

Section 2.
ELEMENTARY IDEAS OF PLANT PHYSIOLOGY.
Characteristics of Plant-Life.

The *Nyâya-vindu-tîkâ* of Dharmottara, the Buddhist scholiast, notices the phenomenon of sleep (contraction of leaves in the night) in certain plants (स्वाप: रात्रौ पत्रसङ्कोच:).

Udayana notices in plants the phenomena of life, death, sleep, waking, disease, drugging, transmission of specific characters by means of ova, movement towards what is favourable and away from what is unfavourable (वृक्षादय: प्रतिनियतभोक्त्रधिष्ठिता: जीवनमरणस्वप्नजागरणरोगभेषजप्रयोग-बीजसजातीयानुबन्धानुकूलोपगमप्रतिकूलापगमादिभ्य: प्रसिद्धशरीरवत् — Udayana, पृथिवीनिरूपणम्). I may add that metaphors drawn from the heliotropic movements of the *Sûryya-mukhî*-flower are among the stock-in-trade of Sanskrit poetry and belles-lettres.

The Jaina writer Guṇaratna, in his commentary on the *Ṣaḍḍarśana-Samuchchaya* (*circa* 1350 A.D.), enumerates the following characteristics of the plant-life: (1) stages of infancy, youth and age; (2) regular growth; (3) various kinds of movement or action connected with sleep, waking, expansion and contraction in response to touch, also movement towards a support or prop; (4) withering on wound or laceration of organs; (5) assimilation of food according to the nature of the soil; (6) growth or decay by assimilation of suitable or unsuitable food as prescribed in the science of the diseases of plants and their treatment (वृक्षायुर्वेद); (7) disease; (8) recovery from diseases or wounds by the application of drugs; (9) dryness or the opposite, due to the sap which answers to the chyle (रस) in animals; and (10) special food favourable to impregnation. (विशिष्टदौहृदादिमत्त्वं विशिष्टस्त्रीशरीरवत् यथा स्त्रीशरीरस्य तथाविधदौहृदपूरणात् पुत्रादिप्रसवनं तथा वनस्पतिशरीरस्यापि तत्पूरणात् पुष्पफलादिप्रसवनं।) Even the *Vanaspatis* (flowerless, but fruit-bearing trees) may be made to flower (*cf.* Vârahamihira's recipes for the treatment of plants for similar purposes; *cf.* Guṇaratna, *Tarkarahasyadîpikâ*, *Jainamâta*, Śloka 49).

Śankara Miśra in the *Upaskâra* notes as an additional characteristic the growth of organs (or tissues) by natural recuperation after wound or laceration (भग्नक्षतसंरोहणे च, *Upaskâra*, Chap. IV., Ahnika 2, Sûtra 5, S. B. H., Vol. VI.).

Guṇaratna gives a list of plants that exhibit the phenomena of sleep and waking (समीप्रपुन्नाटसिडेसरकासुन्दक-बप्पूलागस्त्यामलकीकतिप्रभृतीनां स्वापविबोधतः, *ibid.*). He also notices the sensitiveness to touch of plants like the Mimosa pudica, लज्जावती लता, which show a manifest reaction in the form of contraction, लज्जालुप्रभृतीनांहस्तादिसंसर्गात् यत्र सङ्कोचादिका परिस्फुटक्रिया उपलभ्यते (*ibid.*).

Sexuality.

Very vague ideas were entertained as to the sexual characters of plants. The pollen is called *Rajas, puṣpa*, *prasuna*—names which are also applied to the female menstruum—and Amara expressly states that for females and flowers these elements (and the terms signifying them) are the same (स्त्रीणां सुमनसां पुष्पं प्रसूनं समम्—Amara, *Vanauṣadhivarga*). Charaka (*Dridhavala*), indeed, distinguishes between the male and the female *vatsa* (or *kutaja*), considering the variety that bears white flowers and large fruits as male (बृहत्फलश्वेतपुष्यै: पुमान्, Holarrhena antidysenterica), and that which bears red or yellow flowers and small fruits as female (श्यावारुणानुपुष्पी स्त्री—असितकूटज, Wrightia tinctoria; Charaka, *Kalpasthâna*, Chap. V.; but this is hopelessly wrong. Even these vague ideas were afterwards completely lost, and the *Râjanighantu* tells us of a grotesque division of plants into male, female, and hermaphrodite, based on the slender or stout, the soft or hard, the long or short, the simple or mixed character of the stems and flowers! (*Râjanighantu*, अनूपादि प्रथमो वर्ग: स्त्रीपुंनपुंसकात्वेन त्रैविध्यं स्यावरेष्वपि, etc.).

Consciousness.

The Hindu Scriptures teach that plants have a sort of dormant or latent consciousness, and are capable of pleasure and pain (अन्त:संज्ञा भवन्त्येते सुखदु:खसमन्विता:). Chakrapâni notes in the *Bhânumati* that the consciousness of plants is a sort of stupefied (darkened or comatose) consciousness (वृक्षास्तु चेतनावन्तोऽपि तमश्छन्नज्ञानतया शास्त्रोपदेशविषया एव).

Udayana also notes that plants have a dormant unmanifested consciousness which is extremely dull (अतिमन्दान्त:संज्ञितया, etc.).

The *Mahâbhârata* adds that plants are sensitive to heat and cold, to the sound of thunder, etc., as well as to odours both pleasant and unpleasant :—

उष्मतो म्लायते पर्णं त्वक् फलं पुष्पमेव च ।
म्लायते शीर्यते चापि स्पर्शस्तेनात्र विद्यते ॥
वाय्वग्न्यशनि-निर्घोषैः फलं पुष्पं विशीर्यते ।
श्रोत्रेण गृह्यते शब्दस्तस्माच्छृण्वन्ति पादपाः ।
वल्ली वेष्टयते वृक्षं सर्वतश्चैव गच्छति ।
नह्यदृष्टेश्च मार्गोऽस्ति तस्मात् पश्यन्ति पादपाः ॥
पुण्यापुण्यैस्तथा गन्धैर्धूपैश्च विविधैरपि ।
अरोगाः पुष्पिताः सन्ति तस्माज्जिघ्रन्ति पादपाः ॥
पादैः सलिल-पानाच्च व्याधीनाञ्चापि दर्शनात् ।
व्याधिप्रतिक्रियत्वाच्च विद्यते रसनं द्रुमे ॥
वक्त्रेणोत्पलनालेन यथोर्ध्वं जलमाददेत् ।
तथा पवनसंयुक्तः पादैः पिबति पादपः ॥
सुखदुःखयोश्च ग्रहणात् छिन्नस्य च विरोहणात् ।
जीवं पश्यामि वृक्षाणामचैतन्यं न विद्यते ॥ शान्तिपर्व, महाभारत :

CHAPTER V.

HINDU CLASSIFICATION OF ANIMALS.

Section 1.

CLASSIFICATION OF ANIMALS.

Charaka.

Charaka mentions four primary divisions :—

(1) *Jarâyuja*, born from the uterus, or, rather, placentalia, viviparous (no a-placental mammals were known), *e.g.* man, the quadrupeds, etc.

(2) *Andaja*, born of an ovum (egg), comprising fishes, reptiles, and birds.

(3) *Svedaja* (or *Uṣmaja*), born of moisture and heat, spontaneously or a-sexually generated, *e.g.* worms, mosquitoes, etc.

(4) *Udvijja*, born of vegetable organisms (भूतानां चतुर्विधा योनिर्भवति जरायवण्डस्वेदोद्भिद्:—*Sârîrasthâna*, Chap. III. एकैका योनि: अपरिसंख्येयभेदा भवन्ति भूतानामाकृतिविशेषा परिसंख्येयत्वात् —*Ibid.*).

Praśastapâda.

Praśastapâda begins with two great divisions : (1) Ayonija, animals that are a-sexually generated, of small dimensions (क्षुद्रजन्तु) ; (2) Yonija, sexually generated, *i.e.* from the union of a sperm and a germ element. The latter are subdivided into (*a*) *Jarâyuja*, lit. placentalia, viviparous (no a-placental mammals were known), and (b) *Andaja*, oviparous. Man, the quadrupeds (domesticated and wild), etc., are given as examples of viviparous animals, and birds, *Sarîsripas* (reptiles, etc.) of oviparous animals. Udayana in the *Kiraṇâvalî* notes that *Jarâyu* means the placenta (गर्भवेष्टनचर्म्मपुटकं जरायुः, cf. Śrîdhara in the *Kandalî*, जरायुरिति गर्भाशयस्य अभिधानं तेन वेष्टितं जायते इति जरायुजम्). Udayana adds that the term *Sarîsripa* includes insects and fishes as well as reptiles, these being all oviparous (सरीसृपाः परितः प्रसर्पणशीलाः सर्पकीटमत्स्यादयः—पृथिवीनिरूपणम्).

Patanjali.

The a-sexually generated animals, as we have seen, are also called *Kṣudrajantus* (*lit.* small animals). Pâtanjali in the *Mahâbhâṣya* gives several alternative definitions (or descriptions) of this class of animals. They are defined (1) as animals without bones, अनस्थिकाः क्षुद्रजन्तवः; or (2) as animals that do not possess any blood of their own, येषां स्वं शोणितं नास्ति ते क्षुद्रजन्तवः; or (3) as numbering more than a thousand in a palmful, *i.e.* minute in size; or (4) as not easily crushed; or (5) as comprehending all animals up to the ichneumon (in the animal series), अथवा नकुलपर्यन्ताः क्षुद्रजन्तवः—*Mahâbhâṣya*, 2-4-1.

Suśruta.

Suśruta mentions four great divisions: (1) *Sansvedaja*, born of moisture and heat: this division is mentioned first, as Dalvana notes, because moisture and heat are essential factors in the generation of all forms of animal life, including the classes that follow;

(2) *Jarâyuja*, viviparous or placental; (3) *Andaja*, oviparous; and (4) *Udvijja*, bursting forth (from the ground, or perhaps from some previous unmanifest shape, *e.g.* frogs, coccidæ, etc.). The second, third, and fourth classes are mentioned in the order of their importance. Subsequently the order of enumeration is changed: (1) *Jarâyuja*, (2) *Andaja*, (3) *Svedaja*, (4) *Udvijja*. One reading gives the order: (1) *Svedaja*, (2) *Andaja*, (3) *Udvijja*, and (4) *Jarâyuja*. Some commentators point out that the order in the text (whatever that may be) is intended to indicate the order of creation by Brahmâ.

Suśruta mentions man, *Vyâla* (carnivorous quadrupeds), and *Pasu* (herbivorous quadrupeds) as examples of the viviparous; birds, snakes, and *Sarîsripas* as examples of the oviparous; *Krimis*, *Kîtas*, and *Pipîlikâs* (worms, insects, ants, etc.) as examples of the moisture-born; and frogs and the coccidæ (the coccinella) as examples of the animals that "burst forth" (eruptive or metamorphic?). Dalvana notes that the divisions are really cross-divisions (योनिसंकर), and intended to be such, as the natural divisions of Jiva and species are not all exclusively oviparous or exclusively viviparous. For example, among birds (पक्षिणः, winged animals), bats and *Valâkâs* are viviparous (बलाका जतुकादयः जरायुजाः); indeed, *Valâkâs* are some of them oviparous and some viviparous (पक्षिषु बलाका जरायुजा अराडजाश्च). Among snakes, the *Ahipatâkâs*, a species of non-venomous colubrines snakes, are viviparous (ovo-viviparous?). Among the moisture-born, there are some kinds of ants (पिपीलिकाः) which also lay eggs or burst forth (from the ground, or perhaps from some previous unmanifest shape) (संस्वेदजेभ्वपि काश्चित् पिपीलिका अण्डजा उद्भिज्जाश्च).

The oviparous animals are divided by Suśruta into birds, snakes, *Sarîsripas*, etc. Dalvana notes that the *Sarîsripas* include fishes and *Makaras* (sea-fish with fierce teeth, हिंसदंष्ट्रका:), and the "et cetera" comprehends tortoises and crocodiles (सरीसृपाः शीघ्रगामिनः कृष्णसर्पादयो मीनमकरादयो वा प्रभृतिग्रहणेन कूर्मनक्रादीनां ग्रहणम्)! The "moisture-born" are due to the moisture and heat either of the earth or of organisms (संस्वेदजाः भुवः शरीरस्य च संस्वेदात् ऊष्मणः जाताः). Of these, the *Krimis* (worms) arise from the moisture of the fæces in the bowels (कृमयः कोष्ठपुरीषादिवाप्समम्भवाः—Dalvana); from putrefying dead bodies (शव—Suśruta; *cf.* शरीरे कियत् वेलानन्तरं समुत्पन्नानां कृम्यादीनां कथं चैतन्यम्—Gunaratna, *Tarka-rahasya-dîpikâ* (*Jainamatam*); from decomposing curd or milk (*e.g.* वर्षासु च स्वेदादिना अनतिदवीयसैव कालेन दध्याद्यवयवा एव चलन्तः पूतनादिकृमिरूपा उपलभ्यन्ते—Jayanta, *Nyâya-Manjarî*, Âhnika 7, भूतचैतन्यपक्ष).

The second class, *Kîtas*, noticed among the moisture-born, include the scorpions, the six-spotted venomous insect *ṣadvindu*, etc. (कीटा वृश्चिकषड्विन्दु प्रभृतयः—Dalvana). Of these the scorpions arise from cow-dung, excreta of snakes, rotten wood (कथं गोमयाद् वृश्चिकः जायते—Pâtanjali, *Mahâbhâṣya*, 1-4-3); *cf.* also Suśruta, *Kalpasthâna*, Chap. VII.

The third class, *Pipîlikâs*, ants and the like insects, Dalvana notes, are born of moisture and heat, as well as of eggs, and sometimes burst forth from the ground (भुवमुद्भिद्य जाता उद्भिज्जा—Dalvana). The gnats and mosquitoes (दंशमशकादयः) are also usually placed among the moisture-born. An *anda* (egg) is described as oval, of the form of a *pesî* (अण्डं पेश्याकारवद्वुलं—Dalvana ; *cf.* Śrîdhara, *Kandalî*, अण्डं बिम्बं तेन वेष्टितं जायते तत् अण्डजं, पृथिवीनिरूपणां).

Chhândogya and Śankara.

It may be noted that the *Chhândogya Upaniṣad* classifies animals on the basis of their *vîja* (ovum or seed) as three-fold :—(1) *Andaja*, born of eggs; (2) *Jîvaja*, viviparous; and (3) *Udvijja*. Śankara explains that the *udvijja* animals arise from vegetable organisms (उद्भित् स्थावरं ततो जातम् उद्भिज्जम्), which is also Charaka's view, as we have seen; but unlike Charaka, Śankara holds that the *svedaja* animals must be included partly under the oviparous, and partly under the *udvijja* (vegetable-born) class (अण्डजोद्भिज्जयोरेव यथासम्भवमन्तर्भावः—Chhândogya, Prapâthaka 6, part 3).

Evidently the idea is, that though vegetable organisms may pass off into animal, there cannot be generation without *vîja* (seed or ovum), and inorganic matter without *vîja* (seed or ovum) cannot give rise to animal life. Pâtanjali, in the *Mahâbhâṣya* (*circa* 150 B.C.), mentions the opposed view, which holds that not only animal organisms but also vegetable organisms, *e.g.* grasses, grow from inorganic matter. The Dûrvâ grass, for example, can grow from deposits of the hair of goats and cows, just as scorpions are seen to develop out of cow-dung. Pâtanjali notes the orthodox Sânkhya-Vedânta explanation that these are not cases of growth (or transformation) but merely of coming out (अपक्रामन्ति),

कथं गोमयाद् वृश्चिको जायते गोलोमाविलोमेभ्यः दूर्वा जायन्ते इति अपक्रामन्ति ता वस्तुभ्यः—*Mahâbhâṣya*, 1-4-3.

The Dietary Animals in Charaka and Suśruta.

In noticing different kinds of meat for dietary purposes, Charaka gives a classification of animals (mammals and birds) which has only a practical (therapeutic) significance.

The dietic value of the flesh of any animal was conceived to depend mainly on its habitat and mode of life. Dietary animals (mammals and birds) were accordingly divided into eight classes (अष्टविधा योनिस्तेषाम्) :—

(1) *Prasaha*, carnivorous as well as non-carnivorous (Chakrapâṇî), comprehending land quadrupeds and birds that fall on their food with force.

(2) *Anûpa*, animals that live in marshy or water-logged lands or graze on river-banks.

(3) *Bhûśaya* or *Vileśaya*, animals that live in underground holes.

(4) *Vâriśaya*, aquatic animals, both fresh-water and oceanic.

(5) *Jalachara*, amphibious animals.

(6) *Jângala*, animals that live in dry and elevated (hilly) jungle lands, mostly species of deer.

(7) *Viṣkira*, birds that scatter their food in picking up; and

(8) *Pratuda*, birds that pierce or torment their food (worms and fruits) with the beak.

In the chapter on articles of diet, Suśruta gives a practical classification of (vertebrate) animals for dietary purposes. Animals that find a place in this dietary are first divided into two classes: (1) *Anûpa*, animals that live in marshy or water-logged land (or in water); (2) *Jângala*, animals that live in dry (hilly) jungle land. The Jângalas are divided into five classes, and the Anûpas into eight. The thirteen classes are based on real and natural distinctions of food and habitat; they are for dietary purposes arranged under six conventional (or artificial) classes (त्रयोदशभेदा षट्सु एव अन्तभूंताः । संख्येयम् निर्देशादेव षट्संख्यायां लब्धायां षड्ग्रहणम् तेन षड्वर्गी इति नियमार्थम्—Dalvana, *Sûtrasthâna*, Chap. XXVII.). These thirteen classes of dietary animals may be enumerated as follows:—

  I. *Jângala* animals—*Janghâla, Viṣkira, Pratuda, Guhâśaya, Prasaha, Parṇamriga, Vileśaya* and *Grâmya*, and

 II. *Anûpa* animals—*Kulechara, Plava, Kośastha, Pâdina*, and *Matsya*.

Of these, the *Matsyas* (fishes) are divided into two groups—fresh-water (*lit.* river-water) and sea-water fishes. Among the sea fishes, the *timi* and the *timingala* (whales? तिमिमहत्तमो मत्स्यः तिमिङ्गलस्ततोऽपि महत्तमः—Dalvana) find a place, as also the *makara* (shark, हिंसदंष्ट्राकः—Dalvana).

The *Kośastha* (living in shells—mollusca) are distinguished from the *Matsyas* (fishes). In this class are enumerated *śankhas* (Conchifera), *śankhana* (smaller Conchifera), *śukti* (pearl-mussels), *sambuka* (Helix) with spiral shell (आवर्त्तकोशः—Dalvana), *valluka* (a species of Helix, according to some, अन्य सम्बुकभेदमाहुः—Dalvana), etc. Dalvana adds *vodika, jalaśukti,* and various species of Helix (वोडिकजलशुक्तिशम्बूकभेदा बहुविधा गृह्यन्ते).

The *Pâdinas*, aquatic animals having pedal (or long dorsal) appendages, comprise *kurmas* (oval or oblong-shaped tortoises, turtles), the *kumbhîras* (crocodiles, Emydosauria, Reptilia), *karkatas* (white and black crabs, Crustacea), the *śiśumâra* (a species of the Delphinidæ cetacea), muscular, with a sharp protruding snout, breathing with the blow-hole *out of the water*, probably a dolphin, as the long dorsal fin was taken for a sort of pedal appendage (तुठाकारोर्द्धवक्त्रः वहिर्निःश्वासं मुञ्चति सोऽपि द्विविधः वञ्जुलदीर्घभेदेनः—Dalvana). The *Pâdinas* do not represent any natural division.

Of the other *Anûpa* animals (aquatic or amphibious animals), the *plavas* (*lit.* floating on the water) represent a class of birds (the Natatores and the Grallatores) exemplified by geese, ducks, cranes, etc.

The *Kulecharas* are herbivorous quadrupeds that frequent the banks of rivers and ponds, and comprise the elephant, the rhinoceros, the *Gâvaya* (*Bos gavœus*), the buffalo, various species of deer, etc.

Of the land animals (*Jângala*), three of the subdivisions represent birds, and five, mammals. The land birds are: (1) the *Prasaha* birds, birds of prey proper (Raptores), comprising the vulture, kites, hawks, owls, etc. (Charaka's *Prasaha* is a much wider class); (2) the *Viṣkiras*, birds that scatter their food in picking up; and (3) the *Pratudas*, birds that pierce or torment their food (fruits or worms) with the beak. The last two classes comprehend between them the *Passeres* (proper and so-called), the *Scansores*, the *Rasores* and the *Columbæ*.

The remaining five classes of *Jângala* animals are

mammals, with the exception of several species of *Vileśayas*, which are reptiles. The *Parṇamrigas* (arboreal animals) comprise the apes, sloths, squirrels, as also some of the reptiles and carnivora. Among the *Parṇamrigas*, the *Putighasa* is a kind of tree-cat giving out a pungent odour; the *Madgumuṣika* and the *Brikṣaśâyika* are arboreal rodents; and the *Avakuśa* is a species of cow-tailed monkey (*vide* Dalvana). The *Janghâlas* are wild animals, herbivorous quadrupeds that are strong-legged and quick-footed, comprising various species of deer and antelopes.

The *Grâmyas* (*lit.* living in or about villages, domesticated quadrupeds) comprise the horse, the mule, the ass, the camel, the goat, the sheep, etc. They are non-carnivorous, being distinguished from the carnivorous quadrupeds (क्रव्याद—Suśruta, मांसाद—Charaka). Some are *Ekaśapha* (animals whose hoofs are not cloven) (ग्राम्यशब्देन च एकशफशब्देन च ग्राम्याः—शफः क्षुरः —Dalvana).

The *Guhâśayas* are carnivorous quadrupeds (क्रव्यादाः) living in natural caves or hollows. They comprise the lion, the tiger, the wolf, the hyena, the bear, the panther, the cat, the jackal, the *mrigevaru*, etc. The *vrika* (wolf) is defined as a dog-like animal, small-sized (in comparison with the lion and the tiger). By the cat, here, wild-cats are meant. The *mrigevaru* is described as a jackal-like animal that kills deer.

Finally come the *Vileśayas*, animals that live in holes or burrows, comprising various species of Rodents and Insectivora, and several species of Reptiles.

Snakes in Suśruta-Nâgârjuna.

The Snakes (Ophidæ) are especially noticed by Suśruta-Nâgârjuna in the chapters relating to Toxicology (*Kalpasthâna*, Chap. IV.). Five different genera or families are noticed, of which one is non-venomous and four venomous, including one hybrid and three pure or unmixed families. Of the last, (1) the *Darvîkaras* (कृष्णासर्पे, महाकृष्णा, पद्म, महापद्म, शङ्खपाली—Naia Tripudians, Naia Bungarus) are hooded, swift in their movements, diurnal in their habits, and bear on their hoods or their bodies the marks of chariot-wheels, ploughs, umbrellas, rhombs or cross-bands, goads, etc. (2) The *Mandalîs* (Vipera, Viperidæ?) are thick (पृथवः), slow-moving, nocturnal in their habits, and bear circles or rings on the body (आदर्शमराडल). Charaka adds that they are without hoods. (3) *Rajimats* also are without hoods, and nocturnal, and bear series of dots or marks, and are often of variegated colours on the upper parts and sides. Twenty-six varieties are named of the first, two of the second, and ten of the third.

Of the *Nirviṣas*, non-venomous snakes, twelve varieties are mentioned, including Boidæ (अजगर) and the Colubrine Dendrophis (वृक्षेशय). Of the *Vaikaraṇja* (hybrid) snakes, there are ten varieties, of which three are produced by the union of certain venomous species, and seven are secondary derivative forms.

The *Darvîkaras* are most deadly when young, the *Mandalîs* when middle-aged, the *Rajimats* when aged. Their poisons act differently, and an elaborate description is given of the action of the venom of each of the three venomous families.

Snakes in the Purâṇas.

The *Bhaviṣya Purâṇa* gives the following additional information. The *Nâgas* (Naiæ) copulate in the month of *Jyaistha* or *Âṣâḍha* (May or June), gestate during the rainy months that follow, and bring forth about two hundred and forty eggs in the month of *Kârtika* (November). Most of these are devoured by the parents, but those that are left break forth from the shell in about two months (or one month, according to the *Agni Purâṇa*).

Eggs of a golden hue like that of the (red) flowers of the *Calotropis gigantea* (सुवर्णार्केवर्णनिभ) produce male young ones, those somewhat paler and of an elongated ovoid shape (अकोंदकसुवर्णाभात् दोघेराजीवसन्निभात्) bring forth female snakes, and those of the hue of the *Siriṣa*-blossom hermaphrodite ones. By the seventh day the young snakes turn dark; in a fortnight (or twenty days, according to another account) the teeth come out. The poison is formed in the fangs (दंष्ट्रासु) in three weeks, and becomes deadly in the twenty-fifth night. In six months *Nâgas* shed the skin (कञ्चुक).

In moving on the ground, the folds of the skin on the under surface alternately expand and contract, appearing to put out and draw in fine filament-like legs, about two hundred and forty in number. The joints on the skin (scales or scutes—सन्धयः) are two hundred and forty in number (perhaps the sub-caudals were not counted).

Snakes are killed by men, mongooses, peacocks, *Chakoras* (a kind of partridge), scorpions, boars, cats, and the hoofs of oxen. Escaping death from these enemies, a *Nâga* may live for a hundred and twenty years. The term of life of the non-venomous snake is shorter, about seventy-five years (*Bhavisya Purâna*, पञ्चमकल्प).

The *Agni Purâna* gives the total number of teeth (of a *Nâga*) as thirty-two, of which four (two on either side) are venomous, viz. *Kâlarâtri* and *Yamadutikâ*, which appear to be the names of the fangs, and *Karâlî* and *Makarî*, which seem to stand for two hard (maxillary) teeth accompanying the two fangs (*cf.* also Charaka—*Dridhavala*, *Chikitsâsthâna*, XXIII., विषचिकित्सितम्).

Umâsvati's Classification of Animals.

A more thorough classification of animals is found in the ancient Jaina work, the *Tattvârthâdhigama* of Umâsvati, which the Jaina chronological lists enable us to assign with great probability to the fourth or fifth decennium after Christ (*circa* 40 A.D.). Umâsvati's classification is a good instance of classification by series, the number of senses possessed by the animal being taken to determine its place in the series. Perhaps only senses actively determining the life-habits were counted.

I. First come animals with two senses, viz. touch (as evidenced by contractility of tissue) and taste (as involved in the selection and rejection of food). This division comprises—

    (*a*) *Apâdika* (Vermes without lateral appendages, Scolecids).

(b) *Nûpuraka* (ring-like, with pendants, Vermes with unsegmented lateral appendages, Annelids).

(c) *Gandûpada* (knotty-legged, Arthropoda, including Crustacea, Myriapoda, etc.).

(d) Some forms of Mollusca, *e.g.* Śaṅkha (Conchifera, Lamelli-branchiata), *Śuktika* (Pearl-mussel, Lamelli-branchiata), and *Sambuka* (Helix).

(e) *Jalûkâ*, Leeches (Annelids).

II. Next come the animals with three senses, namely smell in addition to the primordial senses of touch and taste involved in the contraction of tissues and the appropriation of food. Here also well-developed and active senses alone were perhaps intended; rudimentary or dormant senses were not reckoned. This division comprises—

(a) *Pipîlikâ*, Ants (Formicidæ, Hymenoptera).

(b) *Rohiṇikâ*, Red-ants (Formicidæ, Hymenoptera).

(c) *Upachikâ*, *Kunthu*, *Tuburaka*, Bugs and Fleas (Hemiptera, Hemimetabola).

(d) *Trapusavija* and *Karpâsâsthikâ*, Cucumber- and Cotton-weevils and Lice (Aptera, Ametabola).

(e) *Śatapadî* and *Utpataka*, Spring-tails (Aptera-Ametabola).

(f) *Triṇapatra*, Plant-Lice.

(g) *Kâṣṭha-hâraka*, Termites, White ants (Neuroptera, Hemimetabola).

III. Then come the animals with four well-developed and active senses, *i.e.* sight, smell, taste, and touch. This division comprises—

(a) *Bhramara*, *Varaṭa*, and *Sâraṅga*, Bees, Wasps, and Hornets (Hymenoptera, Holometabola).

(b) *Makṣikâ, Puttikâ, Danśa*, and *Maśaka,* Flies, Gnats, Gad-flies, and Mosquitoes (Diptera, Holometabola).

(c) *Vriśchika* and *Nandyâvarta*, Scorpions and Spiders (Arachnida, Arthropoda).

(d) *Kîta*, Butterflies and Moths (Lepidoptera, Holometabola), and

(e) *Patanga*, Grasshoppers and Locusts (Orthopteral Hemimetabola).

IV. Finally come the animals (man and the Tiryyakyonis) with five well-developed and active senses. Omitting man, this division comprises—

(a) *Matsya*, Fishes.
(b) *Uraga*.
(c) *Bhujanga*.
(d) *Pakṣi*, Birds, and
(e) *Chatuṣpada*, Quadrupeds.

Uraga and Bhujanga in popular use mean reptiles; but here evidently Bhujanga is taken to mean oviparous limbed animals (limbed reptiles and Batrachians) and not creatures whose movements are crooked or in the form of a bent bow; and Uraga stands for apodal reptiles, including snakes (Ophidæ).

It will be seen that the first three divisions fall under the Invertebrata, and the fourth is identical with the Vertebrata.

This last division (the Vertebrata) is sub-divided on a different basis, viz. the mode of reproduction. The sub-divisions are three:—

A.—*Andaja*, oviparous (Pisces, Reptilia, and Batrachia), *e.g. Sarpa* (Snakes, Ophidia, Reptilia), *Godha* (Varanidæ Lizards, Reptilia), *Krikalâsa* (Chameleons, Reptilia), *Grihagolika* (Common Lizards, Lacertilia), *Matsya* (Pisces), *Kûrma* (Tortoises, Chelonia, Reptilia), *Nakra* (Crocodiles, Reptilia), *Śiśumâra* (Dolphin or Porpoise, Cetacea), and Birds proper with feather wings—the *Lomapakṣa pakṣis*.

Porpoises are erroneously put here, being really viviparous like other Cetacea. Frogs are not mentioned in this list. The omission is strange. Perhaps (as in Suśruta) frogs were believed to be *Udvijja* (eruptive or metamorphic) and not *Andaja* (oviparous). But Suśruta mentions the frogs after the quadrupedal and centipedal Reptilia (*Kanava, Godheraka, Galagolika,* and *Śatapadî*).

B.—*Jarâyuja*, mammals born with placenta, including all mammals other than the *Potaja* (here *Jarâyuja* is used in a restricted sense): (1) Man, (2) Cow, (3) Buffalo, (4) Goat and Sheep, (5) Horse, (6) Ass, (7) Camel, (8) Deer, (9) Yak (*Chamara*), (10) Hog, (11) Bos Gavæus (*Gâvaya*)—Ungulata, (12) Lion, (13) Tiger, (14) Bear, (15) Panther, (16) Dog, (17) Jackal, (18) Cat (Carnivora), etc.

The Apes, though not expressly mentioned, are also to be included.

C.—*Potaja*, a class of placental mammals comprising the Deciduata with the exception of Man, the Apes, and the Carnivora, *e.g. Śallaka* (Porcupine, Rodentia), *Hasti* (Elephant, Proboscidea), *Śvavit* and *Lâpaka* (Hedgehogs and other creatures that lap up, Insectivora), *Śaśa* and *Śayika* (Hare, Rabbit, and Squirrel, Rodentia), *Nakula* (Ichneumon, which though carnivorous is supposed to come under the Deciduata), *Mûṣik* (Mice, Rodentia), and the *Charma-pakṣa Pakṣis*, so-called birds with leathern wings (Bats, Chiroptera) *e.g.* *Valguli* (Flying-Fox), *Pakṣivirûla* (Flying-Cat, Micro-Chiroptera) and *Jalûkâ* (apparently meaning blood-sucking Bats or Vampires, though these are scarcely found in the Old World).

The *Potaja* class thus comprises the following Deciduata: Proboscidea, Rodentia, Insectivora, and Chiroptera.

The term *Potaja* is intended to signify that these animals are born without the placenta which is thrown off as an afterbirth, whereas such of the *Jarâyujas* as are not *Potajas* are born with the placenta attached to the embryo. But it is not easy to explain why Man, the Apes, and the Carnivora should not also be reckoned among the *Potajas*. An explanation is suggested below (p. 200).

कृम्यादीनां पिपीलिकादीनां भ्रमरादीनां मनुष्यादीनां च यथासंख्यमेकैक-
वृद्धानि इन्द्रियाणि भवन्ति । यथाक्रमम् । तद्यथा कृम्यादीनां अपादिक-
नूपुरक-गण्डूपद-शङ्ख-शुक्तिक-शम्बूक-जलूका-प्रभृतीनां स्पर्शनरसनेन्द्रिये भवतः ।
पिपीलिका रोहिणिका-उपचिका-कुन्थुतुवुरक-तुपुसबीज-कपीसास्थिका-शत-
पद्युतपतक-तृणपत्र-काष्ठहारक-प्रभृतीनां त्रीणि स्पर्शनरसनघ्राणानि । भ्रमर-
वरट-सारङ्ग-मक्षिकापुत्तिका-दंश-मशक-वृश्चिक-नन्द्यावर्त्त-कीट-पतङ्गादीनां
चत्वारि स्पर्शनरसनघ्राणचक्षूंषि । शेषाणां च तिर्यग्योनिजानां मत्स्योरगभु-
जङ्गपक्षि-चतुष्पदानां सर्वेषां च नारकमनुष्यदेवानां पञ्चेन्द्रियाणि । (Umâ-svati, *Tattvarthâdhigaṇa*, Chap. II., Sutra 24).

जरायुजानां मनुष्य-गो-महिषाजाविकाश्व-खरोष्ट्र-मृग-चमर-वराह-गवय-
सिंह-व्याघ्रर्क्ष-द्वीपि-श्व-शृगाल-मार्जारादीनाम् । अण्डजानां सर्प-गोधा-कृकलास-
गृहगोलिका-मत्स्य-कूर्म्म-नक्र-शिशुमारादीनाम् । पक्षिणां च लोमपक्षाणां-हंस-
चाष-शुक-गृध्र-श्येन-पारावत-काक-मयूर-मद्गु-बक-बलाकादीनाम् । पोतजानां

शल्लक-हरि:-श्वाविल्लापक-शश-शायिका-नकुल-भूमिकादीनाम् चर्मपक्षिणां च पक्षाणां जलुका-वलुगुलि-भारख-पक्षिविराळादीनां गर्भेजन्म । (Umâsvati, *ibid.*, Chap. II., Sûtra 34).

SECTION 2.

RECAPITULATION.

The ancient Hindu classification of animals, as gathered from the authorities mentioned above, may be briefly summarised thus:—

A.—*Kṣudrajantus*, boneless and without (red) blood. Invertebrata, divided into—

(a) *Ayonija*, a-sexually generated, *e.g.* the *Svedaja*, born of moisture and heat, and the *Udvijja* (eruptive or metamorphic, *e.g.* the coccinella); and

(b) *Yonija*, sexually generated, *e.g.* the *Andaja*, oviparous.

But some are both a-sexually and sexually generated, being both *Svedajas* and *Andajas*, or *Udvijjas* and *Andajas*.

The *Kṣudrajantus* (Invertebrata) comprise—

(I.) The *Krimis*, Vermes : (a) *Apâdikas* without lateral appendages (*cf.* Scolecids), (b) *Nûpurakas*, Annelids (a section), (c) *Gandûpadas*, Arthropoda (a section).

(II.) The *Jalûkâs*, Leeches, of which twelve species are described, six venomous and six innocuous (*cf.* Suśruta's careful description, *Sûtrasththâna*, Chap. XIII.).

(III.) *Kośasthas*, Shelled Animals, some forms of Mollusca, *e.g.* the *Śankhas* (Conchifera), the

Śuktikas (pearl-mussels), the *Sambukas* (spiral-shelled Helix), the *Voḍikas*, etc.

(IV.) Then the Insects, typified by the Ants, comprising—

    (*a*) *Pipîlikâ, Rohiṇikâ* (ants, Hymenoptera).

    (*b*) *Upachikâ, Kunthu, Tuburaka* (bugs and flies, Hemiptera).

    (*c*) Cucumber- and cotton-lice (Aptera).

    (*d*) *Śatapadî, Utpataka* (spring-tails, Aptera).

    (*e*) *Triṇapatra*, grass- or plant-lice (Aptera).

    (*f*) *Termites* (Neuroptera).

(V.) Insects typified by the Hexopoda, comprising—

    (*a*) *Bhramara, Varaṭa, Sâranga*, bees, wasps, and hornets.

    (*b*) *Makṣikâ, Puttikâ, Danśa, Maśaka*, flies, gnats, gadflies, and mosquitoes.

    (*c*) *Vriśchika* and *Nandyâvarta*, scorpions and spiders (Arachnida, Arthropoda).

    (*d*) *Kîta*, butterflies and moths; and

    (*e*) *Pataṅga*, grasshoppers and locusts.

Suśruta-Nâgârjuna names six varieties of ants, six varieties of flies, five of mosquitoes (including one marine and one mountain kind), eight varieties of *Śatapadîs* (centipedes), thirty varieties of scorpions, and sixteen of spiders (*Lutâs*). Of the *Kîtas*, the glow-worm and the *Tailakita* (lit. oil-worm) are said to be luminous (phosphorescent, *cf. Râjanighantu* खद्योततैलकीटौ).

B.—The *Tiryyakyoni* animals, sexually generated animals other than such of the Ovipara as are included under the *Kṣudrajantu*, in other words, sexually generated animals possessing bones and blood—corresponding to the Vertebrata—comprise the following classes :—

I. *Andaja*, oviparous—

(a) The *Matsyas*, fishes, divided into river-water fishes and sea fishes. Suśruta names eleven species of the latter. The *Timi* (whale ?) is reckoned as a sea-fish. The *Makara* (shark) is also mentioned, but the *Kurmas, Kumbhiras,* and *Śiśumâras* (tortoises, crocodiles, and dolphins) are excluded from the class, as also the so-called shell-fish, being placed among the *Pâdinas* and the *Kośasthas* respectively.

(b) The *Uragas*, apodal reptiles, including the *Sarpas* (snakes, Ophidia). Five classes of snakes are mentioned, one non-venomous, three venomous, and one hybrid. Eighty varieties of snakes are named, but the classification is based on superficial characters, *e.g.* markings on the scales, etc., and do not touch any anatomical peculiarities. The pathological observations regarding the distinct action of the poisons of different orders seem to be good.

(c) *Bhujangas*, oviparous animals with lateral, pedal appendages, both Reptiles and Batrachians. Many of these are quadrupedal and five-clawed (चतुष्पादाः कीटाः पञ्चनखाः—Dalvana).

The *Bhujangas* include :—

    1. *Godha, Grihagolika* and *Krikalâsa* (Varantas lizards, common lizards, and chameleons). Suśruta names four varieties of the

Kanava, a species of chameleon-like lizards (*cf. Lâdyâyana* quoted by Dalvana, *Kalpasthâna*, Chap. VIII.), also six varieties of *Galagolika* (a species of lizards), and five varieties of *Godheraka*, Varanus-like lizards, but smaller in size.

Suśruta mentions the frogs (*Udvijja*, eruptive or metamorphic?) after the quadrupedal and centipedal Reptilia (*Kanava, Godheraka, Galagolika,* and *Śatapadî*). Eight species of frogs are named. The frogs are explained by the mythologist to have arisen from dirty water in the rainy season... प्रावृट्काले ततः (*i.e.* महेश्वरशुक्रात्) मराडोदके जाताः (*cf.* Dalvana, *Kalpasthâna*, Chap. VIII.).

2. *Kûrmas* and *Nakras*, tortoises and crocodiles (Chelonia and Emydosauria, Reptilia). Some species of the former are oval, others elongated (वर्त्तुलदीर्घादिभेदाः).

3. *Śiśumâras*, the Delphinidæ (Odontocete cetacea).

Suśruta's *Pâdinas* (aquatic animals having pedal or long dorsal appendages) are a conventional class formed for practical dietary purposes, and include (2) and (3) and also the *Karkatas*, crabs (Crustacea). Umâsvati's *Bhujanga* class, being a natural sub-division of Vertebrates, does not include Crustacea, which are rightly placed among the Invertebrates.

(d) *Lomapakṣa pakṣi,* winged animals with feathery wings, birds proper. These are oviparous, while the winged animals with leather wings (चर्म्मपक्षपक्षिणः) are placentalia of the Deciduata class (पोतजाः).

The Birds proper are divided into four classes:—

(1) *Plavas,* aquatic or amphibious birds, comprising the Natatores and the Grallatores. Various species are described.

(2) *Viṣkiras,* those that scatter their food in picking up.

(3) *Pratudas,* those that pierce or torment their food (fruits or grains).

> The enumeration of the species under (2) and (3) shows that these two classes included the Passeres (veræ and so-called), the Scansores, the Rasores, and the Columbæ.

(4) *Prasahas,* birds of prey proper (Raptores).

Dalvana's descriptions of deer and birds are precise, turning upon coloration, habits of life, etc., *e.g.* the descriptions of the Ruru, the Kâraṇḍava, and the Kaṅka, expressly quoted from some (unnamed) handbooks:—

कूलेचरमाह ... रुरुः शरदि शृङ्गत्यागी । तल्लक्षणं उच्यते—
"विकटबहुविषाणः शम्बराकारदेहः सलिलतटचारित्वात् सञ्चरेभ्यः विचित्रः ।
त्यजति शरदि शृङ्गं रौति"—इत्यसौ रुरुः स्यात् ।

कारण्डवः शुक्लहंसभेदोऽल्पः अन्ये करहरमाहुः । उक्तञ्च "कारण्डवः काकवक्त्रो दीर्घाङ्घ्रिः कृष्णावर्णभाक्" इति ।

प्रसहानाह ... कङ्कः दीर्घचञ्चुर्महाप्राणः । उक्तं च "कङ्कः स्यात् कङ्कमल्लाख्यो बाणपत्राईपक्षकः । लोहपृष्ठो दीर्घपादः पञ्चाधः पाण्डुवर्णभाक् ।" इति ।

The sources from which Dalvana derives detailed information about these varied forms of animal life are now unavailable, but these extracts abundantly testify to the minute Nature study of the Hindus.

The Hindus had of course no idea of an anatomical classification of birds.

The ancient writer Lâdyâyana had a much better idea of zoological description in reference to the *Kîtas* (insects and reptiles, *vide infra*).

II.—*Jarâyujas* (viviparous, *lit.* placentalia) in the usual wider sense, comprising—

(a) *Charmapakṣa pâkṣis*, leather-winged animals, which are Deciduata (*Potaja*). Charaka calls them *Mrigapakṣiṇa* (mammal birds), and distinguishes them from the birds of prey proper, in his enumeration of the *Prasahas* (*Sutrasthâna*, Chap. XXVII.). The Bats mentioned are :—

(1) *Valguli* (flying-fox).
(2) The *Pakṣi Virâla* (flying-cat, micro-Chiroptera).
(3) The *Bharanda* (a species of micro-Chiroptera, the horse-shoe bat?).
(4) The *Jalukâ* (*lit.* aquatic or amphibious, or more probably leech, bat, blood-sucking or vampire bat?). These are placed among carnivorous animals.

(b) The *Vileśaya Jarâyujas*, mammals that live in holes or burrows, including various species of Rodents and Insectivora, which are named.

Eighteen different varieties of mice are specified (Suśruta, *Kalpasthâna*, Chap. VI.).

(c) *Parṇamrigas*, arboreal mammals, comprising some Rodents (squirrels, etc.), a wild-cat, the sloths, and the apes (वानर).

(d) Non-carnivorous quadrupeds (अक्रव्यादाः) :—

(1) *Janghâlas* (*lit.* strong-legged quadrupeds, frequenting hilly and jungly tracts), comprising various species of deer (non-carnivorous wild animals, अक्रव्याद).

(2) *Kulechara*, mammals grazing on the banks of rivers, and frequenting marshy places, comprising the elephant, the rhinoceros, the gaveya (*Bos gavæus*), the buffalo, the hog, and also several species of deer (which live in well-watered lands). These are also non-carnivorous (अक्रव्याद).

(3) *Grâmyas* (*lit.* living in or near villages), non-carnivorous, domesticated quadrupeds, some with undivided hoof, others with cloven hoof, comprising the horse, the mule, the ass, the camel, the cow, the goat, the sheep, etc. These are all non-carnivorous. The dog and the cat are not mentioned in the list.

(e) Carnivorous quadrupeds, *Guhâśaya* (living in natural caves or hollows, carnivorous *Kravyâda*), comprising the lion, the tiger, the wolf (of the dog class), the hyena, the bear, the panther, the cat, the jackal, etc. The Carnivora were termed

Vyâlas or *Kravyâdas*, and the Herbivore *Pasus* (in a wider sense).

(*f*) Man.

The term *Jarâyuja*, in a wider sense, came to mean "viviparous," and included the above orders of animals. But the Jainas used the term *Jarâyuja* in a narrower sense to mean only those viviparous animals which come out at birth with the placenta (a-deciduata). The Deciduata (including the Proboscidea, the Rodentia, the Insectivora, the Chiroptera, etc.) were termed *Potaja*, *lit.* viviparous animals born without placenta. Man, the apes, and the Carnivora are, however, reckoned with the *Jarâyuja* (viviparous, born with placenta). Perhaps the afterbirth was observed in these cases, whereas the *Potajas* (Deciduata) may have been erroneously conceived to throw off no placenta (गर्भे जन्म, *supra*).

Lâdyâyana appears to have made a special study of the classification of *Kîtas* (Insects and Reptiles), and is quoted by Dalvana as a great authority on the subject.

The various forms (रूप) of *Kîtas* are to be distinguished from one another by peculiarities in the following marks :—

(1) Dottings or markings, (2) wings, (3) pedal appendages, (4) mouth, with antennæ or nippers (मुखसन्दंश—Dalvana), (5) claws, (6) sharp, pointed hairs or filaments, (7) stings in the tail, (8) hymenopterous character (संश्रिद्वै: पक्षरोमभि:), (9) humming or other noise, (10) size, (11) structure of the body, (12) sexual organs (this is how I interpret *linga* here), and (13) poison and its action on bodies.

Cf. कटुभि: बिन्दुलेखाभि: पक्षै: पादै: मुखै: नखै:
शूकै: काटकलांगलै: संश्रिष्टै: पक्षरोमभि: ।
खनै: प्रमाणै: संस्थानै लिङ्गैश्चापि शरीरगै:
विषवीर्य्यैश्च कीटानां रूपज्ञानं विभाव्यते ॥

(Quoted from Ládyáyana by Dalvana, *Kalpasthána*, Chap. VIII.)

CHAPTER VI.

HINDU PHYSIOLOGY AND BIOLOGY.

Section 1.

METABOLISM.

The food that we eat contains five classes of organic compounds. From their radicles or predominant elements, the substances are named Earth-compounds, Ap-compounds, Tejas-compounds, Vâyu-compounds, and Âkâśa-compounds. The Earth-compounds supply the hard, formed matter of the body, the Tejas-compounds give the animal heat (or the metabolic heat), the Vâyu-compounds are the sources of the motor-force in the organism, the Ap-compounds furnish the watery parts of the organic fluids, and the Âkâśa-compounds contribute to the finer etheric essence which is the vehicle of the conscious life

Roughly speaking, the Earth-compounds answer to the nitrogen compounds in the food, the Tejas-compounds to the hydro-carbons (heating-producing), and the Vâyu-compounds to the carbo-hydrates (dynamic). The Ap-compounds are the watery parts of food and drink. The flesh, for example, is a tissue composed principally of the Earth-compounds; the fat, of the Earth- and Ap-compounds; the bones, of Earth-, Vâyu-, and Tejas-compounds. Different operations of the metabolic heat (perhaps different digestive fluids are also meant) are required to digest the different substances in the food.

The course of metabolism is described as follows. The entire alimentary canal is called the Mahâsrotas (the great channel).

The food goes down the gullet by the action of the bio-motor force, the *Prâna Vâyu*.

In the stomach (आमाशय) the food becomes mixed up, first with a gelatinous mucus (फेणीभूतं कफं) which has a saccharine taste, and then gets acidulated by the further chemical action of a digestive juice (विदाहादम्लतां गत:, evidently the gastric juice is meant). Then the bio-motor force, the *Samâna Vâyu*, begins to act, and drives down the chyme, by means of the *Grahani Nâdî*, to the *Pittâsaya* (duodenum, *lit.* bile-receptacle), and thence to the small intestines (the आमपक्वाशय). In these, the bile (or rather the digestive substance in the bile, as opposed to the colouring element) acts on the chyme and converts the latter into chyle (रस), which has at first a *katu* taste (pungency). This chyle contains in a decomposed and metamorphosed condition all the organic compounds, viz. tissue-producing Earth-compounds, water-parts or Ap-compounds, heat-producing Tejas-compounds, force-producing Vâyu-compounds, and lastly, finer etheric constituents which serve as the vehicle of consciousness. The essence of chyle (सूक्ष्मभाग) from the small intestines is driven by the bio-motor force, the *Prâna Vâyu*, along a Dhamanî trunk (*cf.* the thoracic duct), first to the heart (which is a great receptacle of chyle), and thence to the liver (and the spleen); and in the liver the colouring substance in the bile acts on the essence of chyle, especially on the Tejas-substance therein, and imparts to it a red pigment, transforming it into blood; but the grosser part of chyle (स्थूलभाग) proceeds along the Dhamanîs, being driven by the bio-motor force, the *Vyâna Vâyu*, all over the body.

When the blood has been formed, the essence of chyle in the blood, acted on by *Vâyu* (bio-motor force) and Mâmsâgni (the flesh-forming metabolic heat), forms the flesh-tissue, the Earth-compound of the food-substance especially contributing to this tissue. Of the flesh-tissue thus formed, the grosser part goes to feed or replenish the flesh-tissue all over the body. The finer essence of flesh in the blood in the chyle, acted on again by *Vâyu* (bio-motor current) and the fat-forming metabolic heat (मेदोऽग्नि) in the menstruum of lymph (कफं समाश्रित्य), receives viscosity and whiteness, and produces the fatty tissue, the Earth-compounds and Ap-compounds of the food specially contributing to the product. This fat in the chyle (or blood), or rather the grosser part of it, replenishes the fatty tissue of the body, but the finer essence of fat *in* the flesh *in* the blood *in* the chyle, acted on by *Vâyu* (bio-motor current) and the marrow-forming metabolic heat, in the menstruum of lymph (श्लेष्मणावृत), becomes hard (crystalline) and forms bone, the Earth-, Vâyu-, and Tejas-compounds contributing principally to the product. The essence of the fat fills the hollow channels of the bones, and acted on again by bio-motor *Vâyu* and metabolic heat, becomes transformed into marrow. The marrow is similarly transformed into the semen, which is con-

veyed down by means of a pair of *Dhamanîs* or ducts
(द्वे शुक्रवहे), lodged in its receptacles (शुक्रधरा—वृषणौ), and
discharged by means of another pair of ducts (द्वेविसगाय).
The semen, or rather all the elements in their finer
essence, give off *ojas*, which returns to the heart,
the receptacle of chyle and blood, and again floods
the body and sustains the tissues, thus completing the
wheel or self-returning circle of metabolism (परिवृत्तिस्तु
चक्रवत्, *cf.* Charaka and Vâgbhata).

It is to be noted that, throughout, the fluid in the
chyle or blood acts as the menstruum, though occasionally the lymph, which is itself a derivative from the
chyle, is added, as in the case of the fatty tissue and
the bones; and that each preceding element or constituent of the body (धातु—शरीरारम्भक धातु) takes up the
proper organic compounds from the food chyle to form
the next element or tissue. Throughout, also, the
chemical changes are due to the metabolic heat which
breaks up the compounds and recombines, but the
operations, and even the vehicles perhaps, of this heat
are different. For example, these heat-corpuscles in
the biliary ducts produce the bile, but the bile-secretion
is supposed to contain two distinct substances: (1) a
digestive fluid in the duodenum (पित्ताशय), which acts on
the chyme to produce the chyle (अन्नस्य पक्तृ पाचकाख्यं पित्तं);
and (2) a colouring bile-substance in the liver, which
adds a red pigment to the chyle and transforms it into
blood (रञ्जकाख्यं पित्तं). Besides, there are three other biles,
of which the aqueous humour in the eye is supposed to
be one (आलोचकं पित्तं), helping in the formation of visual
images (रूपग्राहकं). This is the view of Dhanvantari and

his school, but Âtreya holds there is no evidence that the bile really performs the first (digestive) function, for this can be accounted for by the animal heat arising from the working of the whole bodily machine.

There are three different hypotheses regarding the course of metabolism and the successive transformations of the chyle (क्षीरदधिन्याय—केदारीकुल्यान्याय—खलेकपोतन्यायेति त्रिधा धातुपोषणक्रमः—Chakrapâni, Bhânumatî, Sûtrasthâna, XIV., 10; also his commentary on Charaka, Sûtrasthâna, XXVIII.), but my account is based on the second hypothesis, which has the preference of Chakrapâni (स्वरसः). It may be added as a curiosity that each element of the body (धातु) under the metabolic heat is supposed to give off a finer essence (सूक्ष्मभाग), which serves as the material of the next succeeding element, and a dross (मल), which forms some of the excreta in the body (including the nails, the hair, etc.), besides retaining its own substance (the gross or main part), which is driven along by the *Vâyus* (bio-motor or vital currents), or by the *Srotas*, to its destination in the body.

Some idea of *circulation* appears to have been entertained, for the heart which receives, and then sends down the chyle through the *Dhamanîs*, gets it back transformed into blood, and the *ojas* also proceeds from the heart and returns to it along with the chyle and the blood.

(*Cf.* Vâgbhata, ताः हृत्स्थाः शिराः रसात्मकं ओजः अभिवहन्यः) । पञ्चभूतात्मके देहे आहारः पाञ्चभौतिकः । विपक्वः पञ्चधा सम्यग् गत्वान् स्वानभिवर्द्धयेत् ।—Susruta, *Sûtrasthâna*, Ch. XLVI.; *cf.* also वियत्पवनजाताभ्यां वृद्धिमाप्नोति मारुतः । आग्नेयमेव यद्द्रव्यं तेन पित्तमुदीर्यते । —*Ibid.*, Ch. XLI. भौमाप्याग्नेयवायव्याः पञ्चोष्माणः सनाभसाः । पञ्चाहा-

रगुणान् म्लान् खान् पार्थिवादीन् पचन्त्यनु । यथाखं ते च पुष्णन्ति पञ्च
भूतगुणान् पृथक् । पार्थिवा: पार्थिवानेव शेषा: शेषांश्च देहगान् । अतिरिक्ता
गुणा रक्ते वहेर्मांसे तु पार्थिवा: । मद्स्पर्शा भुवश्चास्थ्नि पृथिव्यनिलतेजसां ।—
Charaka quoted by Dalvana. आदौ मधुरसमप्पन्नं मधुरीभूतमीरयेत्,
फेणीभूतं कफं यातं विदाहादल्पतां गत: । वायुना समानाख्येन ग्रहण्यामभिनीयते ।
षष्ठी पित्तधरा नाम या कला परिकीर्त्तिता । आमपक्काश्रयान्त:स्था ग्रहणी
साऽभिधीयते । अग्न्यधिष्ठानमन्नस्य ग्रहणाद् ग्रहणी मता । भुक्तमामाशये रुद्धा
सा विपाच्य नयत्यध: । बलवत्यबला त्वन्नमामेव विमुञ्चति ।... अन्नस्य पक्तृ
पित्तन्तु पाचकाख्यं पुररीतम् । दोषधातुमलादीनामुष्मत्यान्नेयशासनम् ।...
तेजोरसानां सर्वेषामम्बुजानां यदुच्यते, पित्तोष्मणा सरागेण रसो रक्तत्वमृच्छति ।
वाय्वग्नितेजसा युक्तं रक्तं मांसत्वमृच्छति । श्लेष्मणां च समाश्रित्य मांसं वाय्वग्नि-
संयुतं, स्थिरतां प्राप्य शौकर्य्यं च मेदो देहेऽभिजायते । पृथिव्यग्न्यनिलादीनां
संघात: श्लेष्मणावृत:, खरत्वं प्रकरोत्यस्य जायतेऽस्थ्नि ततो नृणाम् । करोति तत्र
सौषिर्य्यमस्थ्नां मध्ये समीरण: । मेदसा तानि पूर्य्यन्ते स्नेहो मज्जा तत: स्मृत: ।
तस्मान्मज्ज्ञश्च य: स्नेह: शुक्रे संजायते तत: ।—Charaka-Dridhavala
Samhitâ quoted by Aruna in his commentary on
Vâgbhata.)

यथा केदारनिम्नत्वं कुल्याजलं प्रत्यासन्नां केदारीमाश्रावयति । तथा रस एव
प्रथमं रक्तं श्रावयति । तत्र रक्तस्यानसम्बन्धात् रक्तसादृश्यं रक्तव्यपदेशं च अनु-
भवति । रक्तं च रक्तसमानेन स्तोकेनांशेन अङ्गं पोषयति । ततो रक्तमाश्राव्य
मांसमाश्रावयति, एवमुत्तरोत्तरधातून् रसश्चव श्रावयति । (Chakradatta,
Bhânumati). This passage shows that the "venous
blood" was conceived to be chyle-essence mixed with
blood, and that the circulation of the chyle, so far as it
was held to contribute its quota to the constituent
elements and tissues of the body, was really supposed
to be identical with the circulation of the blood (ततो
रक्तमाश्राव्य मांसमाश्रावयति). This will be abundantly clear
from the following account of the course of the chyle
and the blood :—

तत: सारभूतस्याहाररसस्य द्वौ भागौ भवत: । स्थूल: सूक्ष्मश्च ... तत:

सूक्ष्मोभाग: प्राणवायुनाप्रेरितो धमनीमार्गेण शरीरारम्भकस्य रक्तस्य स्थानं यकृत्-प्लीहरूपं गत्वा तेन सह मिलितोभवति । तत: प्राक्तनरक्तधातौ एव तिष्ठति । ... तत: सारभूतस्य आहाररसस्य द्वौ भागौ भवत: । स्थूल: सूक्ष्मश्च । स्थूलो भागो रञ्जकाख्येन पित्तेन रक्तीकृत: शरीरारम्भकं रक्तं पोषयन् व्यान-वायुना प्रेरितोधमनीभि: सञ्चरन् सकलशरीरगतानि रुधिराणि पुष्णाति । तत: सूक्ष्मोभाग: व्यानवायुनाप्रेरितो धमनीभि: शिराभिश्च शरीरारम्भकाणि मांसानि याति । *et seq.*

This finer essence of chyle which nourishes the flesh is also carried in the blood, on the irrigation channel hypothesis (केदारी-कुल्यान्याय).

Section 2.

THE CIRCULATORY SYSTEM.

The standing puzzle of Hindu anatomy and physiology is the classification of the *Sirâs*, *Dhamanîs*, and *Srotas*, the channels, passages, and ducts in the body including the arteries, veins, nerves, lymphatic vessels, etc. The difficulty was felt by the ancient observers themselves. Some were of opinion that the *Dhamanîs* and *Srotas* are only modifications of the *Sirâs*, and that the division is artificial. Suśruta, however, contends that they are distinct, because they can be traced to different roots and have different functions; they are apt to be confounded only because they are minute, juxtaposed, and similar in function (Suśruta, *Sarîrasthâna*, Chapter IX.). Charaka also accepts the established division, but points out that the numbers as estimated are conjectural (अनिर्देश्यमत:परं तर्कमेव, *Sarîrasthâna*, Chapter VII.).

The *Sirâs*, *Dhamanîs*, and *Srotas* form networks

(जालानि) of cords, fibres, passages, which in the fœtus take their rise from the umbilical cord, and proceed upwards to the heart and head, downwards to the kidneys and rectum, and outwards to the trunk and limbs. These three classes comprise all the vehicles or conductors of the fluids, secretions, and currents in the bodily system.

The *Śrotas* (currents). This is a peculiarity of Hindu physiology. The chyle, the blood, the *Vâyu*, the metabolic fluid (पित्त), the lymph, the fat, the marrow, in every part of the body, is supposed to be connected by means of subtle currents (*Śrotas*) with the same kind of fluid (or tissue) in every other part. Without supposing such special connections, many pathological phenomena cannot be explained.

The *Sirâs* are divided into four groups: (1) the arteries for conducting the blood, (2) the lymphatics for conducting the lymph, (3) a class of bile-ducts, and (4) a class of ducts for the *Vâyus*, the currents which work the automatic and reflex machinery of the living organism. In each group there are 10 trunk *Sirâs*, which sub-divide into 175 cords, and further ramify minutely all over the body, even as a network of minute fibrils covers the leaf of a tree.

The functions of the different groups of *Sirâs* are to conduct or transmit the (arterial) blood, the lymph, the bile, and the (vital) *Vâyu* currents respectively to the different parts of the body. The *Sirâs* are compared to the conduits of the flowing water in a pleasure-house (a garden), or the channels of irrigation that flood a field. The conduction (or transmission) of the fluids and currents is effected by an alternate dilation and contraction of the vessels, the systolic movement differing according to the nature of the fluid propelled:

सप्त शिराशतानि भवन्ति याभिरिदं शरीरमाराम इव जलहारिणीभिः केदारइव च कुल्याभिरुपचिह्यते अनुगृह्यते च आकुञ्चनप्रसारणादिभिर्विशेषैः । द्रुमपत्तसेवनीनामिव तासां प्रताना: । तासां नाभिमूलं ततश्च प्रसरत्यूर्ध्वं अधस्तिर्य्यक् च । तासां मूलशिराश्चत्वारिंशत् । तासां वातवाहिन्यो दश पित्तवाहिन्यो दश कफवाहिन्यो दश दश रक्तवाहिन्यः—Suśruta, *Śârîrasthâna*, Chap. VII.

The *Dhamanîs* in the foetus take their rise from the umbilical cord, thus bringing nourishment from the mother. They are divided into three groups: (*a*) ten trunks or cords going up to the heart, and thence to the head, (*b*) ten going down to the intestines, kidneys, and rectum, and (*c*) four branching obliquely or sidewise, and ramifying over the whole body. In a general way, it may be stated that the *Dhamanîs* comprise (1) the veins, (2) the nerves (including the sympathetic system), (3) the chyle-ducts (including the thoracic duct?) as distinguished from the other lymphatics, which are mostly classed as *Sirâs*, (4) the ducts for urine, sweat, and other secretions, and (5) lastly, certain classes of bile-ducts and conductors of *Vâyu* currents, possibly those connected with the venous system and the chyle-ducts.

The first group of *Dhamanîs*:—Special features: Each of the ten ascending *Dhamanîs*, on reaching the heart, trifurcates, and proceeds to the head. Of these fibres, one pair is engaged in conducting each of the four sensory currents (those of sound, colour, taste, and smell) *from the sense-organs, as Charaka and Suśruta must have supposed, to the heart, which is for them the seat of consciousness* (हृदयं विशेषेण चेतनास्थानम्, Suśruta, *Śârîrasthâna*, Chap. IV.; हृदयं चेतनाधिष्ठानमेकम्, Charaka, *Śârîrasthâna*, Chap. VIII.). Other *Dhamanîs*, also in pairs, are engaged in conducting automatic (or voluntary) motor currents (*e.g.* the currents concerned in respiration, yawning, sleeping and waking), or the secretions of the lachrymal and mammary glands.

The second group of *Dhamanîs* :—Special functions : The descending *Dhamanîs* go down to the intestines, kidneys, bladder, and rectum, and their special function is to convey, in pairs as before, urine and other secretions and excreta. They also convey the chyle from the small intestines to the ascending as well as the ramifying *Dhamanîs*. In addition, some of them convey sweat to the ramifying *Dhamanîs*.

The third group :—Special functions : The remaining four *Dhamanîs* ramify obliquely over the body into millions of fibres and fibrillæ, which terminate in the pores of the skin. From all parts of the periphery they conduct the sensory currents of touch to the central organ of the heart (including the internal organic sensations). Being connected with the pores of the skin, they conduct sweat outwards, and the influences of baths, embrocations, and fomentations inwards.

Other *Dhamanîs* serving as chyle-ducts and as (venous) blood-vessels.—Besides the special functions performed by the three groups, there are two characteristic functions common to certain classes of *Dhamanîs* which are found in all the three groups, viz. the conduction of chyle and of (venous) blood, *i.e.* of impure blood before it gets its red pigment from the liver. It may also be added that the three principal elements of the body—*Vâyu* (vital current), *Pitta* (bile, or rather the fluid animal heat which produces metabolism, पाक, and flows to all the parts of the body by means of connective passages), and *Kapha* (lymph)—make use of the *Dhamanîs* as well as the *Sirâs* and *Srotas*, *i.e.* of all manner of conductors in the organism (*cf.* Charaka, वातपित्तश्लेष्माणां पुनः सर्वशरीरचराणां सर्वाणि स्रोतांसि अयनभूतानि— *Vimânasthâna*, Chapter V.).

The functions of the *Sirâs* may therefore be stated as follows:—

(1) The conduction of blood from the liver and spleen, red blood (what may be called the arterial blood of this system of physiology), to the heart, head, trunk, limbs, etc.

(2) Common functions of all connective passages, viz. the conduction of *Vâyu* (vital current), *Pitta* (metabolic fluid), and *Kapha* (lymph).

The different classes of *Dhamanîs*, with their functions, are:—

(1) The nerves: (*a*) eight sensory (central) nerves for the four special senses other than touch; (*b*) twelve motor nerves partly for voluntary and partly for automatic movements; and (*c*) the nerves of touch and organic sensation, including the sympathetic nerves.

(2) and (3) The chyle-ducts and the conductors of (venous) blood before it is transformed into blood in the liver (and the spleen).

(4) The classes of *Dhamanîs*, which, in common

with the *Sirâs* and *Srotas*, conduct *Vâyu, Pitta,* and *Kapha*, the prime movers of the organic life.

The Vascular System.

The anatomical arrangement of the *Sirâs* and *Dhamanîs* in Charaka and Suśruta is so obscure that only a rough outline of its general features can be attempted. In fact, Charaka contents himself with giving the number of *Sirâ* cords as 700, and of *Dhamanî* cords as 200. He also estimates the ramifications as numbering 3,056,900.

The carriage of the blood and the lymph is accomplished by two sets of vessels, *Sirâs* and *Dhamanîs*, the first standing for "arteries" (with capillaries) and lymphatics (other than chyle-ducts), and the second for "veins" and chyle-ducts (as well as certain passages for sweat, etc.).

The navel in the fœtus is taken to be the source and origin of the entire vascular system, whether for the blood or the lymph. Vâgbhata takes the heart to be the origin of the *Sirâs*.

From this central alimentary tract two sets of vessels (*Sirâs* and *Dhamanîs—Rasavâhinyah*) issue for the flow of the chyle and other lymph, and two sets (*Sirâs* and *Dhamanîs*, "arteries" and "veins"— *Raktavâhinyah*) for the flow of the blood.

The Lymph (and Chyle): Distribution.—The chyle is conducted by the chyle-bearing *Dhamanîs* (*Rasavâhinyah*), and the lymph (other than chyle) by the lymph-bearing *Sirâs* and *Dhamanîs* (*Kaphavâhinyah*).

The lymph-bearing *Sirâs* comprise 10 branches at the origin, and ramify into 175—viz., 25 in each leg, 25 in each arm, 8 in the pelvic cavity, coccyx, penis, etc., 2 in each side, 6 in the back, 6 in the abdomen, 10 in the breast, 14 in the neck, 2 in the ears, 9 in the tongue, 6 in the nose, and 10 in the eyes.

The chyle is carried by another system of vessels (*Rasavâhinyah Dhamanyah*). The chyle-ducts issue from the Navî (possibly the receptaculum chyli in this case). A *Dhamanî* trunk descends to the small intestine, and, taking up the chyle, proceeds upwards towards the heart (thoracic duct?). Two chyle-ducts as well as two lymph-ducts (*Dhamanîs—Rasavâhinyah* and *Kaphavâhinyah*) proceed from the heart, and ramify over the head and trunk. Similarly two chyle-ducts and two lymph-ducts proceed from the intestinal tract and ramify over the pelvic region. Four obliquely branching *Dhamanîs* (bearing chyle, sweat, and internal secretions) also spread from the central tract, and ramify in numberless minute channels over the limbs and the body.

The Blood-vascular System.—There are two classes of blood conductors: (1) *Sirâs*, which break up into capillaries (*Pratân*) and distribute "pure" blood from the liver (and spleen) to the heart, and from the heart to the rest of the body (*asrigvahâscha rohinyah sirâh nâtyuṣnaśîtalâh*,—Suśruta, Sarîrasthâna, Chap. VII.; *cf.* Vâgbhata : *daśa mûlaśîrâh hritsthâh*, Chap. III., Sârîrasthâna), and (2) *Dhamanîs* (*Raktavâhinyah*), which proceed, two from the intestinal tract (portal vein and inferior vena cava), and two from the heart (superior vena cava and pulmonary artery?).

The "venous" blood (chyle-mixed blood) proceeds from the alimentary tract (gastric and intestinal vessels), along a *Dhamanî* trunk (portal vein?) to the liver (and spleen), where the chyle gets a red pigment and is turned into (pure) blood. From the liver and spleen, *Sirâs* ("arteries") proceed to the heart. The liver (and spleen, a minor blood-vascular gland) and the heart are the centres of origin of the *Sirâs* ("arteries"), and distribute pure blood by their means over the entire body.

Arrangement of the blood-bearing *Sirâs* and *Dhamanîs.* — Two blood-bearing *Dhamanî* trunks ("veins") proceed from the heart (superior vena cava and pulmonary artery?), and two proceed from different regions of the alimentary tract (portal vein and inferior vena cava?). Ten *Sirâs* bearing pure blood proceed from the alimentary tract to the liver and spleen, which are joined on to the heart by means of both *Sirâs* and *Dhamanîs.* The ten *Sirâs* are subdivided into 175 branches, which are distributed over the body in the same way as the lymph-bearing *Sirâs* (*vide supra*).

It is clear that Charaka and Suśruta had no idea of the part played by the lungs in the purification of the blood. The liver converts the "venous" blood in this system into true ("arterial") blood, and along with the spleen serves as a basis of discrimination between a *Sirâ* and a *Dhamanî*, thus illustrating Suśruta's statement that the distinction between these two kinds of blood-vessels must be accepted as real, inasmuch as they have different sources and different functions.

तासान्तु नाभिप्रभवानां धमनीनामूर्ध्वंगा दश दश चाधोगामिन्यस्तत्-सक्तियेग्गाः जद्ध्वगास्तु हृदयमभिप्रपन्ना स्तिधा जायन्ते । अधोगमास्तु पित्ताशय-मभिप्रतिपन्नास्तत्रस्थमेवान्नपानरसं विपक्कं औष्ण्याद् विरेचयन्त्यः अभिवहन्त्यः शरीरं तर्पयन्ति चोद्ध्वगतानां तिर्यग्गतानां रसस्थानमभिपूरयन्ति (Suśruta, Śârîrasthâna, Chap. IX.). तत्र पांचभौतिकस्य आहारस्य सम्यक् परिणतस्य यस्तेजोभूतः सारः परमसूक्ष्मः स रस इष्यते । तस्य च हृदयं स्थानम् । स हृदयाच्चतुर्विंशतिः धमनीरनुप्रविश्य जद्ध्वगा दश दश चाधोगामिन्यस्तत्-सक्तियेग्गाः कृत्स्नं शरीरं अहरहस्तर्पयति । तस्य शरीरमनुधावतोऽनुमानाद् गतिरुपलक्ष्यितव्या । स खल्वाप्योरसः यकृत्प्लीहानौ प्राप्य रागमुपैति । (Ibid., Chap. IV.). रञ्जिततेजसाश्चाप: शरीरस्थेन देहिनो रक्तमित्यभिधीयते । (Ibid., Sutrasthâna, Chap. XIV.). सप्तशिराशतानि भवन्ति । याभिरिदं शरीरम् आराम इव जलहारिणीभिः केदार इव कुल्याभिरुपस्निहयते आकुञ्चनप्रसारणादिभिर्विशेषैः । नाभ्यां सक्ता निबद्धास्ताः प्रतन्वन्ति समन्ततः । तासां मूलशिराः चत्वारिं शतासां वातवाहिन्यो दश पित्तवाहिन्यो दश कफवा-हिन्यो दश दश च रक्तवाहिन्यः । तासान्तु वातवाहिनीनां वात स्थानगतानां पञ्चसप्ततिशतं भवति । रक्तवाहिन्यश्च यकृत्प्लीहोरेव । तत्र वातवाहिन्यः शिराः एकस्मिन् सक्थ्नि पञ्चविंशतिः । एतेन इतरसक्थिबाहू च व्याख्यातौ । विशेषतस्तु कोष्ठे पृष्ठे चोदरे वक्षसि जत्रुणः जद्ध्वं । एवं रक्तवहाः कफवहाश्च । धातूनां पूरणं वर्णं स्पर्शज्ञानमसंशयम् । स्वाः शिराः सर्वद्रव्यं कुर्य्याच्चान्यान् गुणानपि (Śârîrasthâna, Chap. VIII.). द्वितीया (कला) रक्तधरा नाम । तस्यां शोणितं विशेषतस्तु शिरासु यकृत् प्लीहोष्ठ भवति (Ibid., Chap. IV.). षष्ठी (कला) पित्तधरा नाम । चतुर्विधमन्नपानमुपयुक्तमामाशयात् प्रच्युतं पक्काश-योपस्थितं धारयति । स्रोतस्तद् विज्ञेयं शिराधमनीवर्ज्जितं । ... तानि (स्रोतांसि) प्राणान्नोदकरसरक्तमांसमेदोमूत्रपुरीषशुक्रार्तववहानि । तत्र प्राणवहे द्वे । तयोर्मूलं हृदयं रसवाहिन्यश्च धमन्यः । उदकवहे द्वे । तयोर्मूलं तालु क्लोम (Kloma, gall-bladder) च । तत्र विद्धस्य पिपासा । अन्नवहे द्वे । तयोर्मूलं आमाशयः अन्नवाहिन्यश्चधमन्यः । रसवहे द्वे । तयोर्मूलं हृदयं रसवाहिन्यश्च धमन्यः । रक्तवहे द्वे । तयोर्मूलं यकृत्प्लीहानौ रक्तवाहिन्यश्च धमन्यः । मांसवहे द्वे । तयोर्मूलं स्नायुत्वचं रक्तवाहिन्यश्च धमन्यः ।

Section 3.

THE NERVOUS SYSTEM IN CHARAKA.

The Nerves.—*Dhamanîs* as nerves: The anatomy of the nervous system in Charaka and Suśruta can be more clearly and confidently restored. The *Dhamanîs* that ascend from the heart divide into thirty cords, of which twenty, *i.e.* ten pairs, are cranial nerves, and the other ten, or five pairs, are engaged in conveying vital currents, metabolic fluid, lymph, blood, and chyle.

The cranial nerves are: (1) four pairs of sensory nerves carrying sensory impulses from the sense-organs to the heart, viz. the optic, auditory, olfactory, and gustatory nerves, and (2) six pairs of motor (or mixed nerves), *e.g.* three pairs of motor nerves for the eye (Motores oculorum, Pathetic and Abducentes) working the Levator Palpebræ and other muscles of the orbit; one pair of motor nerves for articulation (the Hypoglossal); one pair of motor nerves for the larynx (the Pneumo-gastric), and another pair connected with mammæ and (in the case of the male) the seminal duct. It is further stated that other motor or sensori-motor impulses are carried by some of these cranial nerves, viz. those which produce sighs and sobs, yawning, laughter, and hunger. Evidently some of the functions of the pneumogastric and the spinal accessory nerves are intended, as also of the phrenic and other nerves of the cervical plexus.

Of the thirty descending *Dhamanîs*, ten (or five pairs) are conductors of blood, chyle, vital current, metabolic fluid, and lymph, and the remaining twenty are spinal nerves (specially the nerves of the sacro-coccygeal and sacral plexuses, if not also of the lumbar plexus). The obliquely branching *Dhamanîs*, so far as they are nerves, comprise the brachial and the lumbar plexus, and divide and sub-divide hundred-fold, thousand-fold, till they ramify into fibrillæ round the pores of the skin. They carry to the heart cutaneous sensations, external as well as internal. A fibril (सूक्ष्मनाड़ी) is said to be as minute as the thousandth part of a hair (लोम्नः सहस्रभागेन तुल्यासु प्रचरत्ययुः—*Panchadaśî*).

अदृश्यगाः शब्दरूपरसगन्धप्रश्वासोच्छ्वासविजृम्भितक्षुइसितकथितरुदितादीन्-
विशेषान् अभिवहन्त्यः शरीरं धारयन्ति । तासु हृदयमभिप्रतिपन्नास्तिस्रोधा जायन्ते
तास्त्रिंशत् । तासानु वातपित्तकफशोणितरसान् द्वे द्वे वहतस्ता दश । शब्द-
रूपरसगन्धान् अष्टाभिर्गृह्णाति । द्वाभ्यां भाषते । द्वाभ्यां घोषं करोति । द्वाभ्यां
स्वपिति । द्वाभ्यां प्रतिबुध्यते । द्वे च अश्रुवाहिन्यौ । द्वे स्तनसंश्रिते । ते एव
शुक्रं नरस्य स्तनाभ्यां अभिवहतः ।

तिर्य्यग्गानानु चतसृणां धमनीनां एकैका शतधा सहस्रधा चोत्तरोत्तरं
विभज्यन्ते तास्त्वसंख्येयाः ।

ताभिरिदं शरीरं गवाक्षितं तासां मुखानि रोमकूपप्रतिबद्धानि । यैः
स्वेदमभिवहन्ति रसञ्चापि सन्तर्पयन्ति अन्तर्बहिश्च । तैरेव चाभ्यङ्गपरिषेकावगा-
हालेपनवीर्य्याणि अन्तःशरीरमभिप्रतिपद्यन्ते । त्वचि विपक्कानि तैरेव स्पर्शसुख-
मसुखं वा गृह्णाति । तासु रताश्वतसोधमन्यः सर्वाङ्गताः सविभागा व्याख्याताः ।
(Suśruta, Śārîrasthâna, Chap. IX.).

SECTION 4.

THE NERVOUS SYSTEM AFTER THE TANTRAS—PSYCHO-PHYSIOLOGY.

In Charaka and Suśruta (as in Aristotle) the heart is the central organ and seat of consciousness; but in the Tantric writings (as in Galen) the seat of consciousness is transferred to the brain or rather the cerebro-spinal system. The soul (the *Jiva*) has its special seat within the *Brahmarandhra* above the foramen of Monro and the middle commissure, but traverses the whole cerebro-spinal axis, up and down, along the *Suṣumna* (the central passage of the spinal cord). The *Brahmadanda* (vertebral column) contains the *Suṣumna*, the *Brahma Nâḍî*, and the *Manovahâ Nâḍî*. The cerebro-spinal axis with the connected sympathetic system contains a number of ganglionic centres and plexuses (*Chakras, Padmas*) from which nerves (*Nâḍîs, Śirâs,* and *Dhamanîs*)[1] radiate over the head, trunk, and limbs.

Section 5.

GANGLIONIC CENTRES AND PLEXUSES (SYMPATHETIC-SPINAL SYSTEM).

Beginning with the lower extremity, the centres and plexuses of the connected spinal and sympathetic systems may be described as follows :—

(1) The *Adhâra Chakra*, the sacro-coccygeal plexus, with four branches, eleven *angulis* (about nine inches) below the solar plexus (*Kanda, Brahmagranthi*); the source of a massive pleasurable æsthesia, voluminous organic sensations of repose. An inch and a half above

---

[1] The writers of the Yoga and Tantra schools use the term *Nâdî*, by preference, for nerves. They also mean cranial nerves when they speak of *Śirâs*, never using the latter term for arteries, as in the older medical literature.

it, and the same distance below the membrum virile (*Mehana*), is a minor centre called the *Agni-sikhâ*.

(2) The *Svâdhisthâna Chakra*, the sacral plexus with six branches (पत्राणि, दलानि—leaves), concerned in the excitation of sexual feelings with the accompaniments of lassitude, stupor, cruelty, suspicion, contempt.

(3) The *Nâvikanda* (corresponding to the solar plexus, *Bhânubhavanam*), which forms the great junction of the right and left sympathetic chains (*Pingalâ* and *Idâ*) with the cerebro-spinal axis.

Connected with this is the *Manipuraka*, the lumbar plexus with connected sympathetic nerves, the ten branches of which are concerned in the production of sleep and thirst, and the expressions of passions like jealousy, shame, fear, stupefaction.

(4) The *Anâhata Chakra*, the cardiac plexus of the sympathetic chain, with twelve branches, connected with the heart, the seat of the egoistic sentiments, hope, anxiety, doubt, remorse, conceit, egoism, etc.

(5) The *Bhâratîsthâna*, the junction of the spinal cord with the medulla oblongata, which, by means of nerves like the pneumo-gastric, etc., regulates the larynx and other organs of articulation. This also comprises the laryngeal and pharyngeal plexuses.

(6) The *Lalanâ Chakra*, opposite the uvula, which has twelve leaves (or lobes), supposed to be the tract affected in the production of ego-altruistic sentiments and affections like self-regard, pride, affection, grief, regret, respect, reverence, contentment, etc.

(7) The sensori-motor tract, comprising two Chakras, (*a*) the *Âjnâ Chakra*, *lit.* the circle of command (over

movements), with its two lobes, and (*b*) the *Manaschakra*, the sensorium, with its six lobes (five special sensory for peripherally initiated sensations, and one common sensory for centrally initiated sensations, as in dreams and hallucinations).

The *Âjnâvahâ Nâḍîs*, efferent or motor nerves, communicate motor impulses to the periphery from this *Âjnâ Chakra*, this centre of command over movements; and the afferent or sensory nerves of the special senses, in pairs, the *Gandhavahâ Nâḍî* (olfactory sensory), the *Rupavahâ Nâḍî* (optic), the *Śavdavahâ Nâḍî* (auditory), the *Rasavahâ Nâḍî* (gustatory), and the *Sparaśavahâ Nâḍî* (tactile), come from the periphery (the peripheral organs of the special senses) to this *Manaschakra*, the sensory tract at the base of the brain. The *Manaschakra* also receives the *Manovahâ Nâḍî*, a generic name for the channels along which centrally initiated presentations (as in dreaming or hallucination) come to the sixth lobe of the *Manaschakra*.

(8) The *Somachakra*, a sixteen-lobed ganglion, comprising the centres in the middle of the cerebrum, above the sensorium; the seat of the altruistic sentiments and volitional control, *e.g.* compassion, gentleness, patience, renunciation, meditativeness, gravity, earnestness, resolution, determination, magnanimity, etc.; and lastly

(9) The *Sahasrâra Chakra*, thousand-lobed, the upper cerebrum with its lobes and convolutions, the special and highest seat of the *Jiva*, the soul.

गुह्यलिङ्गान्तरे चक्रमाधाराख्यं चतुर्दलम् । परम: सहज: ... आनन्द: ... स्यादैशानादिदले फलं । स्वाधिष्ठानं लिङ्गमूले षट्पर्णं चक्रमस्यच । पृष्ठादिषु दलेषु फलानि एतानि प्रश्रय: क्रूरता ... मूर्च्छा ... अवज्ञा स्यादविश्वास:

कामशक्ते रिदं गृहम् । नाभौ दशदलं चक्रं मणिपूरसंज्ञं । सुषुम्नित्र तृष्णा स्यादीर्षा ... लज्जा भयं घृणा मोह: ... क्रमात् पूर्वादि दलेषु स्यात् भानुभवनञ्च तत् ।

हृदये अनाहतं चक्रं । दलैर्द्वादशभिर्युतं । लौल्यं कापट्यं वितर्कोऽप्यनुतापिता आशा ... चिन्ता ... दम्भोवैकल्प्यं विवेकोऽहंकृतिस्तथा फलान्येतानि । कखठेऽसि भारतीस्थानं षोडशच्छदं तत्र प्रणव उद्‌गीष्म: सप्त स्वरा षड्जादय: । ललनाख्यं घटिकायां चक्रं द्वादशपत्रकं । दमोमानस्तत: स्नेह: शोक: खेदश्च सम्भ्रमश्चोर्मि: श्रद्धा तोषोऽपराधिता फलानि ललनाचक्रे । भ्रूमध्ये द्विदलं चक्रं आज्ञासंज्ञं फलानि च आविर्भावा: सत्त्वरजस्तमसां । तत्र चास्ति मनश्चक्रं षड्दलं तत्फलानि तु स्वप्नो रसोपयोगश्च घ्राणं रूपोपलम्भनं स्पर्शीनं शब्दबोधश्च पूर्वादिषु दलेषु । ततोऽपि षोड्शदलं सोमचक्रं । दलेषु षोडश तस्य कला: षोडश संस्थिता: । कृपाघ माहैवं धैर्यं वैराग्यं धृतिसम्पदौ हास्यं रोमाञ्चं विनयो ध्यानं सुस्थिरता तत: । गाम्भीर्य्यमुद्यमोऽच्छोभौदार्य्यंकायहे क्रमात् । फलान्युद्यन्ति जीवस्य पूर्वादिदलगामिन: । चक्रे सहस्रपत्रन्तु ब्रह्मरन्ध्रे । सुषुम्नया ब्रह्मरन्ध्रमारोह्यावरोहति । जीव: प्राणसमारूढो रज्ज्वा कोलाटिको यथा । ब्रह्मरन्ध्रे स्थितो जीव: सुधया संप्लुत: । ... आधाराद्द्व्यङ्गुलादूर्ध्वं मेहनाद्द्व्यङ्गुलादध: अग्निशिखा (चक्रं) चक्रात् तस्मात् नवाङ्गुल: देहस्य कन्दोऽसि । उत्सेधायामाभ्यां चतुरङ्गुल: ब्रह्मयन्त्रिरितिप्रोक्त: ।
(संगीतरत्नाकर as summarised in Dâmodara's Sangitadarpaṇa; *vide* Sangita-ratnâkara, पिराडोत्पत्तिप्रकरण, verses 116-144)
दीर्घास्थिर्मूर्द्धपर्य्यन्तं ब्रह्मदण्डेति कथ्यते तस्यान्ते सुषिरं सूक्ष्मं ब्रह्मनाडीति सूरिभि: (उत्तरगीता)-तत् कर्णिकायां विश्वव्यापिशाखासहस्रवत्या मनोवहनाड्या मूलं तिष्ठति । तस्या अलाबुलतिकायाइव अधऽर्ध्मुखे एकाशाखा सुषुम्ना इति गीयते । स वैमनोवहा नाडी चित्तस्थानं भवति (विज्ञानभिक्ष, योगवार्त्तिक) सुषुम्ना चोद्‌र्ध्वगामिनी ज्ञाननाडी भवेत् (*Jnâna Sankalinî Tantra*). For functions of *Âjnâvahâ Nâḍî* and *Manovahâ Nâḍî*, also see Śankara Miśra's *Upaskâra*.

The cerebro-spinal axis and the heart: their respective relations to the conscious life.—Vijnânabhikshu, in the passage just quoted, identifies the *Manovahâ Nâḍî* (vehicle of consciousness, चित्तस्थान) with the cerebro-spinal axis and its ramifications, and compares the figure to an inverted gourd with a thousand-branched stem hanging down. The *Suṣumna*, the central passage of the spinal cord, is the stem of this gourd (or a single branch). The writers on the Yoga (including the authors of the various Tantric systems) use the term somewhat differently. On this view, the *Manovahâ Nâḍî* is the channel of the communication of the *Jiva* (soul) with the *Manaschakra* (sensorium) at the base of the brain. It has been stated that the sensory currents are brought to the sensory ganglia along afferent nerves of the special senses. But this is not sufficient for them to rise to the level of discriminative consciousness (सविल्वकज्ञानम्). A communication must now be established between the *Jiva* (in the *Sahasrâra Chakra*, upper cerebrum) and the sensory currents received at the sensorium, and this is done by means of the *Manovahâ Nâḍî*. When sensations are centrally initiated, as in dreams and hallucinations, a special *Nâḍî* (*Svapnavahâ Nâḍî*), which appears to be only a branch of the *Manovahâ Nâḍî*, serves as the channel of communication from the *Jiva* (soul) to the sensorium. In the same way, the *Âjnâvahâ Nâḍî* brings down the messages of the soul from the *Sahasrâra* (upper cerebrum) to the *Âjnâ Chakra* (motor tract at the base of the brain), messages which are thence carried farther down, along efferent nerves, to various parts of the periphery. I may add that the special sensory nerves, together with the *Manovahâ Nâḍî*, are sometimes generally termed *Jnânavahâ Nâḍî*, lit. channel of presentative knowledge. There is no difficulty so far. The *Manovahâ Nâḍî* and the *Âjnâvahâ Nâḍî* connect the sensori-motor tract at the base of the brain (*Mânaschakra* and *Âjnâchakra*) with the highest (and special) seat of the soul (*Jiva*) in the upper cerebrum (*Sahasrâra*), the one being the channel for carrying up the sensory, and the other for bringing down the motor messages. But efforts of the will (*Âjnâ*, *Prayatna*) are conscious presentations, and the *Manovahâ Nâḍî* must therefore co-operate with the *Âjnâvahâ* in producing the consciousness of effort. Indeed, attention, the characteristic function of *Manas*, by which it raises sense-presentations to the level of discriminative consciousness, implies effort (*Prayatna*) on the part of the soul (*Âtman, Jiva*), an effort of which we are conscious through the channel of the *Manovahâ Nâḍî*. But how to explain the presentation of effort in the motor nerves? Śankara Miśra, the author of the *Upaskâra* on *Kanâda's Sûtras*, argues that the *Nâḍîs* (even the volitional or motor nerves) are themselves sensitive, and their affections are conveyed to the sensorium by means of the nerves of the (inner) sense of touch (which are interspersed in minute fibrillæ among them). The consciousness of effort, then, in any motor nerve, whether *Âjnâvahâ* (volitional-motor) or *Prâṇavahâ* (automatic-motor), depends on the tactile nerves (or nerves of organic sensation) mixed up with it. Thus the assimilation of food and drink by the automatic activity of the *Prâṇas* implies an (automatic) effort (जीवनयोनिप्रयत्न) accompanied by a vague organic consciousness, which is due to the fact that minute fibres of the inner touch-sense are interspersed with the machinery of the automatic nerves (the *Prânavahâ Nâḍîs*).

यद्यपीन्द्रियं मनो न साक्षात् प्रयत्नविषयः तथापि मनोवहनाडीगोचरेण प्रयत्नेन मनसि कर्म्मे द्रष्टव्यं । नाड्यास्तु त्वगिन्द्रियग्राह्यत्वमङ्गीकर्त्तव्यं । अन्यथा प्राणवहनाडीगोचरेण प्रयत्नेन अशितपीताद्यभ्यवहरणमपि न सम्भवेत् । तज्जदिन्द्रियप्रदेशेन मनःसंयोगमन्तरेण सुखदुःखे न स्यातामेव । यदि मनसि कर्म्मे न भवेत् न भवेच्च पादे मे सुखं शिरसि मे वेदना इत्याद्याकारोऽनुभवः । (Śankara Miśra's *Upaskâra*, on Sûtras 14, 15, Âhnika 2, Chap. V.).

The Heart. The heart in the older schools is considered to be the seat of waking consciousness; for the heart expands during waking life and contracts during sleep.

Sleep (स्वाप) again is of two kinds, (1) dreaming sleep (*swapna, supti*), when the external senses are withdrawn into the heart, but the representative-presentative faculty (मनः, चित्तं) wakes, and (2) dreamless sleep (*suṣupti*), when this last faculty is likewise merged in the mere automatic activity of life.

हृदयं पंकजाकृति । सुषिरं स्यादधोपंकचं एतच्च चेतनास्थानं । निमीलति स्वपित्यात्मा जागर्त्ति विकशत्यपि । द्वेधा स्वप्नसुषुप्तिभ्यां स्वापः । बाह्येन्द्रियाणि चेत् लीयन्ते हृदि जागर्त्ति चित्तं सुप्तिस्तदोच्यते । मनश्चेत् लीयते प्राणे सुषुप्तिः स्यात्तदात्मनः—(*Sangîta-ratnâkara*).

Section 6.

NERVE-CORDS AND FIBRES (SYMPATHETIC-SPINAL SYSTEM).

Nerve-cords and fibres—Cranial and spinal nerves, and the connected sympathetic nerves.—With the writers on the Yoga, all the *Sirâs*, and such of the *Dhamanîs* as are not vehicles of vital current, metabolic

Q

226 THE POSITIVE SCIENCES OF

fluid, lymph, chyle or blood, are cranial nerves, and proceed from the heart through the spinal cord to the cranium. These cranial nerves include pairs for the larynx and the tongue, for the understanding and use of speech, for the raising and lowering of the eyelids, for weeping, for the sensations of the special senses, etc.—a confused and unintelligent reproduction of Suśruta's classification. But the enumeration of the spinal nerves with the connected sympathetic chain and ganglia, is a distinct improvement on the old anatomists. The following plan attempts to give a rough idea of the relative position of the principal nerves of the sympathetic-spinal system.

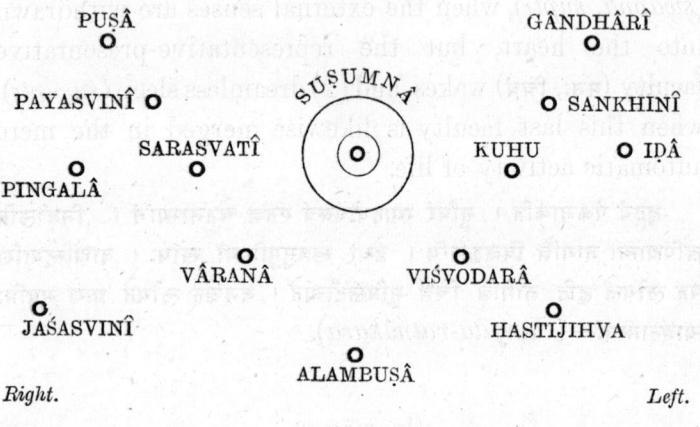

```
              PUṢÂ                                GÂNDHÂRÎ
               O                                      O
                              SUṢUMNÂ
   PAYASVINÎ O                                 O SANKHINÎ
                  SARASVATÎ     (o)      KUHU
                       O                   O      O IḌÂ
   PINGALÂ
       O
                  VÂRAṆÂ           VIŚVODARÂ
                    O                  O
   JAŚASVINÎ                                   HASTIJIHVA
       O                                           O
                         ALAMBUṢÂ
                            O
Right.                                                   Left.
```

The *Suṣumnâ* is the central cord in the vertebral column (ब्रह्मदण्ड, मेरु). The two chains of sympathetic ganglia on the left and the right are named *Iḍâ* and *Pingalâ* respectively. The sympathetic nerves have their main connection with *Suṣumnâ* at the solar plexus (भानुभवन, नाभिचक्र in the कन्द, नाभिकन्द or ब्रह्मग्रन्थि). Of the seven hundred nerve-cords of the sympathetic-spinal system (भूरितरा: Sangîta-ratnâkara), the fourteen most important are:—

(1) *Suṣumnâ*, in the central channel of the spinal cord.

(2) *Iḍâ*, the left sympathetic chain stretching from under the left nostril to below the left kidney, in the form of a bent bow.

(3) *Pingalâ*, the corresponding chain on the right.

(4) *Kuhu*, the pudic nerve of the sacral plexus, to the left of the spinal cord.

(5) *Gândhârî*, to the back of the left sympathetic chain, supposed to stretch from below the corner of the left eye to the left leg. It was evidently supposed that some nerves of the cervical plexus came down through the spinal cord and joined on to the great sciatic nerve of the sacral plexus.

(6) *Hastijihvâ*, to the front of the left sympathetic chain, stretching from below the corner of the left eye to the great toe of the left foot, on the same supposition as before. Pathological facts were believed to point to a special nerve connection between the eyes and the toes.

(7) *Sarasvatî*, to the right of *Suṣumnâ*, stretching up to the tongue (the hypo-glossal nerves of the cervical plexus).

(8) *Puṣâ*, to the back of the right sympathetic chain, stretching from below the corner of the right eye to the abdomen (a connected chain of cervical and lumbar nerves).

(9) *Payasvinî*, between Puṣâ and Sarasvatî, auricular branch of the cervical plexus on the right.

(10) *Sankhinî*, between Gândhârî and Sarasvatî, auricular branch of the cervical plexus on the left.

(11) *Jaśasvinî*, to the front of the right sympathetic chain, stretching from the right thumb to the right leg (the radial nerve of the brachial plexus continued on to certain branches of the great sciatic).

(12) *Vâranâ*, the nerves of the sacral plexus, between Kuhu and Jasaśvinî, ramifying over the lower trunk and limbs.

(13) *Viśvodarâ*, the nerves of the lumbar plexus, between Kuhu and Hastijihvâ, ramifying over the lower trunk and limbs.

(14) *Alambuṣâ*, the coccygeal nerves, proceeding from the sacral vertebræ to the urino-genitary organs.

(*Vide* Sangîta-ratnâkara, खराध्याय, पिण्डोत्पत्तिप्रकरणम्— Ślokas 144–156. Also, the Yogârṇava.)

Section 7.

AUTOMATIC AND REFLEX ACTIVITY OF THE ORGANISM—THE FORTY-NINE *VÂYUS*.

Charaka describes *Vâyu* as that which keeps the machine of the body at work, the prime-mover, the impelling force which sets in motion the organs (including the senses and the mind), which arranges the cells and tissues, and which unfolds or develops the fœtal structure out of the fertilised ovum. Charaka and Suśruta notice the five chief *Vâyus* with their functions in the maintenance of the animal life. Suśruta mentions *Prâṇa* as having its course in the mouth, and concerned in deglutition, hiccough, respiration, etc., *Udâna* as concerned in articulation and singing, *Samâna* as digesting the food in the stomach in conjunction with the animal heat, *Vyâna* as coursing all over the body, driving the chyle and causing the flow of blood and sweat, and *Apâna* as having its seat in the intestinal region, and sending down the urino-genital secretions. (Suśruta—*Nidânasthâna*, Chapter I.)

In the mediæval physiology the number of *Vâyus* is given as 49. As in Charaka and Suśruta, the *Vâyus* are regarded as the moving or impelling forces that work the organism and all its automatic and reflex machinery. The *Âjnâvahâ Nâḍîs* (efferent nerves) are only channels for the conduction of commands of the self or the will (स्वात्मप्रयत्न); the *Vâyus*, on the other hand, are forces (or currents) that maintain the automatic, reflex, or instinctive activities of the organism. The ten chief *Vâyus* with their functions are enumerated thus :—

(1) *Prâṇa*, which works the ideo-motor verbal mechanism and vocal apparatus, the respiratory system, the muscles engaged in coughing, sighing, etc.

(2) *Apâna*, which ejects the excretions and wastes, the urine, the fæces, the sperm and germ-cells, etc.

(3) *Vyâna*, whose work is extension, contraction, and flexion of the muscles, tendons, and ligaments; the stored-up energy of the muscles.

(4) *Samâna*, the force which, in conjunction with animal heat, works the machinery of metabolism, in the maintenance of the organic life. It drives or propels

the chyle, blood, and every other current (*Srota*) or circulating fluid in the body.

(5) *Udâna*, concerned in maintaining the erect posture of the body.

(6) *Nâga*, which is concerned in involuntary retching, vomiting.

(7) *Kûrma*, which works the automatic movement of the eyelids, winking, etc.

(8) *Krikara*, concerned with the appetites of hunger and thirst.

(9) *Devadatta*, which brings about yawning, dozing, etc.

(10) *Dhananjaya*, which is concerned with coma, swooning, trance.

वायुः तन्वयन्लधरः प्रवर्तकः चेष्टानां, प्रष्टोता मनसः, सर्व्वेन्द्रियाणां उद्योतकः, सर्वशरीरधातुव्यूहकरः, सन्धानकरः शरीरस्य, प्रवर्त्तको वाचः, हर्षोत्साहयोर्योनिः, खेष्मा बहिर्मेलानां, कर्त्ता गर्भकृतीनां । प्राणापानोदानसमानव्यानात्मा (चरक सूत्रस्थान, Chap. XII.) तेषां मुख्यतमः प्राणः शब्दोच्चारणिःश्वासोच्छ्वास-काशादिकारणं, अपानः ... अस्य मूत्रपुरीषादिविसर्गः कर्म्म कीर्त्तितं । व्यानः ... प्राणापानधृतित्यागग्रहणाद्यस्य कर्म्म च । समानोऽपि अखिलं व्याप्य शरीरं वह्निना सह । द्विसप्तति सहस्रेषु नाडीरन्ध्रेषु संचरन् भुक्तपीतरसान् सम्यगानयन् देहपुष्टिकृत् । उदानः कर्म्मास्य देहोन्नयनोत्क्रमणादि प्रकीर्त्तितं । त्वगादिधातूनाश्रित्य पंचनागादयःस्थिताः उद्गारादि निमेषादि क्षुत्पिपासादिकं क्रमात् । तन्द्राप्रभृति मोहादि तेषां कर्म्म प्रकीर्त्तितं । (संगीतरत्नाकर ।)

Cf. the summary in Raja Sourîndra Mohan Tagore's edition of the *Sangîta-darpaṇa*.

शब्दोच्चारणं (बाइनिष्पत्तिकारणं) निश्वासः उच्छ्वासः (अनमुखश्वासः) तन्द्रादीनां कारणं (साधनं) प्राणवायुः । विण्मूत्रशुक्रादिवहत्वमपानस्य कर्म्म । आकुञ्चनप्रसारणादि व्यानस्य कर्म्म ज्ञेयं । अशितपीतादीनां समतानयनद्वारा शरीरस्य पोषणं समानस्य कर्म्म । उदानवायुः ऊर्ध्वनयनमेव अस्य कर्म्म नागादयः नागकूर्मकृकरदेवदत्तधनञ्जयरूपाः पञ्च वायवः । एतेषां कर्म्माणि

च यथाक्रमं उद्गारोन्मीलनक्षुधाजननविजृम्भनमोहरूपाणि । (*Sangita-darpaṇa*, Chap. I., Ślokas 43–48). *Cf.* the extract in Śankara.

प्राण: प्राग्वृत्तिरुच्छ्वासादिकर्मा । अपान: अवाग्वृत्तिरुत्सर्गादिकर्मा । व्यान: तयो: सन्धौ वर्तमान: वीर्यवत्कर्महेतु: । उदान: ऊर्ध्ववृत्ति: उत्क्रान्त्यादि हेतु: । समान: समं सर्वेषु अङ्गेषु य: अन्नरसान् नयति । इति । (*Śārīraka Bhāṣya*, Chap. II., Pāda 4, Sūtra 2).

Section 8.

FŒTAL DEVELOPMENT (AFTER SUSRUTA).[1]

The ovum fertilised by the sperm-cell and developing under the influence of animal heat forms successive layers and tissues, even as layers of cells and fibres are formed in wood. First are formed seven layers, epithelial and dermal (*Saptatwachah*), then follow the several tissues (*Kalâh*), the flesh, the vascular tissue, the fat and marrow, the lymphatic and (glandular) tissue, the intestinal tissues, the biliary and the seminal vessels. These tissues are regarded by some as modifications of the original dermal layers of the ovum (*cf.* the layers of the blastoderm and their relation to the tissues in Embryology). The tissues are supposed to be developed successively, one out of another, by chemical action or metabolism (*pâka*), *e.g.* chyle is transformed into blood, blood into flesh, flesh into fat, fat into bone, bone (in reality, fat in the bones) into marrow, marrow into sperm-cell. The organs are next formed out of the tissues. The liver, gall-bladder (*kloma*), spleen, and

---

[1] Reproduced from my monograph in Dr. Ray's "Hindu Chemistry," Vol. II.

lungs are referred to the blood; the intestines to the blood, lymph, and bile; the kidneys to the blood and fat; the testicles to the blood, lymph, and fat; the heart to the blood and lymph; and the tongue to the lymph, blood, and flesh. *Vâyu*, with the accompaniment of animal heat, impels the "currents" (*śrotâmsi*) in the system; *Vâyu* acting on the flesh gives rise to the muscles; and it is *Vâyu*, again, which, with the essence of fat (or marrow), produces the nerves, arteries, and tendons (Suśruta, *Śârîrasthâna*, Chap. IV., and *Sûtrasthâna*, Chap. XIV.).

The following parts (tissues and organs) in the fœtus are in a special sense modifications of the four organic substances (compounds) contributed by the sperm-cell of the male parent: hair, nails, teeth, bones, nerves, veins and arteries, tendons and ligaments, and the sperm-cell; the following are modifications of the four organic substances derived from the mother: skin, blood, flesh, fat, the heart, liver and spleen, kidneys, stomach, intestines, etc. (Charaka, *Śârîrasthâna*, Chap. III.).

The rudiments of the head and the limbs begin to appear in the third month, and are developed in the fourth; the bones, ligaments, nails, hair, etc., become distinct in the sixth. In the second month the sexual character is indicated by the shape of the fœtus, the shape of a round joint (?) indicating the male sex, and an elongated shape, as of a muscle (?), the female sex. (*Cf.* Charaka, *Śârîrasthana*, Chap. IV.—द्वितीयेमासि घनः सम्पद्यते पिण्डः पेश्यर्बुदंवा । तत्र घनः पिण्डः पुरुषः स्त्री पेशी अर्बुदं नपुंसकः Chakrapâni notes घनः कठिनः । पिण्डो ग्रन्थ्याकारः । पेशी दीर्घमांसपेश्याकारा । अर्बुदं वर्त्तुलोन्नत *loc. cit.*)

Section 9.

HEREDITY.

Transmission of specific characters—what parental characters are transmitted to offspring.—The question is raised in Charaka (and earlier still in the *Brâhmanas*) how specific characters are transmitted—why the offspring is of the same species as the parental organism, say, the human or bovine species, the equine species (Charaka), or the Asvattha species, Ficus religiosa (Śankara, Brihadâranyaka-bhâsya). Species (योनयः) may be compared to so many moulds, as it were, into which the ovum is cast, even as molten metals are cast in moulds. This is of course only an illustrative analogy; the cause has to be investigated.

Now Charaka and Suśruta, following Dhanvantari, hold that the fœtus, or rather the fertilised ovum, develops by palingenesis (instead of epigenesis); in other words, all the organs are potentially present therein at the same time, and unfold in a certain order. As the sprouting bamboo-seed contains in miniature the entire structure of the bamboo, as the mango-blossom contains the stone, the pulp, the fibres, which appear separated and distinct in the ripe fruit, though from their excessive minuteness they are undistinguishable in the blossom, even such is the case with the fertilised ovum.

गर्भस्य हि सम्भवतः ... सर्वाङ्गप्रत्यङ्गानि युगपत् सम्भवन्ति इत्याह धन्वन्तरिः । गर्भस्य सूक्ष्मत्वात् नोपलभ्यन्ते वंशाङ्कुरवत् चूतफलवच्च तद्यथा चूतफले परिपक्के केशरमांसास्थिमज्ञानः पृथक् दृश्यन्ते कालप्रकर्षात् । तान्येव तरुणे नोपलभ्यन्ते सूक्ष्मत्वात् । तेषां केशरादीनां कालः प्रव्यक्ततां करोति एतेनैव वंशाङ्कुरोऽपि व्याख्यातः । एवं गर्भस्य तारुण्ये सर्वेषु अङ्गप्रत्यङ्गेषु सत्सु सौक्ष्म्याद-

नुपलब्धिः तान्येव फलप्रकर्षात् प्रव्यक्तानि भवन्ति । (Suśruta, *Śarira sthâna*, Chap. III.).

The inheritance of specific characters is explained in accordance with this view. Charaka assumes that the sperm-cell of the male parent contains minute elements derived from each of its organs and tissues. (*Cf.* Darwin's gemmule and Spencer's "ids.") Śankara similarly states that the sperm-cell (or the seed in the case of a plant) represents in miniature every organ of the parent organism, and contains *in potentia* the whole organism that is developed out of it (शरीरधानवात्मा शुक्रभूतः अङ्गादङ्गात् सम्भवति । Charaka, *Śarirasthâna*, Chap. IV.; *cf.* Śankara on *Brihadâraṇyaka*).

But if this is so, why are not congenital deformities of the parent, or constitutional diseases contracted in later life, invariably inherited? Congenital blindness, deafness, dumbness, stammering, lameness, or deformity of the spinal column or of the bony framework, or dwarfish stature, or constitutional diseases like madness, leprosy, or skin diseases in the parent, do not necessarily produce corresponding deformities or infirmities in the offspring. It cannot therefore be that the fertilised ovum represents in miniature every organ and tissue of the parental organisms. The solution of this difficulty Charaka ascribes to Âtreya. The fertilised ovum, it is true, is composed of elements which arise from the whole parental organism (समुदायात्मक, समुदायप्रभव), but it is not the developed organs of the parents, with their idiosyncrasies or acquired characters, that determine or contribute the elements of the sperm-cell (or seed). The parental Vîja (seed, germ-plasm) contains the whole parental organism in miniature (or *in potentia*), but it is independent of the parents' developed organs, and is not necessarily affected by their idiosyncracies or deformities. In fact, the parental Vîja (seed, germ-plasm) is an organic whole independent of the developed parental body and its organs. In the parental Vîja an element representing a particular organ or tissue may happen (for this is accidental, दैव) to be defective or undeveloped, or otherwise abnormally characterised, and in this case the corresponding organ or tissue of the offspring will be similarly characterised. When constitutional diseases, acquired in later life, are found to be inherited, Âtreya would suppose that the Vîja of the parent has been affected, and this would explain the fact of the inheritance. In the case of leprosy, for example, it is transmitted to the offspring only when the germ-plasm (the Vîja or the fertilised ovum) is infected with the virus of the disease by reason of the leprosy of the parent (*vide* Charaka's report of Âtreya's theory, *Sârîrasthâna*).

एवमयं नानाविधानां एषां गर्भकराणां भावानां समुदायादभिनिवर्त्तते गर्भः ।
यद्ययमेषां नानाविधानां गर्भकराणां भावानां समुदायादभिनिवर्त्तते गर्भः कथमयं
सन्धीयते । यदि चापि सन्धीयते कस्मात् समुदायप्रभवः सन् गर्भो मनुष्यविग्रहेण
जायते मनुष्यश्च मनुष्यप्रभवः । उच्यते । ... तत्र चेत् इष्मेतत्तस्मात् मनुष्योमनुष्य-
प्रभवः तस्मादेव मनुष्यविग्रहेण जायते यथा गौगींप्रभवः यथा चाश्वः अश्वप्रभवः
इत्येवं यत्तुक्तं अग्रे समुदायात्मक इति तद्युक्तं । यदि च मनुष्यः मनुष्यप्रभवः
कस्मात् जडान्धकुब्जमूकवामनमिन्मथ्यङ्गोन्मत्तकुष्ठकिलासेभ्यो जाताः पितृसदृशा
न भवन्ति *et seq.* ...... यच्चोक्तं यदि च मनुष्यो मनुष्यप्रभवः कस्मान्न
जडादिभ्यो जाताः पितृसदृशरूपा न भवन्तीति तत्रोच्यते यस्य यस्यहि अङ्गावयवस्य
बीजे बीजभाव उपतप्तो भवति तस्य तस्य अङ्गावयवस्य विकृतिः उपजायते ।
नोपजायते च अनुपतापात् तस्मात् उभयोपपत्तिरप्यत्र । सर्वस्य च आत्मज्ञानीन्द्रि-

यानि तेषां भावाभावहेतुः दैवं । तस्मात्नैकान्ततो जडादिभ्यो जाताः पितृसदृशरूपा भवन्ति । (चरक, शारीरस्थान, तृतीयपरिच्छेद) दम्पत्योः कुष्ठबाहुल्याहुष्टशोणित-शुक्रयोः । यदपत्यं तयोर्जीतं ज्ञेयं तदपि कुष्ठितं ।

N.B.—The seventh tissue (the *Śukradharâ kalâ*, sperm-bearing or reproductive) contains the parental Vîja, which is a minute organism (समुदायात्मक) deriving its elements from the parental organs, but distinct from the latter, and independent of their peculiarities, and it is the combination and characters of these constituent elements of the parental Vîja in the reproductive tissue that determine the physiological characters and predispositions of the offspring. We may call this Âtreya's *germ-plasm* theory, for it is an advance on the conception of gemmules and of ids, but in Âtreya's version the " germ-plasm " is not only representative of the "somatic" tissues, but also generates and is generated by the latter. This mutual interaction of the " germ-plasm " and " somatic tissues " is a distinctive feature of Âtreya's hypothesis, the value of which will be differently estimated by different schools of biologists.

I may also add that the continued identity of the germ-plasm (बीज) from generation to generation, though it follows as a corollary from this doctrine of a distinct reproductive tissue, even when conceived to be affected by somatic processes, as Âtreya and Charaka conceive it to be, is nowhere expressly deduced. On the other hand, Âtreya and Charaka emphasise the influence of abundant or defective nutrition, and of the constituents of the food, etc., on the characters of the Vîja in the reproductive tissue, especially as regards the sexual character, the stature, and the colour-pigment

(वर्णो) of the offspring. But though the influence of nutrition on the Vîja is thus freely admitted in a general way, it is expressly stated that the peculiar characters or idiosyncracies of the elements that combine to form the Vîja must be regarded as a matter of chance (दैव), in other words, the truly congenital variations are accidental.

Section 10.

THE SEX QUESTION.

Influence of nutrition on the ovum, especially as regards the sex, stature, and colour-pigment of the resulting offspring.—In a general way, ghee and milk for the male, and oil and beans for the female parent, are favourable to the Vîja. The sexual character of the offspring depends in part on a periodicity to which the life-history of the ovum in the female parent is conceived to be subject—a law of alternate rhythmic change (not unlike what we now know to regulate the development of several orders of bacteria or unicellular organisms), a law under which the fertilisation of the ovum on the fourth day after the menstrual discharge, or on the alternate days succeeding, is favourable to the foetus developing the male sexual character, and on the fifth, seventh, and alternate following days to the foetus assuming the female sex. The *Prayogachintâmaṇi* states that the latter occurs on even days, and the former on odd days. Another factor is the relative predominance of the sperm and the germ cells in the fertilised ovum. Excess of the sperm-cell produces the male, that of the germ-cell the female. For male offspring of tall stature, fair complexion, and energetic temperament, wheat-pulp with honey, ghee (clarified butter), and milk should be taken by the female parent. Generally speaking, the adoption of the food, clothing, habits of people of any particular clime are supposed to be favourable to the production of their characteristic stature and complexion. As to sex, the fœtus for a time remains indeterminate, and then takes on a definite male or female character, but before this stage is reached the development of the sex can be modified to some extent by food and drugs (पुंसवनमौषधं). As for the colour-pigment, it is the animal heat (तेजोधातु) which is its source; but where the *Âkâśa* and *Ap* particles predominate (in the food) the animal heat (of the metabolic processes) produces a fair complexion; where Earth and *Vâyu* particles predominate in the food, blackness is the result; and where the different *Bhutas* are combined in nearly equal proportion in the food, the metabolic heat produces a dark pigment. In the later literature, ghee (clarified butter) habitually taken by the female during gestation is supposed to produce a fair complexion, and rice (or wheat) and salads a dark complexion. Charaka also holds that mental impressions of the parent are powerful factors in the determination of the characters of the offspring.

यथाहि बीजमनुपतप्तं उप्तं खां खां प्रकृतिं अनुविधीयते ब्रीहिर्वा ब्रीहित्वं यवोवा यवत्वं तथा स्त्रीपुरुषौ अपि यथोक्तं हेतुविभागं अनुविधीयते । . . . तस्मादापन्नगर्भी स्त्रियमभिसमीक्ष्य प्राग् व्यक्तीभावात् गर्भस्य पुंसवनमौषधमस्यै दद्यात् । . . . स्नानात् प्रभृति युग्मेषु अहःसु संगमेतां पुत्रकामौ तौ अयुग्मेषु दुहितृकामौ । . . . उपाचरेच्च मधुरौषधसंस्कृताभ्यां घृतक्षीराभ्यां पुरुषं स्त्रियन्तु तैलमाषाभ्यां । साचेत् एवमाशासीत् बृहन्तमवदातं हर्यक्षं ओजस्विनं शुचिं

सखसम्पर्वं पुत्रमिच्छेयमिति । शुद्धस्नानात् प्रभृति अस्यै मधुसर्पिभ्यां संसृज्य
श्वेतायाः गोः खरूपवत्सायाः पयसा आलभ्य राजते कांस्ये वा पात्रे काले काले
सम्राहं सततं प्रयच्छेत् पानाय । ... या येषां जनपदानां मनुष्याणां अनुरूपं
पुत्रमाशासीत सा तेषां जनपदानां मनुष्याणां आहारविहारोपचारपरिच्छदान्
अनुविधीयख इति वाच्या स्यात् ।

न खलु केवलमेतदेव कर्म्मे वर्णानां वैशेष्यकरं अपितु तेजोधातुरपि उद्-
कान्तरीक्षधातुः प्रायः अवदातवर्णीकरो भवति । पृथिवीवायुधातुः प्रायः कृष्ण-
वर्णीकरः । समसर्वधातुः प्रायः श्यामवर्णीकरः । आधिक्ये रेतसः पुत्रः,
कन्या स्यात् आर्त्तवेऽधिके ।

Section 11.

LIFE.

These activities maintain the life of the organism, but what is this life itself?

The *Chârvâkas* (materialists and sensationalists) answer that life (as well as consciousness) is a result of peculiar chemical combinations of dead matter (or the four elements) in organic forms, even as the intoxicating property of spirituous liquors results from the fermentation of unintoxicating rice and molasses. Similarly, the instinctive movements and expressions of new-born babes (sucking, joy, grief, fear, etc.) can be explained mechanically as due to external stimuli as much as the opening and closing of the lotus and other flowers at different hours of the day (or night), or the movement of iron under the influence of the loadstone. In the same way, the spontaneous generation of living organisms is frequently observed, *e.g.* the case of animalcules which develop in moisture or infusions, especially under the influence of gentle warmth (स्वेदज, उष्मज, दंशमशकादयः), or of the maggots or other worms which in the rainy season, by reason of the atmospheric moisture, are developed in the constituent particles of curds and the like, which begin to live and move in so short a time.

Gotama, in his *Sûtras*, reports the Chârvâka explanation of instinctive emotional expressions in babes: पद्मादिषु प्रबोधसम्मीलिनवत् तड्डिकारः—Sûtra 20, Âhnika 1, Chapter III.; *cf.* the explanation of the movement preparatory to sucking : अयसो हयस्कान्ताभिगमनवत् तदुपसर्पणं —Sûtra 23, *ibid.* Jayanta, in the *Nyâya-manjarî*, reports the Chârvâka explanation of consciousness (and life).

मदशक्तिवत् विज्ञानं । पृथिव्यादीनि भूतानि चत्वारि तत्त्वानि । तेभ्य एव देहाकारपरिणतेभ्यः मदशक्तिवत् चैतन्यमुपजायते ।

For spontaneous generation, *vide* Jayanta's report :—
वर्षासुच खेदादिना अनतिदवीयसैव कालेन दध्याद्यवयवा एव चलन्तः पूतनादिक्रिमिरूपा उपलभ्यन्ते ।—*Nyâya-manjarî*, Âhnika 7, भूतचैतन्यपक्षः ।

The Sânkhya view of consciousness—Reply to the materialists :—

The intoxicating power in liquor is a force, *i.e.* a tendency to motion, and this is the resultant of the tendencies (or subtile motions) present in the particles of the fermented rice, molasses, etc. A motion, or a tendency to motion, can in this way be the resultant of several other motions or tendencies. But consciousness (चैतन्य) is not a motion, and cannot be the resultant of (unconscious) natural forces or motions. Neither can the consciousness of the Self, or of the organism as a whole, be supposed to be the resultant of innumerable consciousnesses vested in the innumerable constituent particles of the body. One central abiding intelligence is a simpler and therefore more legitimate hypothesis than an assemblage of consciousnesses latent in different Bhûtas or particles, *cf.* Vijnâna-bhiksu's comment on the Sûtra. मदशक्तिर्वचेत् प्रत्येकपरिदृष्टे सांहत्ये तदुद्भव: (Sûtra 22, Chapter III.) ननु यथा मादकताशक्ति: प्रत्येकद्रव्यावृत्तिरपि मिलितद्रव्ये वर्त्तते एवं चैतन्यमपि स्यादिति चेन्न प्रत्येकपरिदृष्टे सति सांहत्ये तदुद्भव: सम्भवेत् । प्रकृते तु प्रत्येकपरिदृष्टत्वं नास्ति ... ननु समुच्चिते चैतन्यदर्शनेन प्रत्येकभूते सूक्ष्मचैतन्यशक्तिरनुमेया इति चेन्न । अनेकभूतेषु अनेकचैतन्यशक्तिकल्पनायां गौरवेण लाघवादेकस्यैव नित्यचित्स्वरूपस्य कल्पनौचित्यात् । *Cf.* also भूतगतविशेषगुणानां सजातीयकारणगुणजन्यतया कारणे चैतन्यं विना देहे चैतन्यासम्भवात् । (*ibid.*).

मद्ये मदशक्तिर्न गुणा: । मद्यारम्भकानां पिष्टगुडमध्वादीनां यत् यस्य कर्म तै कर्मभिरारब्धं स्वस्वकर्मविरोधिकर्मे यदुच्यते प्रभाव इति । चैतन्यादिकं न कर्म । (Gangâdhara's *Jalpakalpataru* (1867, Calcutta), explaining the distinction between property (गुण) and power (प्रभाव), a technical term in medicine, which denotes a form of motion (कर्म) *Sûtrasthâna*, Jalpakalpataru).

The Sânkhya view of Prâna (life) :—

Life, according to the Sânkhya, is not a *Vâyu* (bio-mechanical force) nor any mere mechanical motion resulting from the impulsion of *Vâyu*. The five vital operations, Prâna, Apâna, etc., are called *Vâyus*, but this is only a metaphor. Life is in reality a reflex activity, a resultant of the various *concurrent* activities of the *Antahkaranas*, *i.e.* of the sensori-motor (ज्ञानेन्द्रिय कर्मेन्द्रिय), the emotional (मन:) and the apperceptive reactions of the organism (for some add अहङ्कार).

Vijnâna-bhiksu notes that this explains the disturbing (elevating or depressing) effect on the vitality of pleasurable or painful emotions, like love (काम), which

R

are activities of *Manas*, one of the *Antahkaranas* concerned in the reactions of the living organism. On the Sânkhya view, then, *Prâna* or life is not a *Vâyu*, nor is it evolved from the Bhutas, inorganic matter. *Prâna* is only a complex reflex activity (सम्भूयैका वृत्ति) resulting from the operations of the psycho-physical principles or forces in the organism. *Cf.* Śankara reporting the Sânkhya view—करणानि नियतवृत्तयः सन्तः सम्भूयैकां प्राणाख्यां वृत्तिं प्रतिपद्यन्ते ।—*Śârîraka-bhâṣya*, Chapter II., Pada 4, Sûtra 9. सामान्यकरणवृत्तिः प्राणाद्या वायवः पञ्च ।—Iśvarakriṣṇa, Kârikâ. Also Sûtra 31, Chapter II., where Vijnâna-bhikṣu notes :—

वायुवत् सञ्चारात् वायवः प्रसिद्धाः । अस्माकं नायं नियमः यदिन्द्रियवृत्तिः क्रमेणैव भवति नैकदा । जातिसाङ्कर्य्यस्य अस्माकं अदोषत्वात् । सामग्रीसमवधाने सति अनेकैरपीन्द्रियैः एकदैकवृत्युत्पादने बाधकं नास्ति।—Vijnâna-bhikṣu, *Pravachana-bhâṣya*, Chapter II., Sûtras 31, 32. मनोधर्म्मस्य कामादेः प्राणक्षोभतया सामानाधिकरण्येनैव औचित्यात् ।—*ibid.*

The Vedântic View of Prâṇa.

The Vedântists are believers in an independent vital principle. They agree with the Sânkhyas in holding that *Prâna* is neither a *Vâyu* nor the operation of a *Vâyu*. But neither is life a mere reflex or resultant of concurrent sensori-motor, emotive and apperceptive reactions of the organism. You may put eleven birds in a cage, and if they concurrently and continually strike against the bars of the cage in the same direction, the cage may move on under this conjoint action. But the sensory and motor activities cannot in this way originate the vital activity of the organism. For the deprivation of any one or more of the senses does not mean a deprivation of life, and above all there is this radical distinction : there is sameness of kind (समजातीयत्व) between the motions of the individual birds and the resultant motion of the cage, but the sensations do not explain life. *Life* (Prâna) must therefore be recognised as a separate principle, just as the *Manas* and the *Antahkaranas* generally are in the Sânkhya Philosophy. Life is a sort of subtle rarefied "ether-principle" (अध्यात्मवायु) pervasive of the organism—which is not gross *Vâyu*, but is all the same subtilised matter, like the Manas itself, for, in the Vedânta, everything other than the Self (आत्मा) is "material" (जड).

This Life is prior to the senses, for it regulates the development of the fertilised ovum, which would putrefy if it were not living, and the senses with their apparatus develop subsequently out of the ovum (न वायुक्रिये पृथगुपदेशात्), Chapter II., Pada 4, Sûtra 9 ; *vide* Sarîraka-Bhâsya Sankara ; also Vâchaspati Miśra, Bhâmatî :—

सिद्धान्तस्तु न समानेन्द्रियवृत्तिः प्राणः । स हि मिलितानां वा वृत्तिर्भवेत् प्रत्येकं वा । न तावत् मिलितानां । एकद्वित्रिचतुरिन्द्रियाभावे तदभावप्रसङ्गात् । न खलु चूर्णेहरिद्रासंयोगजन्माऽरुणगणस्तयोरन्यतराभावे भवितुमर्हेति । न च वहुविछिन्नसाध्यं शिविकोद्वहनं द्वित्रिविछिन्नसाध्यं भवति । न च त्वगेकसाध्यं । तथा सति सामान्यवृत्तित्वानुपपत्तेः । अपि च यत् सम्भूयकारकाणि निष्पादयन्ति तत् प्रधानव्यापारानुगुणावान्तरव्यापारेणैव । यथा वयसां प्रातिस्विको व्यापारः पिञ्जरचालनानुगुणः । इहतु श्रवणाद्यवान्तरव्यापारोपेतः प्राणा न सम्भूय प्राण्यु-रिति युक्तं प्रमाणाभावादत्यन्तविजातीयत्वाच्च श्रवणादिभ्यः प्राणनस्य । . . . तस्मादन्यो वायुक्रियाभ्यां प्राणः । . . . वायुरेवायमध्यात्मतामापन्नः मुख्योऽपि प्राणः ।

—Sankara, *ibid. Cf.* also, ज्येष्ठश्च प्राणः शुक्रनिषेककालादारभ्य तस्य वृत्तिलाभात् । नचेत् तस्य तदानीं वृत्तिलाभः स्यात् शुक्रे पूयेत न सम्भवेद्वा श्रोत्रादीनान्तु कर्णशष्कुल्यादिस्थानविभागनिष्पत्तौ वृत्तिलाभान्न ज्येष्ठत्वं ।—Sankara, on Sûtra 9, Pâda 4, Chapter II.

CHAPTER VII.

ON THE SCIENTIFIC METHOD OF THE HINDUS.

The Doctrine of Scientific Method.—A study of the Hindu Methodology of Science is absolutely essential to a right understanding of Hindu positive Science, its strength and its weakness, its range and its limitations. Apart from this rigorous scientific method, Hindu Chemistry, for example, would be all practical recipe, or all unverified speculation. This, however, would be a very inadequate and indeed erroneous view of this early achievement of the human mind. That the whole movement was genuinely and *positively* scientific, though arrested at an early stage, will appear from the following brief synopsis of the Hindu Methodology of Science.

Criterion or Test of Truth, after the Buddhists.— The ultimate criterion of Truth is found, not in mere cognitive presentation, but in the correspondence between the cognitive and the practical activity of the Self, which together are supposed to form the circuit of consciousness. That knowledge is valid which prompts an activity ending in fruition. (*Cf.* the distinction between सम्वादिज्ञान and विसम्वादिज्ञान । Also compare प्रमाणतोऽर्थप्रतिपत्तौ प्रवृत्तिसामर्थ्यात् अर्थवत् प्रमाणम्—Vátsyáyana.) Truth, the Buddhists contend, is *not* self-evidence, *not* the agreement between ideas, *nor* the agreement of the idea with the reality beyond, if any, for this cannot be attained direct, but the harmony of experience (सम्वाद), which is implied when the volitional reaction, that is prompted by a cognition and that completes the circuit of consciousness, meets with fruition, *i.e.* realises its immediate end (with this compare Sríharsha, Khandana Khanda Khádya, on the relation of प्रमा to लोकव्यवहार). This is the material aspect of Truth. The formal aspect is given in a principle which governs all presentations in consciousness, and which combines the three moments of Identity, non-Contradiction, and Excluded Middle in every individual cognitive operation [तदुक्तं तत् परिच्छिनत्ति (identity) अन्यद् व्यवच्छिनत्ति (non-contradiction) तृतीयप्रकाराभावं च सूचयति (excluded middle) इति एकप्रमाणव्यापारः—Jayanta, Nyáyamañjarí, प्रमाणद्वैविध्यखण्डनम्].

Perception.—The conditions of Perception, and its range and limits, were carefully studied. The minima sensibile (*e.g.* the minimum visibile, the Trasarenu, the just-perceptible mote in the slanting sunbeam), the infra-sensible (अनुद्भूतरूप, सूक्ष्म, sometimes termed अतीन्द्रिय), the obscured (अभिभूत, *e.g.* a meteor in the mid-day blaze), and the potential (अनुद्भूतवृत्ति), are distinguished; but finer instruments of measurement were wanting, and this was a principal cause of arrested progress. It may be noted that the measurement of the relative pitch of musical tones was remarkably accurate (*vide* my Paper on Hindu Mechanics and Physics).

Observation (दर्शन—*Váchaspati and Udayana*)— The entire apparatus of scientific method proceeded on the basis of observed instances carefully analysed and sifted. This was the source of the physico-chemical theories and classifications, but in Anatomy the Hindus went one step farther; they practised dissection on dead bodies for purposes of demonstration. Ingenious directions are given, *e.g.*, the body must be first disembowelled and wrapped round with the *kusa* and other grasses, then kept immersed in still water for seven days, after which the medical student should proceed to remove the layers of the skin with a carefully prepared brush made of the fresh elastic fibres of green bamboos, which will enable the tissues, vessels and ducts to be observed. Post-mortem operations as well as major operations in obstetric surgery (the extraction of the fœtus, etc.) were availed of for embryological observations (*e.g.*, it is stated that the rudiments of the head and the limbs begin to appear in the fœtus in the third month, and are developed in the fourth; the bones, ligaments, nails, hair, etc., becoming distinct in the sixth), and also embryological theories, *e.g.*, the indication of sexual character in the second month by the shape of the fœtus, the shape of a *round* joint indicating the male sex, and an *elongated* shape the female sex (*cf.* Charaka, Sútrastháne, Chap. IV.—द्वितीये मासि घनः सम्पद्यते पिण्डः पेश्यर्बुदं वा । तत्र घनः पिण्डः पुरुषः स्त्री पेशी अर्बुदं नपुंसकम् । Chakrapáni notes : घनः कठिनः । पिण्डो ग्रन्थ्याकारः । पेशी दीर्घमांसपेश्याकारा । अर्बुदं वर्तुलोन्नतम् *loc. cit.*). In Phonetics (as in the Prátisákhyas, *circa* 600 B.C.), in Descriptive and Analytical Grammar (as in Pánini), and in some important respects in Comparative Grammar (as in Hemachandra's Grammar of the Prákrita

Dialects), the observation was precise, minute, and thoroughly scientific. This was also the case in Materia Medica and in Therapeutics, especially the symptomology of diseases. In Meteorology the Hindus used the rain-gauge in their weather forecasts for the year, made careful observations of the different kinds of clouds and other atmospheric phenomena (*e.g.*, they estimate the heights of clouds, the distance from which lightning is ordinarily visible or the thunder is heard, the area of disturbance of different earthquakes, the height to which the terrestrial atmosphere extends, etc.; *vide* Varáhamihira, Śrípati, and the authorities quoted by Utpala). In Astronomy the observation was, generally speaking, very defective, as in the determination of the solar and the planetary elements, and this was probably due to the lack of practical interest, but the determination of the lunar constants entering into the calculation of lunar periods and eclipses, matters in which the Hindus had a practical ceremonial interest, reached a remarkable degree of approximation (much above Græco-Arab computations) to the figures in Laplace's Tables, which can only be explained by the circumstance that in the case of these constants the Hindus carried out for more than a thousand years a systematic process of verification and correction by comparison of the computed with the observed results (like the navigator's correction of the course of the ship at sea), a process which was termed दृग्गणितैक्य. In Zoology the enumeration of the species of Vermes, Insecta, Reptilia, Batrachia, Aves, etc., makes a fair beginning, but the classification proceeds on external characters and habits of life, and not on an anatomical basis. In Botany the observation was mainly in the interests of Materia Medica, and the classification was as superficial as possible. (*Vide* my Paper on the Hindu Classification of Plants and Animals.)

Experiments.—Experiments were of course conducted for purposes of chemical operations in relation to the arts and manufactures, *e.g.* Metallurgy, Pharmacy, Dyeing, Perfumery and Cosmetics, Horticulture, the making and polishing of glass (lenses and mirrors of various kinds are mentioned, the spherical and oval वृत्त and वर्तुल being well known—Pliny indeed mentions that the best glass ever made was Indian glass). And the results of such experiments were freely drawn upon for building up scientific hypotheses and generalisations. But of experiment as an *independent* method of proof or discovery the instances recorded in books are rare. I may note one interesting example in Udayana's Kiranávali, relating to the weight of air. Udayana argues that air must be a distinct and independent Bhúta, for if air were a form of the Earth-Bhúta, it would have weight, and it has none. To prove the absence of weight, he refers to an experiment. A small bladder made of a thin membrane, filled with air, will not cause a greater descent in the scale than the same bladder weighed empty. Hence the air possesses no weight. Then Udayana makes an interesting statement. It may be objected, he says, by one who accepts the weight of air, that this argument is inconclusive; for a counter-experiment may be suggested. The balloon filled with smoke (or gas, धूम) rises in the air, whereas the air-filled balloon comes down. This would go to show that air has weight. Udayana replies that this would only show that both smoke (or gas, धूम) and air have no weight. The Hindus appear to have been ignorant of the principle of Archimedes. Vallabhácháryya, in the Lílávatí, it is true, speaks of a peculiar resistance to sinking (or gravity) exercised by water, which explains the tendency in certain objects to float or to come up to the surface of the water, but the description does not show that he had any clear ideas on the subject. Mathuránátha, again, states that the determination of the degree of purity (the carat) of gold by rubbing against the assaying-stone and observing the character of the yellowish streak against the black smooth background, is only an indirect means of ascertaining weight (गुरुत्ववैलक्षण्य, *lit.* specific gravity)—which seems to suggest that there was a more direct means of arriving at the latter. Probably this refers to the common Indian method of comparing the lengths and weights of wires of uniform thickness that can be formed by drawing different pieces of gold through the same diamond bore. I think it may be regarded as fairly certain that the Hindus were ignorant of Archimedes' discovery, an ignorance which, at any rate, they could not have well borrowed from the Greeks, no more than they could have thus borrowed their knowledge of things unknown to the Greeks themselves.

[*Cf.* Udayana, Kiranávali :—वायुनिरूपनम्, किं च (वायो:) पृथिवीत्वे गुरुत्वमपि स्यात् । न च पवनापूरितस्य चर्म्मपुटकादे: अपूरणदशात:

अधिकं अवनमनम् । उद्वीयमानस्य धूमापूरितेन इदम् अनैकान्तिकं इति चेत्
न । अलं धूमदशायां तत्रापि गरिमविशेषहेतोरवनतिविशेषस्य अप्रतीतेः ।
—*cf.* Vallabháchárya, Lílávatí—गुरुत्वविशेषेऽपि पाषाणलावु-
प्रभृतिषु मज्जनोन्मज्जननियमवत् अदृष्टहेतुकतासाम्येऽपि पतनोत्पतननियमो
भविष्यतीति चेत् न । जलाधोगमनं जलेन धारणं पतनप्रतिबन्ध उन्मज्जनं
एतच्च जलस्य योगस्य कस्यचिदेव पतनप्रतिबन्धसामर्थ्यात् । दृष्टहेतुकमेव
मज्जनच्च उन्मज्जनच्च ।] *Cf.* Mathuránátha, सन्निकर्षवादरहस्य on
Gaṅgeśa's Tattvachintámani—तस्य (निकषोपलस्य) न सुवर्ण-
पीताभिव्यञ्जकत्वं किन्तु पीतद्वारा गुरुत्ववैलक्षण्यव्यञ्जकत्वमेव तस्य ।

Fallacies of Observation.—Mal-observation and Non-observation :—These were carefully studied in relation to errors of observation, and hallucination (भ्रम, अध्यास, आरोप), which were ascribed to three causes : (*a*) Dosha, दोष, defect of sense organ, as of the eye in jaundice, or of the skin in certain forms of leprosy (leading to tactile insensibility, *cf.* Suśruta), or defect of necessary stimulus, *e.g.* too faint light, or undue distance or nearness, in vision; (*b*) Samprayoga, सम्प्रयोग, presentation of a part or an aspect instead of the whole; and (*c*) Sanskára, संस्कार, the disturbing influence of mental predisposition, *e.g.* expectation, memory, habit, prejudice, etc.

The Doctrine of Inference.—Anumána (Inference) is the process of ascertaining, not by perception or direct observation, but through the instrumentality or medium of a mark, that a thing possesses a certain character. Inference is therefore based on the establishment of an invariable concomitance (Vyápti, व्याप्ति) between the mark and the character inferred. The Hindu Inference (Anumána) is therefore neither merely formal nor merely material, but a combined Formal-

Material Deductive-Inductive process. It is neither the Aristotelian Syllogism (Formal-Deductive process), nor Mill's Induction (Material-Inductive process), but the real Inference which must combine formal validity with material truth, inductive generalisation with deductive particularisation.

An inference admits of a rigorous formal statement —in the shape of five propositions for dialectical purposes (*i.e.* in demonstrating to others)—or of three propositions when the inference is for oneself (स्वार्थानुमान) :—

(1) The probandum, the statement of the proposition to be established (प्रतिज्ञा, साध्यनिर्देश), *e.g.* yonder mountain is "fiery"; (2) the reason, the ascription of the mark (हेतु, लिङ्गव्यपदेश), *e.g.* for it smokes; (3) the general proposition, stating the invariable concomitance which is the ground of the inference—clenched by an example, *e.g.* whatever smokes is "fiery," as an oven (उदाहरण); (4) next, the application, the ascertainment of the existence of the mark in the present case (उपनय), *e.g.* yonder mountain smokes; (5) finally, the conclusion, the probandum proved (निगमन), *e.g.* yonder mountain is "fiery."

1. Yonder mountain is "fiery."
2. For it smokes.
3. Whatever smokes is "fiery," as an oven.
4. Yonder mountain does smoke.
5. Therefore yonder mountain is "fiery."

For inference for oneself only the first three or the last three propositions are held to be sufficient.

The Hindu Anumána, it will be seen, anticipates J. S. Mill's analysis of the syllogism as a material inference, but is more comprehensive; for the Hindu Udáharaṇa, the third or general proposition with an example, combines and harmonises Mill's view of the major premise as a brief memorandum of like instances already observed, fortified by a recommendation to extend its application to unobserved cases, with the Aristotelian view of it as a universal proposition which is the formal ground of the inference. This Formal-Material Deductive-Inductive process thus turns on one thing—the establishment of the invariable concomitance (व्याप्ति) between the mark and the character inferred—in other words, an inductive generalisation. The question is—what is our warrant for taking the leap from the observed to unobserved cases? Under what conditions are we justified to assert a Universal Real proposition on the basis of our necessarily limited observation?

The Chárváka View.—Among the Chárvákas there were two classes, the cruder school of materialists who accepted perception (प्रत्यक्ष) as a valid source of knowledge, as well as the reality of natural law (स्वभाव), and the finer school of sceptics, who impugned all kinds of knowledge, immediate as well as mediate, and all evidence, Perception as well as Inference; *vide* Jayanta's reference in the Nyáyamañjarí to सुशिक्षितचार्व्वाकाः; also चार्व्वाकधूर्त्तेस्तु अयातत्त्वं व्याख्यास्याम इति प्रतिज्ञाय प्रमाणप्रमेयसंख्यालक्षणनियमाशक्यकरणीयत्वमेव व्याख्यातवान्— Áhnika 1, Mañjarí.

The Chárvákas hold that the principle of causality

which the Buddhists assume to be a ground of an induction (व्याप्ति), is itself an induction (a case of Vyápti), which amounts to reasoning in a circle (चक्रक); that every inference is based on an unconditional invariable concomitance, which itself must be inferred, as universal propositions cannot be established by our limited perceptions, and thus there is a *regressus ad infinitum* (अनादिपरम्परा), and that the *nexus* between cause and effect, or between the sign and the thing signified (*e.g.* smoke and fire), is only a mental step or subjective association based on former perception, a mental step which by accident is found justified by the result in a number of cases.

The Buddhists: their Analysis and Vindication of Inference.—The Buddhists, however, take their stand on the principle of the Uniformity of Nature (प्रतिबन्ध, स्वभावप्रतिबन्ध, Nyáya-Vindu). This uniformity, for scientific purposes, has to be divided into two different relations: (1) the uniformity of succession in the relation of cause and effect, *e.g.* of smoke to fire (कार्य्य-कारणभाव, तदुत्पत्ति, Nyáya-Vindu); (2) the uniformity of co-existence (in the form of co-inherence in the same substrate) in the relation of genus and species, *e.g.* the relation of invariable concomitance expressed in the proposition " all *Sinsapás* are trees," which is not a relation of causality, but of co-existence or co-inherence in the same substrate (*i.e.* the co-inherence of the generic qualities of a tree with the specific characters of a Sisu-tree in this particular individual before me, a Sisu-tree), a relation which may be termed essential identity (तादात्म्य, स्वभाव—Nyáya-Vindu). To these two the Buddhists add a third ground of inference, non-perception of the perceptible (अनुपलब्धि, दृश्यानुपलब्धि), which is employed in inferring the absence (प्रतिषेध) of a thing from the non-perception of the thing or of something else. In all cases of inference based on the Uniformity of Nature, the relation is that of inseparableness or non-disjunction between the mark and the character inferred. The question is: how is this inseparableness (अविनाभाव) ascertained, and what is the warrant of our belief in it in these cases?

Ascertainment of Inseparableness or Non-disjunction: Buddhist Account.—First take the case of causation. The cause is the invariable antecedent of the effect. What is meant is that (*a*) a specific cause (or sum of causal conditions) is invariably followed by a specific effect, and (*b*) a specific effect (with all the distinctive and relevant accompaniments, कार्यविशेष) is invariably preceded by a specific cause (कारणविशेष). It is not that clouds always lead to rain, or that floods in the river-valley always imply rain in the hills higher up. But this particular conjunction of antecedent circumstances (*e.g.* the appearance of a particular kind of clouds accompanied by flashes of lightning, the roll of thunder and flights of Valákás—driven by the wind from a particular quarter of the horizon, and ascending in black masses, etc.) is as a rule the precursor of a particular assemblage of rain effects (rain with particular accompaniments). Again, this particular kind of flood (overflowing of the river-banks accompanied by muddy discoloration of the water, rapid currents, the bearing down of tree-trunks, etc.) is always preceded by rain in the hills higher up (though, no doubt, other cases of floods in a river may be due to a breach in an embankment or the melting of the snows). In other words, the Buddhists (and the earlier Nyáya schools) avoid the difficulty arising from the plurality of causes by taking into consideration the accompanying phenomena, which, if properly marked, would always point to a specific cause of a specific effect, and *vice versa*.

I quote Nyáya authorities, but this device to obviate the plurality of causes is common to the early Nyáya and the Buddhistic systems.

पूर्ववत् । यत्र कारणेन कार्य्यमनुमीयते । उदाहरणम्—
मेघोन्नत्या भविष्यति वृष्टिरिति कारणेन कार्य्यानुमानम् । कथं पुनरस्य प्रयोगः । वृष्टिमन्तः एते मेघाः गम्भीरध्वनिवत्त्वे सति बहुवलाकावत्त्वे सति अचिरप्रभावत्त्वे सति उन्नतिमत्त्वात् वृष्टिमन्मेघवत् ।

शेषवत् (यत्र कार्य्येन कारणमनुमीयते)—उदाहरणम्—
उपरिवृष्टिमद्देशसम्बन्धि नदीस्रोतः शीघ्रत्वे सति पूर्णफलकाष्ठादिवहनत्वे सति पूर्णत्वात् पूर्ववृष्टिमन्नदीवदिति । (Udyotakara, Chap. I., Áhnika 1, Sútra 5.) Váchaspati puts this clearly:—
यद्यपि कारणमात्र व्यभिचरति कार्य्योत्पादं तथापि यादृशं न व्यभिचरति तत्र निपुणेन प्रतिपन्न भवितव्यम् । अन्यथा धूममात्रमपि वह्निमत्त्वा व्यभिचरतीति न धूमविशेषो गमको भवेत् । In other words, a single condition called a cause is not invariably succeeded by the effect, nor does the effect-phenomenon in general point to any particular cause as antecedent, for there may be a plurality of causes of a general effect. The skilful observer will therefore select the full complement of causal conditions which is invariably succeeded by the effect, and also the specific effect (*e.g.* धूमविशेष) which points to a specific causal antecedent. Compare also

Jayanta: "We infer an effect from a specific assemblage of causes"—न च कारणमात्रस्य हेतुत्वं ब्रुमो येनास्य व्यभिचारः स्यात् । अपि च विशिष्टमेव कारणं हेतुः । न च कारणविशेषो दुरवगमः । गम्भीर-गर्ज्जितारम्भनिर्भिन्नगिरिगह्वराः रोलम्बगवलव्यालतमालमलिनत्विषः . . . वृष्टिं व्यभिचरन्तीह नैव प्रायः पयोमुचः । अनभ्युपगमे चैवमनुमानस्य जीवितम् । न स्याड्रुमविशेषाणामपि बोद्धुमशक्तितः । Similarly, we infer a specific cause from a specific assemblage of effects:—शेषवदिति यत्र कार्येण कारणमनुमीयते यथा नदीपूरेण उपरितने देशे वृष्टिरिति । वृष्टिमत्पृष्टदेशसंसृष्टा ईयं नदी फेनिलकलुषत्वादिविशिष्टपूरो-पेतत्वात् । यत्तु सेतुभङ्गहिमविलयनादिनापि नदीपूरोपपत्ति दृष्टा इति तत्रापि उच्यते—

प्रमातुरपराधोऽयं विशेषं यो न पश्यति ।
नानुमानस्य दोषोऽस्ति प्रमेयाव्यभिचारिणः ॥

(Nyáyamañjarí, Áhnika 2, on Gotama Sútra 5, Áhnika 1, Chap. I.)

A specific assemblage of causes, therefore, has only one specific assemblage of effects, and *vice versa*. Of course, the observer is to find out the essential or relevant features (as distinguished from the irrelevant ones) which, being included, will enable him to specify the particular cause of the particular effect.

Now, this being premised to be the exact meaning of the inseparableness or non-disjunction in the case of cause and effect, we come to the question with which we started—how is this relation to be ascertained or established between two phenomena or assemblages of phenomena? Obviously, mere observation of their agreement in presence (अन्वय) and their agreement in absence (व्यतिरेक) is no help in the matter. Take a concrete example. The ass is customarily employed to bring the fuel with which fire is lighted. In a hundred cases you have observed the ass among the antecedents of smoke. In a hundred cases you may have observed that when there is no ass there is no smoke. This is no warrant for concluding a relation of cause and effect between an ass and smoke. It may be that you happen to have never observed smoke without an antecedent ass, or an ass without smoke following. Even this is of no avail. It is not agreement (unbroken and uniform though it be) in presence or in absence, or in both, that can settle the matter. There is one and only one way of ascertaining the causal relation. Suppose A with certain accompaniments is found to precede B immediately. Now, if A disappearing B disappears, even though all other antecedents remain and there is no other change in the case, then and then only can the causal relation be ascertained. It is not a mere table of positive instances or negative instances (अदर्शनान्न दर्शनात्); it is this Method, which we may term the Method of Subtraction (the Method of Difference in its negative aspect), that is the only exact and rigorous scientific Method. Such was the statement of the earlier Buddhists (*cf.* Udyotakara's and Váchaspati's report of the Buddhist doctrine of Inference—स हि प्रतिबन्धी न दर्शनमात्रावसेय:).

तस्मात् तादात्म्यतदुत्पत्तिनिबन्धनः एव प्रतिबन्धः । यदाह कार्य्यकारण-भावाद्वा स्वभावाद्वा नियामकात् । अविनाभावनियमोऽदर्शनान्न दर्शनात् —a Buddhist Káriká quoted in Váchaspati, Udayana. Sríharsha, Mádhava, etc.—कार्य्यकारणभावश्च इदम्—अस्मिन् सति भवति—सत्सु अपि तदन्येषु अस्मिन्नसति न भवति—एवमाकारः । न अन्वयव्यतिरेकाभ्यामतिरिच्यते । . . . (एवं तादात्म्यमपि विपर्य्यये बाधक-प्रमाणोपपत्त्या निश्चेतव्यम् । . . . तस्मात् तादात्म्यतदुत्पत्तिभ्यामेव प्रतिबन्धो

S

नान्यत: ।—Váchaspati, Tátparyyatiká, Chap. I., Áhnika 1, Sutra 5, अनुमानलक्षणम्—व्याभिग्रहोपाय:)

But the canon in this form is not sufficiently safeguarded against possible abuse. Two points have to be emphasised : (1) It must be carefully observed that no other condition is changed, (2) that the appearance and disappearance of A must immediately precede the appearance and disappearance of B. The definition of a cause is based on two fundamental characters : (1) the unconditional invariableness of the antecedence, and (2) the immediateness of the antecedence. The canon of the Method of Difference must therefore be stated in such a form as to emphasise each of these aspects. And one main difficulty in the practical application of the canon is that, along with the introduction or sublation of an antecedent, some other phenomenon may be introduced or sublated unobserved. As a safeguard against this radical vitiation of the Method, the later Buddhists formulated the canon of a modified Method, termed the Pañchakáraní, a Joint Method of Difference, which combines the positive and the negative Methods of Difference (the Method of Addition and the Method of Subtraction) in a series of five steps, and which equally emphasises the unconditionality and the immediateness of the antecedence as essential moments of the causal relation. This is neither agreement in presence nor agreement in presence as well as absence (the foundation of J. S. Mill's Joint Method of Agreement), but the Joint Method of Difference. The Pañchakáraní runs thus :—

The following changes being observed, everything

else remaining constant, the relation of cause and effect is rigorously established :—

 First step—The "cause" and the "effect" phenomena are both unperceived.

 Second step—Then the "cause" phenomenon is perceived.

 Third step—Then, in immediate succession, the "effect" phenomenon is perceived.

 Fourth step—Then the "cause" phenomenon is sublated or disappears.

 Fifth step—Then, in immediate succession, the "effect" phenomenon disappears.

Throughout, of course, it is assumed that the other circumstances remain the same (at least the relevant or material circumstances).

This Pañchakáraní, the Joint Method of Difference, has some advantages over J. S. Mill's Method of Difference, or, what is identical therewith, the earlier Buddhist Method; and the form of the canon, bringing out in prominent relief the unconditionality and the immediateness of the antecedence, is as superior from a theoretical point of view to J. S. Mill's canon, and is as much more consonant than the latter to the practice of every experimenter, as the Hindu analysis of Anumána as a Formal-Material Deductive-Inductive Inference is more comprehensive and more scientific than Aristotle's or Mill's analysis of the Syllogism (or Mediate Inference).

But even the Pañchakaraní is no sufficient answer to the question with which we started. The Pañchakáraní is only a method ; it shows only how in a particular case the relation of cause and effect is to be established (प्रतिवन्धग्रहोपाय). But we want more than this—we require a warrant for the process. The Buddhists therefore supply the following proof of the Method : Doubt is legitimate, but there is a limit to doubt. When doubt lands you in an unsettlement of a fundamental ground of practice, and would thus annul all practical exercise of the will, the doubt must cease ; else the doubt would be suicidal or sophistical. In this particular case, when the Pañchakáraní is satisfied, the antecedent in question must be the cause, for there is no other antecedent to serve as cause ; the proof is indirect but rigid. If this be not the cause, there is no cause of the phenomenon. It was not, and it begins to be, without a cause ; which would be a contradiction of the rational ground of all practice, for all volitional activity proceeds by implication on the principle of causality. If things could happen without a cause, all our motives to action would be baffled. The link between a presentation and the instinctive volitional reaction would snap, and the circuit of consciousness would be left incomplete. In fact, the Buddhists go farther ; they hold causal efficiency (अर्थक्रिया) to be of the essence of empirical (relative) Reality. The proof of the Joint Method of Difference, then, lies in a strict application of the principle of causality in its negative form (viz., there can be no phenomenon without a cause), and the truth of this last is guaranteed by the same ultimate criterion of empirical (relative) Reality as the truth of Perception itself, viz. the correspondence between the rational and the practical activity of the self.

But invariable concomitance (or non-disjunction), the Buddhists argue, has another form, *e.g.* the relation of the genus to the species. We may have perceived a hundred instances of the association of certain characters with certain others ; we may also have never perceived the former when the latter were absent ; but this would not enable us to generalise and establish invariable and unconditional co-existence. We must be first satisfied that there is identity of essence (तादात्म्य, स्वभाव). It is only when we perceive that the characters of a *Sin*sapá are co-inherent with the generic characters of a tree in the same individual object (a *Sin*sapá-tree before me), and when we further perceive that the characters are held together by the relation of identity of essence, that we can say that all *Sin*sapás are trees. For as there is identity of essence, a *Sin*sapá would not be a *Sin*sapá if it were not a tree ; it would lose its self-identity, which is a contradiction. Hence the relation of identity of essence (तादात्म्य, स्वभाव), as in the relation of the species to the genus, is the sole ground for establishing uniformity of co-existence (प्रतिबन्ध, स्वभावप्रतिबन्ध).

For the Buddhist Method of Induction in its later form, the Pañchakáraní, *vide* Sarvadarsana Sangrahá— Buddhist reply to the Chárváka attack on Inference :—

यदभ्यधायि अविनाभावो दुर्बोध इति तदसाधीयः । तादात्म्यतदुत्पत्तिभ्याम्-विनाभावस्य सुज्ञानत्वात् । तदुक्तं—कार्य्यकारणभावात् वा स्वभावात् वा नियामकात् । अविनाभावनियमोऽदर्शनान्न न दर्शनात् । As for the Nyáya view, अन्वयव्यतिरेकौ अविनाभावनिश्चायकौ इति ।—the

Buddhist objects: ननु पक्षे साध्यसाधनयोर्व्यभिचारो दुरवधारणः भवेत् । भूते, भविष्यति, वर्त्तमाने अनुपलभ्यमाने च व्यभिचारशङ्कायाः अनिवारणात् ।—the Nyáya retorts: ननु तथाविधस्थले तावकेऽपि मते व्यभिचारशङ्का दुष्परिहरा ज्ञात ।—the Buddhist answers: मैवं वोचः, विनापि कार्य्यं कार्य्यमुत्पद्यताम् इत्येवं विधायाः शङ्कायाः व्याघाता-वधिकृतया निवृत्तत्वात् । तदेव हि आशङ्क्येत यस्मिन्नाशङ्क्यमाने व्याघातादयः नावतरेयुः । तदुक्तं व्याघातावधिराशङ्का इति । तस्मात् तदुत्पत्तिनिश्चयेन अविनाभावो निश्चीयते । तदुत्पत्तिनिश्चयश्च कार्य्यहेत्वोः प्रत्यक्षोपलम्भानुपलम्भ-पञ्चकनिबन्धनः । कार्य्यस्य उत्पत्तेः प्रागनुपलम्भः, कारणोपलम्भे सति उपलम्भः, उपलम्भस्य पश्चात् कारणानुपलम्भात् अनुपलम्भः इति पञ्चकारण्या धूम-धूमध्व-जयो कार्य्यकारणभावः निश्चीयते । तथा तादात्म्यनिश्चयेन अपि अविनाभावः निश्चीयते । यदि शिंशपा वृक्षत्वम् अतिपतेत् स्वात्मानमेव जह्यात् इति विपक्षे बाधकप्रवृत्तेः । अप्रवृत्ते तु बाधके भूयः सहभावोपलम्भेऽपि व्यभिचारशङ्कायाः को निवारयिता । शिंशपावृक्षयोश्च तादात्म्यनिश्चयः वृक्षोऽयं शिंशपा इति सामानाधिकरण्यबलात् उपपद्यते तस्मात् कार्य्यात्मानौ कारणम् आत्मानम् अनुमापयत इति सिद्धम् । Sarvadarśana Saṅgrahá, Bauddha-Darśanam; *vide* also Śridhara, Kandalí.

The Nyáya Doctrine of Inference.—The Nyáya easily demolishes the Buddhist contention about identity of essence. The Nyáya writers, being realists, do not impugn the reality of the genus (जाति) like the nominalists or the nominalistic conceptualists; but they point out that the inseparableness (or non-disjunction) in such cases can only be established by the experience of unbroken uniformity (अव्यभिचारित्व, *i.e.* by अन्वयव्यतिरेकौ, दर्शनादर्शने). Uniform agreement in presence with uniform agreement in absence—not the mysterious identity of essence irresistibly perceived in any individual case or cases—is the only basis for constituting genera and species in natural classification. Indeed, some of the later Nyáya writers point out that individuals do not always possess in nature all the characters that go to form the definition of the class to which they are referred.

Similarly, as regards the relation of cause and effect, a *nexus* is sometimes fancied to be perceived, a power in the cause to produce the effect (शक्ति), or an ultimate form (जातिसौक्ष्म्य), which is supposed to be present whenever the effect (quality or substance) is produced (*cf.* Bacon's view of the "Forms" of Simple Qualities). All this is neither a matter of observation nor of legitimate hypothesis. There is nothing except the invariable time-relation (antecedence and sequence) between the cause and the effect. But the mere invariableness of an antecedent does not suffice to constitute it the cause of what succeeds; it must be an unconditional antecedent as well (अन्यथासिद्धिशून्यस्य नियतपूर्ववर्तिता, being the definition of कार्यकारणभाव). For example, the essential or adventitious accompaniments of an invariable antecedent may also be invariable antecedents; but they are not unconditional, but only collateral and indirect. In other words, their antecedence is conditional on something else (न स्वातन्त्र्येण). The potter's stick is an unconditional invariable antecedent of the jar; but the colour of a stick, or its texture or size or any other accompaniment or accident which does not contribute to the work done (so far as we are considering it), is not an unconditional antecedent, and must not therefore be regarded as a cause. Similarly, the co-effects of the invariable antecedents, or what enters into the production of these co-effects, may themselves be invariable antecedents; but they are not unconditional, being themselves conditioned by those of the antecedents of which they are effects. For example, the sound produced by the stick or by the potter's wheel invariably precedes the jar, but it is a co-effect, and Ákása (ether) as the substrate and Vayu (air) as the vehicle of the sound enter into the production of this co-effect; but these are not "unconditional" antecedents, and must therefore be rejected in an enumeration of conditions or causes of the jar. Again, the conditions of the conditions, the invariable antecedents of the invariable antecedents, are not unconditional. The potter's father is an invariable antecedent of the potter who is an invariable antecedent of the jar, but the potter's father does not stand in a causal relation to the potter's handiwork. In fact, the antecedence must not only be unconditionally invariable, but must also be immediate (अव्यवहितपूर्वकालावच्छेदेन कार्यदेशे सत्त्वम्). Finally, all seemingly invariable antecedents which may be dispensed with or left out are *ipso facto* not unconditional, and cannot therefore be regarded as causal conditions. In short, nothing that is unnecessary is unconditional. For this class, *vide* Visvanátha :—नियतावश्यकपूर्वभाविनः अवश्यक्लृप्तनियतपूर्ववर्त्तिन एव कार्य्य- सम्भवे । तद्भिन्नम् (अतिरिक्तं) अन्यथासिद्धं—Visvanátha, Siddhánta-Muktávali, on Sloka 20. For example, it is the custom to point to spatial position or direction with the fingers; but finger-pointing, though invariably present, is not causally related to the perception of direction or spatial position, because we can imagine such perception without finger-pointing (अन्यथासिद्धतया अङ्गुल्या निर्देशस्य दिक्प्रत्यक्षत्वेन न स्वाभाविकः सम्बन्धः, Váchaspati, Tátparyyatíká, Chap. I.,

Áhnika 1, Sútra 5. This shows that the doctrine of अन्यथासिद्धिशून्य was long anterior to Gangesa).

[Viśvanátha in the Bháshá-Parichchheda mentions five kinds of अन्यथासिद्ध, conditional antecedents—(1) येन सहपूर्व्वभाव: ; (2) यस्य वा कारणमादाय (पूर्व्वभाव:) ; (3) अन्यंप्रति पूर्व्वभावे ज्ञाते यत्पूर्व्वभावविज्ञानम् ; (4) जनकं प्रति पूर्व्ववर्त्तिताम् अपरिज्ञाय यस्य (पूर्व्ववर्त्तिता) न गृह्यते ; and (5) अथापि यत् नियतावश्यकपूर्व्वभाविन: अतिरिक्तम् भवेत् (एतेषु पञ्चसु आवश्यकत्वसौ—Slokas 19 and 20), यस्य स्वातन्त्र्येण अन्वयव्यतिरेकौ न स्त: किन्तु खकारणमादायैव अन्वयव्यतिरेकौ गृह्यते तदन्यथासिद्धम्—Siddhánta-Muktávali, *loc. cit.*—The Dinakarí points out that the first two cases are comprehended under the formula इतरान्वयव्यतिरेकप्रयुक्तान्वयव्यतिरेकशालित्वम् । There are several classifications of these irrelevant antecedents (अन्यथासिद्ध); I quote one of the best known.]

The unconditional (अन्यथासिद्धिशून्य), as interpreted in this comprehensive sense, is a far more fruitful conception than Mill's, and is well adapted to its work—the elimination of the irrelevant factors in the situation. In the end, the discrimination of what is necessary to complete the sum of causes from what is dependent, collateral, secondary, superfluous, or inert (*i.e.* of the relevant from the irrelevant factors), must depend on the test of expenditure of energy. This test the Nyáya would accept only in the sense of an operation analysable into molar or molecular motion (परिस्पन्द एव भौतिको व्यापार: करोत्यर्थे:—अतीन्द्रियस्तु व्यापारो नास्ति—Jayanta, Mañjarí, Áhnika 1), but would emphatically reject if it is advanced in support of the notion of a mysterious causal power or efficiency (शक्ति). With the Nyáya all energy is necessarily kinetic. This is a peculiarity of the Nyáya—its insisting that the effect is only the sum or resultant of the operations of the different causal conditions—that these operations are kinetic, being of the nature of motion, in other words, holding firmly to the view that causation is a case of expenditure of energy, *i.e.* a re-distribution of motion, but at the same time absolutely repudiating the Sánkhya conception of power or productive efficiency as metaphysical or transcendental (अतीन्द्रिय), and finding nothing in the cause other than an unconditional invariable complement of operative conditions (कारणसामग्री), and nothing in the effect other than the consequent phenomenon which results from the joint operations of the antecedent conditions. (समुदितसकलकारकनिकरपरिस्यन्द एव—Jayanta. सामग्री कार्यं—सामग्रीकार्यत्वे तु कार्यमस्तु किमन्तरालवर्तिन्या शक्त्या—Jayanta, *ibid.*, Áhnika 1, शक्तिनिराकरणम् । It may be noted that the Nyáya, while repudiating transcendental power (Śakti) in the mechanism of Nature and natural causation, does not deny the existence of metaphysical conditions like merit (धर्म), which constitute a system of moral ends that fulfil themselves in and through the mechanical system and order of Nature—*vide* Jayanta, अतीन्द्रियं किमपि कारणं कल्पितमेव धर्मादि—Áhnika 1, शक्तिनिराकरणम् ।)

The causal relation, then, like the relation of genus to species, is a natural relation of concomitance (व्याप्तिः स्वाभाविकः सम्बन्धः—Váchaspati) which can be ascertained only by the uniform and uninterrupted experience of agreement in presence and agreement in absence, and not by deduction from a certain *a priori* principle like that of Causality or Identity of Essence.

Nyáya objection to the Buddhist Method of Difference as a means of ascertaining Causality.—Take for example the Buddhist deduction of Causality in any particular conjunction by means of the negative Method of Difference, or of the Pañchakáraní. The ascertainment of the causal relation by these Methods is open to the following objections: (1) The unconditionality of the antecedent cannot possibly be ascertained. As the Chárváka rightly points out, the Methods enable you to eliminate irrelevant antecedents that are or can be perceived; but the introduction or sublation of latent or undetected antecedents can be imagined, against which the Method of Difference is powerless. In the case of the production of smoke, for example, by fire— what if I say that an invisible demon intervenes in every case between the fire and the smoke, that this demon (पिशाच) is the immediate antecedent and real cause of the latter, and that the fire is an accident which in every such case is brought about by its own causal antecedents? In saying this I do not go counter to the principle of causality, and am landed in no contradiction (व्याघात) such as strikes at the very roots of all practice, or baffles the completed circuit of consciousness, however much I may violate probability.

(2) In the second place, even supposing that the fire in this particular case (which satisfies the Method of Difference rigidly) is ascertained to be the cause of the smoke, how can I know that fire is the cause in other cases, or that there is no other cause? You will perhaps argue that if there were an *indefinite* number of causes of the same specific phenomenal effect, it would

violate the principle that phenomena are all conditioned, *i.e.* exist only under certain conditions (कादाचित्कत्व), which is more comprehensive than the principle of causality, and the contradiction of which equally overthrows all rational practical activity. Yes, I accept the conditionality of phenomena, but this is not violated by supposing that one specific assemblage of phenomena has more than one cause. It is true that if you suppose such plurality of causes you cannot establish the invariableness of the particular conjunction (green-wood fire and smoke) which your Method of Difference fixes upon as a case of cause and effect; in other words, with your special principle of Causality so restricted, and without any general principle of Uniformity of Nature to fall back upon, you cannot ascertain from the present case, or from any number of similar cases that you may have observed, that *all* green-wood fires are followed by smoke, or that in a given case smoke has been preceded by fire—*i.e.*, you are helpless in demonstrating (or ascertaining indubitably) the relation of cause and effect. But this is an objection against your own position, not mine. Why not admit at once that certain phenomena are naturally connected (as invariable concomitants or antecedents) with other phenomena, and take your stand on observed concomitance (uniform and uninterrupted experience of agreement in presence as well as absence) without assuming causality as an *a priori* principle and making deductions therefrom, and without the trouble of ascertaining the relation of cause and effect in every individual case? I am free to admit that theoretical objections of irresistible force (like those of the Chárváka sceptics) can be urged against this ascertainment of universal invariable and unconditional concomitance (व्याप्तिग्रहोपाय) on the basis of mere observation. Doubts of this kind can no more be laid by my view of the matter than by your canons of causality and essential identity (तदुत्पत्ति and तादात्म्य). Ultimately we all have to fall back on the rational practice of thinking persons (प्रेक्षावन्तः), and such persons are always content to act on practical certitude instead of hankering after an unattainable apodictic certainty in the affairs of life (प्रामाणिकलोकयात्रामनुपालयता यथादर्शनं शङ्कनीयम्). This same practical certitude is also the ultimate warrant of the Deductive-Inductive Inference by which we ascertain the characters of things without direct perception and through the medium or instrumentality of a mark.

[To the earlier Buddhist canon of the Method of Subtraction, *i.e.* the negative Method of Difference, Udyotakara and Váchaspati, of the Nyáya school, pertinently and acutely object as follows :—

सत्यं यत् किञ्चित् क्वचित् दृष्टं तस्य यत्र प्रतिबन्धः, तद्विदः तस्य तत् गमकं तत्र इति अनुजानीमः । स एव तु प्रतिबन्धो न तावत् तदुत्पत्त्या सम्भवति । का पुनरियं तदुत्पत्तिः । धूमस्य किं वह्यनन्तरं भावः । स तादृशः अस्ति रासभस्यापि । तत्प्रतिवद्धोऽपि धूमः स्यात् । अथ तदनन्तरमेव भावः, न च रासभानन्तरं भवन्नपि तदनन्तरमेव भवति, तस्मिन् सति अपि असति अग्नौ तदभावात् । असति अपि तस्मिन् सत्यादेर्न्यनवति वह्नौ तदभावात् । अथ यद्यपि धूमस्य वह्निभावानुविधानं तत्रोपलभ्यं, तथापि देशान्तरादिषु तदभावोऽस्य कुतस्यः । तथा हि भूयो भूयो रासभे दृष्टे धूमोदृष्टः, तदभावे च अदृष्टः, न स तत्कार्यः । तज्जातीयस्यैव धूमस्य रासभे विना सति वह्नौ भावात्, एवं सत्यपि अग्नौ पिशाचेन जनितो धूमः, क्वचिद्देशादौ तज्जातीय एव रासभवदह्व्यभावेऽपि पिशाचादेव भविष्यति, इति अवश्यं शङ्कया भाव्यं नियामकं अपश्यताम् । न च

सति भावमात्रे नियामकं, तस्य रासभादिषु अविशेषात् । तदनन्तरमेव इति च अवधारणस्य शङ्कायामभावात् । अवधारणेन तु शङ्कापनयने परस्पराश्रयप्रसङ्गात् ।

Buddhist reply :—स्यादेतत् । यो यो धूमोदृष्टः स सर्वस्तावत् आर्द्रेन्धनसहित वह्न्यनन्तरमेव, न पिशाचानन्तरं । स च कादाचित्कतया निमित्तमपेक्षमाणो यदनन्तरमेव गम्यते तदेव अप्रतीतव्यभिचारं निमित्तं करोति, न तु प्रतीतव्यभिचारं रासभादि । नापि सर्वेषाऽनुपलम्भःपिशाचादिः । यदि न तन्निमित्तं कस्मात् विनाऽपि वह्निं क्वचित् धूमो न उपलभ्यते । अय असौ (पिशाचः) सर्वथा वह्निसहितः तथा सति आर्द्रेन्धनवत् कथं वह्निरपि न कारणं । कारणं चेत् कथं तमन्तरेण धूमभावशङ्का । Now the phenomenon that is contingent (कादाचित्क) cannot be uncaused—अकारणस्य हि कार्यस्य नित्यं सत्त्वं असत्त्वं वा स्यात्, अनपेक्षत्वात् न कादाचित्कात्वम् । And with the limitation of a specific effect, there must be only one specific cause, for an unrestricted plurality of causes would amount to the denial of uniformity in causality (i.e. of the *unconditional invariable* antecedence)—

नापि अनेकं कारणं, सकारणत्वप्रसङ्गादेव । वह्न्यनन्तरमेव भाव इति हि धूमस्य वह्निकार्यत्वम् । स चेत् अवह्रेरपि अनन्तरं, न एवकारार्थः स्यात्, इति न वह्रेः कार्यम् । एवम् अन्यस्यापि न कार्यं । न हि अन्यानन्तरमेव भवति, वह्रेरपि अनन्तरं भावात्, ततश्च अहेतुको धूमः स्यात् । तथा च कादाचित्कत्व-व्याहतिः ।

Nyāya rejoinder :—सत्यम् । यद्यपि विना वह्निं नोपलम्भो धूमः, यद्यपि च पिशाचान्तरं नोपलभ्यते तेषामनुपलम्भः, तथाऽपि पिशाचकार्यं एव धूमः । तत्र तत्र वह्निः कुतश्चित् सहेतोः उपनिपतितः, रासभ इव, न धूमस्य जनकः । तेन तद्भावेऽपि तज्जातीय एव कारणभेदजन्मा कदाचित्, कादाचित्को धूमः स्यात् । इति अनिवृत्तिरेव शङ्कायाः । न च दृष्टसम्भवे नादृष्टं कल्पयितुं युक्तम् इति शक्यं भवद्विवेक्तुम् । अनुपलम्भिलक्षणप्राप्तस्य अशक्यनिराकरणात्वात् (vide Nyāya-Vindu) । न च अनुपलब्ध्यन्तराणि अपि तन्निषेधे प्रभवन्ति । तस्मात् अनन्तरमेव इति अवधारणाभावात् नैवं कार्येकारणभावावधारणं युक्तम् । न च यदन्यसहितानन्तरं उपलम्भे तत्, तदन्यरहितात् तस्मात् भवन् भिन्नजातीयं भवति । उक्तं हि रासभसहितात् वह्निः यादृशो धूमः

तादृश इव तद्रहितात् वह्ने रिति । तस्मादेवंविधा शङ्कापिशाची खनिवारकं
तदुत्पत्तिनिश्चयमास्कन्दती न शक्या निवारयितुम् ।

The Nyáya proceeds to point out that what is
contingent need not necessarily be produced by a cause.
It is enough if there is natural connection with something else, a relation of antecedence and succession (or
concomitance), without any element of productive
efficiency or causation.

अपि चास्तु तदुत्पत्तिनिश्चयः तथाऽपि कस्मात् कारणमन्तरेण न कार्यं
भवति । तथा च सति अनपेक्षतया कादाचित्कात्वविहतिः इति चेत् । अस्तु
तर्हि सम्बन्धः स्वाभाविकतया अन्यानपेक्षः अव्यभिचारी गमकान्वाङ्गम् । स च
यो वा स वा भवतु । कृतं कार्य्यकारणभावावधारणायासेन । यथा चैतत् तथा
अग्रे दर्शयिष्यामः ।—Váchaspati, Tátparyyatíká, Chap. I.,
Áhnika 1, Sútra 5, व्याप्तिग्रहोपायविचारः ।]

*The Nyáya Analysis of the Causal Relation con-
tinued: Co-effects.*—In the enumeration of different
varieties of irrelevant antecedents (अन्यथासिद्ध), we have
already noticed that co-effects of the same cause are
apt to be confounded as cause and effect. In some
cases the co-effects may be simultaneous, *e.g.* the case
of the ascending and the descending scale in a balance,
which are co-effects of gravity (*vide* Pártha-sárathi
Misra on Kumárilá, Sloka-Vártika—तुलानमनोन्नमनयोस्तु न
मिथः कार्य्यकारणत्वम्, उभयोरेककारणत्वात्,—Sloka 157, Súnya-
Váda). In other cases the co-effects may be successive
effects of the same cause, and here the risk is great
of mistaking the antecedent co-effect to be the cause of
the succeeding co-effect, *e.g.* the case of ants moving
in a line to carry their eggs upward, which is observed
before the summer rains, where the movement of ants
and the rains are not cause and effect, but successive

effects of the same cause, viz. the heat (उष्मा), which disturbs the elements, viz. the earth and the atmosphere (महाभूतक्षोभ); the ants being affected by this heat earlier than the atmospheric movements which bring the clouds and the rain.

(Udyotakara and Váchaspati : न च पिपीलिकानाड़ सञ्चरणं वर्षस्य कारणमनुपलब्धसालयात् । असत्यपि तस्मिन् वर्षस्योत्पत्तेः । वर्षमूल-कारणस्य तु महाभूतक्षोभस्य पिपीलिकानाड़सञ्चरणं पूर्व्वंकार्य्यम् । दृश्यमानाः खलु पिपीलिका भौमेनोष्मणा खानि अण्डानि भूमिष्ठानि उपरिष्टात् नयन्ति —Tátparyyatíká, II., 2, Sútra 37.)

Synchronousness of Cause and Effect.—This is resolved into a case of simultaneous co-effects of the same ultimate cause, *e.g.* the ascent of one scale and the descent of the other in the balance, which are not related as cause and effect, but are simultaneous effects of gravity. In other cases the synchronousness is only apparent, the interval between the antecedent and the consequent being too small (सूक्ष्मकाल) to be apprehended (यौगपद्याभिमान), *e.g.* in the case of the needle piercing a hundred soft lotus-petals laid one upon another, where the steps are really successive; or the illumination of the whole room by the light of a lamp, where the succession is unperceived owing to the inconceivable velocity of light (*cf.* Kumárilá, Sloka-Vártika—हेतुहेतुमतां सिद्धं यौगपद्यनिदर्शनम्,—यत् प्रदीपप्रभाद्युक्तं, सूक्ष्मकालोऽस्ति तत्र नः । तुल्यस्तु यथा वेधः पद्मपत्रशते तथा । Sunya-váda, Sloka 156–157.—I quote Mimánsá authorities, but the view is common to the Mimánsá and the Nyáya-Vaiseshika).

The Time-relation in a Chain of Causes and Effects.—A careful study of the time-relation in a chain of causes and effects is a peculiarity of the Vaiseshika system (and the later Nyáya). A moment (ultimate unit of time, Kshana, क्षण) is defined to be the time-interval between the completion of the sum of conditions and the appearance of the effect. The Vaiseshika conceives the unit to be determined by reference to the division of one atom from another (विभागानुतृपाञ्जविभाग प्रागभाव-सम्बद्धकर्मावच्छिन्न: काल: क्षण:—Sapta-Padárthí, Siváditya— *i.e.* the ultimate unit of time is the time during which motion exists in an atom prior to its division from another atom, in a case of division due to motion). The Sánkhya, we have already seen, determines this ultimate unit by reference to the motion of a Tanmátra.

The number of such units will determine the time-interval between a given set of physical conditions and a particular effect, for between a so-called sum of causes and a so-called sum of effects there intervenes a series of atomic (or molecular) motions, with conjunctions and disjunctions which form the causal chain. However crude in the practical application, the fundamental idea is, in connection with the principle of work and energy (for which both the Sánkhya and the Nyáya-Vaiseshika furnish a rudimentary basis), immensely suggestive of a possible Time Calculus.

Plurality of Causes.—This will be discussed when we consider the relation of Vyápti to the principle of Causality.

The Nyáya Ground of Inference—Vyápti नियतसाहचर्य्यं. —Inference, then, in the Nyáya, depends on the ascertainment, not of the causal relation, nor of the relation of genus to species, but of a natural relation, between two phenomena, of invariable and unconditional concomitance (उपाधिविधुरः स्वाभाविकः सम्बन्धः व्याप्तिः—Udyotakara and Váchaspati). Of the two phenomena so connected, one is called the Vyápya or Gamaka (the sign, mark, or indicator), and the other Vyápaka or Gamya (the thing signified, marked, or indicated). In the relation of fire and smoke, for example, smoke is the Vyápya or Gamaka (sign or mark); and fire, the Vyápaka or Gamya (the thing signified or marked). Now the relation of Vyápti between A and B may be either unequal or equipollent (विषमव्याप्ति or समव्याप्ति). When A is the sign of B, but B is not the sign of A, the Vyápti is one-sided or unequal, and here a Vyápti is said to exist between A and B, but not between B and A. For example, smoke is a sign of fire, but fire is not universally a sign of smoke. When, therefore, the relation of Vyápti is an unequal one, as between smoke and fire, it is expressed in the proposition—Wherever the Vyápya (sign or mark, *e.g.* smoke) exists, the Vyápaka (the thing signified or marked, *e.g.* fire) also exists. From this it follows by necessary implication (a sort of अर्थापत्ति) that whenever the Vyápaka (*e.g.* fire) is absent, the Vyápya (*e.g.* smoke) is also absent (व्यापकाभावे व्याप्याभावः). Again, the Vyápti may be a mutual or equipollent one, *i.e.* A and B may be signs of each other, *e.g.* green-wood fire and smoke. Here each in turn is Vyápya and Vyápaka, and this is expressed in the two propositions:—(1) Wherever there is smoke there is green-wood fire, and (2) wherever

there is green-wood fire there is smoke. By necessary
implication it follows—(1) Where there is no green-
wood fire there is no smoke; (2) where there is no
smoke there is no green-wood fire. We have seen that
a Vyápti exists between smoke and fire, for wherever
there is smoke there is fire, but we cannot say that a
Vyápti exists between fire and smoke, for we cannot
say that wherever there is a fire there is smoke. The
combustion of an iron ball (अयोगोलक), for example, is a
case of fire without smoke. But it would be correct to
say that a Vyápti exists between green-wood fire and
smoke, as well as between smoke and green-wood fire.
The question, therefore, is: what is the relation
between fire and smoke? The relation between fire
and smoke is a conditional relation; *i.e.* on condition
that the fire is green-wood fire, it would be a sign of
smoke. In other words, a Vyápti implies unconditional
invariable concomitance, and the relation between fire
and smoke is not therefore a Vyápti (natural unconditional concomitance), for fire requires a "condition,"
Upádhi, viz. green-wood, to be followed by smoke.
Smoke, on the other hand, requires no "condition" to
indicate fire. For the purposes of Inference, therefore,
relations between phenomena may be considered as of
two kinds: (1) Contingent conditional relations,
holding good on the fulfilment of a certain condition or
Upádhi, and (2) Vyápti, or unconditional invariable
relation, between a mark and that which it marks, a
relation without any Upádhi or determining condition
(उपाधिविधुरः सम्बन्धः). It is this latter kind of relation that
serves as the ground of inference. If we can ascertain

that a Vyápti exists between A and B, then A is a sign of B, and an inference of the presence of B from the presence of A, and of the absence of A from the absence of B, would be warranted. The question, therefore, is, how to ascertain the relation of Vyápti between two phenomena.

Ascertainment of Vyápti according to the early Nyáya (व्याप्तिग्रहोपाय).—Briefly speaking, the observation of agreement in presence (अन्वय) as well as agreement in absence (व्यतिरेक) between two phenomena, with the non-observation of the contrary (व्यभिचारादर्शनम्), is the foundation of our knowledge of Vyápti (दर्शनादर्शने —Váchaspati). This suggests a natural relation (स्वाभाविकसम्बन्ध—Váchaspati) of invariable concomitance (नियतसाहचर्य्य—Váchaspati) between the phenomena, which is fortified by our non-observation (अदर्शन) of the contrary (व्यभिचार). But this does not establish the unconditionality of the concomitance (उपाधिविधुरसम्बन्ध), which is essential to a Vyápti. We have therefore to examine the cases carefully to see if there is any determining condition (Upádhi—*i.e.* some hidden or undetected but really operative or indispensable accompaniment) which conditions the relation between the supposed sign or mark (Gamaka) and the supposed signate (thing signified, Gamya). Now let us consider what constitutes an Upádhi. It is a circumstance which always accompanies, and is always accompanied by, the supposed signate (the thing signified, Gamya), but does not invariably accompany the supposed sign or mark (Gamaka). If, therefore, in the set of positive instances where both the sign and the signate are present, nothing else is constantly present, there can be no Upádhi. Or, again, if in the set of negative instances where both the sign and the signate are absent, no other material circumstance is constantly absent, there is no Upádhi. This follows from the very definition of an Upádhi. It is impracticable to fulfil these requirements rigorously. Still, every one of the accompanying circumstances (of course the likely ones) may be taken successively, and it may be shown that the comcomitance continues even when the suspected Upádhi (शङ्कितोपाधि) is absent, and therefore it cannot be the Upádhi. And this is to be fortified by the observation of uniform and uninterrupted agreement in absence (Vyatireka) between the two concomitant phenomena. In this way, when we have disproved all suspected Upádhis, we conclude by establishing the Vyápti. It is true that we may still go on doubting; but doubt has a certain limit for the "experimenter" and the thinking person (परीक्षक, प्रेक्षावान्). When doubt overthrows the foundation of all rational practice (प्रामाणिकलोकयात्रा), or leads to a stoppage or arrest of all practical activity (लोकव्यवहार), it stands *ipso facto* condemned, and must be abandoned (व्याघातावधिराशङ्का—Śríharsha and Udayana; व्याघात is mentioned by Váchaspati). Thus it is that Vyápti is ascertained. In this way we observe innumerable instances of Vyápti. Now, by means of repeated observations of this kind (भूयोदर्शन) we have established the principle of the Uniformity of Nature (स्वभावप्रतिबन्ध), and also of Causality; and these two principles thus ascertained may be made use of in their turn as the basis of an argumentation or deduction (Tarka, Úha, तर्क) to confirm a particular Vyápti in a particular case. Tarka or Úha, then, is the verification and vindication of particular inductions by the application of the general principles of Uniformity of Nature and of Causality, principles which are themselves based on repeated observation (भूयोदर्शन) and the ascertainment of innumerable particular inductions of uniformity or causality (भूयोदर्शनजनितसंस्कारसहितम् इन्द्रियमेव स्वाभाविकसम्बन्धग्राहि—Váchaspati). Thus Tarka also helps in dispelling doubt (सन्देह). Sríharsha, however, questions the validity of this verification—*cf.* the well-known couplet ending तर्कः शङ्कावधिः कुतः ।

It will be seen that the process of disproving all suspected Upádhis (उपाधिशङ्कानिरास), in the early Nyáya, answers exactly *as a process* to Mill's Method of Agreement. In fact, the disproof of a suspected Upádhi by pointing to instances of agreement in presence (अन्वय), even in the absence of the Upádhi, fortified as this is by the instances of agreement in absence (व्यतिरेक), virtually amounts to Mill's Joint Method of Agreement. But the fundamental difference is this: Mill's Method of Agreement is formulated in view of the phenomena of causation (including co-effects, etc.), and, as usually enunciated, confessedly breaks down in dealing with cases of Uniformities of Co-existence unconnected with Causation; the Nyáya Method, based on the disproof of suspected Upádhis, is a more daring and original attempt, and is far more comprehensive in scope, being applicable to all Uniformities of Co-existence and of Causation alike. And this the Nyáya successively accomplished by introducing the mark of unconditionality (उपाधिविधुरता).

into the relation of Vyápti (Concomitance), even as the same mark of unconditionality (अन्यथासिद्धिशून्यता) had been previously introduced into the definition of Causality (कार्य्येकारणभाव). The difference between the early Nyáya and the Buddhist systems may be briefly put thus:—The former relied on empirical induction based on uniform and uninterrupted agreement in Nature, and accordingly regarded the Method of Agreement as the fundamental Method of Scientific Induction, founding Inference on Vyápti, to which they subordinated Causality in the doctrine of Method; the latter assumed two *a priori* principles, viz. causality and identity of essence, deduced the canon of the Method of Difference by an indirect proof from the principle of Causality, and made this Method the foundation of all scientific Induction of Causality, just as they based all natural classification of genera and species on their *a priori* principle of Identity of Essence.

Texts from the early Nyáya :—

(*a*) Method of Agreement and the Joint Method without the device of the Upádhi :—

Cf. Jayanta on साहचर्य्ये—तस्मिन् सत्येव भवने न विना भवनं ततः। अयमेवाविनाभावो नियमः सहचारिता। 'तस्मिन् सत्येव,' "only this remaining throughout," while others change—implying the Method of Agreement. The set of positive instances, in which this antecedent alone is constant, must be supplemented by a set of negative instances (agreement in absence) :—व्यतिरेकनिश्चयमन्तरेण प्रतिबन्धग्रहणानुपपत्ते:। नियमश्चायं उच्यते यत् तस्मिन् सति भवनं ततो विना न भवनं इति भूयोदर्शनम्। तच्च तस्मिन् सति भवनं इत्यन्वयमात्रपरिच्छेदात् अगृहीतो नियमः स्यात्। ततो

विना न भवनम् इतयस्य अर्थस्य अपरिच्छेदात् इति—Jayanta, Áhnika 2, व्यतिरेकव्याप्तिनिश्चयावश्यकत्वम् ।

(b) Doctrine of the Upádhi: unconditional concomitance distinguished from conditional :—

यो वा स वा अस्तु सम्बन्ध: यस्य असौ स्वाभाविको नियत: स एव गमक:, गम्यश्च इतर: सम्बन्धीति युज्यते । तथा हि धूमादीनां वह्न्यादिसम्बन्ध: स्वाभाविक: । नतु वह्न्यादीनां धूमादिभि: । उपलभ्यन्ते ते हि विनापि धूमादिभि: । यदातु आर्द्रेन्धनादिसम्बन्धम् अनुभवन्ति तदा धूमादिभि: सह संवध्यन्ते । तस्मात् वह्न्यादीनाम् आर्द्रेन्धनाद्युपाधिकृत: सम्बन्धो न स्वाभाविक: । ततो न नियत: । स्वाभाविकस्तु धूमादीनां वह्न्यादिसम्बन्ध उपाधे: अनुपलभ्यमानात् क्वचित् व्यभिचारस्य सदर्शनात् अनुपलभ्यमानस्यापि कल्पनानुपपत्ते: । अतो नियत: सम्बन्ध: अनुमानाङ्गम् ।

(c) Concomitance sufficient without causal *nexus*:—

The Buddhist objects: In Nature everything is connected with everything else. Hence, if there were no *nexus* of causality between antecedent and consequent, everything might follow from everything else. The Nyáya replies: You admit uniformities (of coexistence, etc.) other than causal; so you confess that a natural fixed order can exist without the causal *nexus*....

(d) An Upádhi, how established and how disproved :—

The Nyáya then proceeds to show how an Upádhi is established, or how disproved by observation :—

तत्र वहे: अनार्द्रेन्धनस्य विना धूमम् अयोगोलकादौ दर्शनात् आर्द्रेन्धनोपाधि: अस्य धूमेन सम्बन्ध: न तु स्वाभाविक इति निश्चीयते । धूमविशेषस्य तु विना वह्निम् अनुपलम्भात्, उपाधिभेदस्य च अदृश्यमानस्य कल्पनायां प्रमाणाभावात्, विशेषस्मृत्यपेक्षस्य च संशयस्य अनुपलम्भपूर्वं अनुत्पादात्, उत्पादे च अतिप्रसङ्गात् प्रेक्षावत् प्रवृत्त्युच्छेदात्, स्वाभाविक: सम्बन्ध: अवधार्य्यते ।

(e) General Method of Induction by exhaustion

of the Upádhi, more comprehensive than Mill's Joint Method :—

For the definition of an Upádhi, *vide* Śríharsha and Udayana : अव्याप्तसाधनो यः साध्यसमव्याप्तिः उच्यते स उपाधिरिति । Hence, to avoid an Upádhi (which is साध्यसमव्याप्तिः), the constant presence of anything relevant other than the sign and the signate in the positive instances (of agreement in presence, अन्वय), and the constant absence of any such thing in the negative instances (of agreement in absence, व्यतिरेक) must be safeguarded against. This amounts to Mill's Joint Method.

(*f*) Suspicion of non-perceptible Upádhi—Limits of legitimate doubt :—

न च अदृश्यमानोऽपि दर्शनानर्हतया साधकबाधकप्रमाणाभावेन संदिह्यमान उपाधिः स्वाभाविकत्वं प्रतिबध्नाति इति साम्प्रतम् । अवश्यं शङ्कया भवितव्यं नियामकाभावादिति दत्तावकाशा खलु इयम् प्रमाणमर्य्यादातिक्रमेण शङ्का पिशाची लम्बप्रसरा न क्वचित् नास्तीति नेयं क्वचित् प्रवर्त्तते । सर्व्वैव कस्यचित् कथञ्चित् अनर्थस्य शङ्कास्पदत्वात् । अनर्थशङ्कायाश्च प्रेक्षावतां निवृत्त्यङ्गत्वात् । अन्यथा स्निग्धान्नपानोपयोगेषु अपि मरणादिदर्शनात् । तस्मात् प्रामाणिकलोकयात्राम् अनुपालयता यथादर्शनं शङ्कनीयम् । ... तस्मादुपाधिं प्रयत्नेन अन्विष्यन्तोऽनुपलभमाना नास्तीति अवगम्य स्वाभाविकत्वं सम्बन्धस्य निश्चिनुमः ।—

(*g*) Tarka, Úha : Deductive verification of particular inductions by applying the two fundamental inductions of Uniformity of Nature and Causality :—Doubt finally dispelled :—

Now innumerable particular uniformities of this kind (Vyáptis) are observed, and as a result of this repeated observation a belief in the Uniformity of Nature (स्वभावप्रतिबन्ध), as well as in the principle of Causality (कार्य्यकारणभाव), is generated in the mind, a belief which has evidential value and validity. It is not intuition (न मानसम्) but a mental pre-disposition based on uniform and uninterrupted experience (भूयोदर्शनजनित-संस्कारसहितम् इन्द्रियमेव स्वाभाविकसम्बन्धग्राहि—यत्र भूयोदर्शनम् असाधारणम् इति प्रमाणान्तरं जातम्). Then, armed with these new resources, the belief in uniformity and in causality as general principles, we proceed to fortify our particular inductions (Vyáptis), whether of Uniformity of Nature or of Causality, by indirect deduction from these general principles:—We argue: If, under these observed circumstances, A were not the mark of B, the principle of Uniformity of Nature would be violated—Nature would not be uniform—or, if under these observed circumstances A were not the cause of B, the principle of Causality would be violated, the phenomenon B would be without a cause;—and such indirect proof (तर्कं, अह) gives us the overwhelming probability which we call practical certitude, and on which every reasonable man (every thinking and judging person) proceeds to act in due natural course.—स्वभावतश्च प्रतिबद्धा हेतवः स्वसाध्येन, यदि साध्यमन्तरेण भवेयुः, स्वभावादेव प्रच्यवेरन्निति तर्कसहायः अनिरस्तसाध्यव्यतिरेकवृत्तिसंदेहा यत्र दृष्टाः, तत्र स्वसाध्यम् उपस्थापयन्त्येव ।—Vácbaspati, I., 1, Sútra 5; *cf.* also I., 1, Sútra 40 : अह: कारणस्योपपत्त्या संभवेन ज्ञायते । कारणासम्भवे कार्यस्य असत्त्वात् ।

Instances of Vyápti (uniformity) not comprehended under Causality, or the relation of genus and species:— The Nyáya points out that the relations of cause and effect and of genus and species do not exhaust the grounds of Inference. There are cases of Inference based on Vyápti (*i.e.* on invariable and unconditional concomitance) which come neither under Causality (तदुत्पत्ति) nor under Identity of Essence (तादात्म्य).

Váchaspati notes that to-day's sunrise and yesterday's sunrise, the rise of the moon and the tide in the ocean, the relative positions of the stellar constellations, are instances of Vyápti (invariable concomitance) between phenomena which are neither related as cause and effect nor as genus and species. Jayanta adds the conjunction of sunset with the appearance of the stars; of ants moving in procession (with their eggs) with the approach of the rains; of the rising of the constellation Agastya (Canopus) above the horizon with the drying-up of rivers; of the spring-tide with the full moon; and dismisses as sophistical and far-fetched the Buddhist attempt to explain all these cases by means of causality. We have seen that the Nyáya and the Mimánsá reduce most of these conjunctions to cases of co-effects of the same cause, co-effects which may be either simultaneous or successive.

अपि च अद्यतनस्य सवितुरुदयस्य ह्यस्तनेन सवितुरुदयेन, चन्द्रोदयस्य च समानकालेन समुद्रवृद्ध्या ... न कार्यकारणभाव: तादात्म्यं वा । अथच दृष्टो-गम्यगमकभाव: ।—Váchaspati, Tátparyyatíká, I., 1, Sútra 5; *cf.* also Jayanta, Nyáyamañjarí : अन्येषामपि हेतूनां भूयां जगति दर्शनात् । सूर्यास्तमयमालोक्य कल्प्यते तारकोदय: । पूर्णचन्द्रोदयादृष्ट्वेदिरम्बुधेर-वगम्यते । उदितेनानुमीयन्ते सरित: कुम्भयोगिन: । शुष्यतपुलिनपर्यन्त-विश्रान्तखगपङ्क्तय: । पिपीलिकाण्डसञ्चारचेष्टानुमितवृष्टय: । भवन्ति पथिका: पर्णकुटीरकरणोद्यता: ।

Vyápti between Cause and Effect—Relation of Causality to Vyápti :—

On the Buddhist (and early Nyáya) view that one specific assemblage of "effect" phenomena has one specific assemblage of causal conditions, there would be two aggregates—the sum of causal conditions (कारणसामग्री)

and the sum of effects (कार्य्यसामग्री). For example, fire requires green-wood to complete the sum of causal conditions to give rise to smoke with some particular marks (धुमविशेष—बहुलपाशुतादिधर्म्मे विशिष्ट, Jayanta, II.; compare Gaṅgeśa, कृष्णागुरुप्रभववह्निमानयं कटुकासुरभिपाशुरधूमवत्त्वात् ।—Chintámaṇi, Anumána, Viruddha-Siddhánta). Here, between an effect and a single condition (termed a cause) there is a relation of Vyápti. The effect is Vyápya or Gamaka (the sign or mark); the cause (or condition) is Vyápaka or Gamya (the thing signified). In other words, the presence of the effect indicates the presence of the causal condition, and the absence of the causal condition will by implication indicate the absence of the effect. Smoke of this particular kind is supposed to be an effect of which there is one and only one assemblage of causal conditions (fire and green-wood); hence, where there is smoke there is fire, and when there is no fire there is no smoke.

Now introduce the complication of the plurality of causes:—Fire, for example, is the effect of several assemblages, *e.g.* (1) blowing on heated grass; (2) focussing rays through a lens on a combustible like paper or straw; (3) friction with the fire-drill, etc. Here each assemblage is regarded as a sum of causes. But in this case there is no Vyápti between the effect "fire" and any particular assemblage of causal conditions, say of the lens or the fire-drill; for the presence of fire does not indicate the presence of the lens or the fire-drill assemblage, nor does the absence of either of the latter in particular indicate the absence of fire. Indeed, in such a case the effect "fire" is not a mark or sign

(Gamaka or Vyápya) of any one in particular of the different possible causal assemblages, though each of these particular assemblages of causal conditions is a mark or sign (Gamaka or Vyápya) of fire.

The plurality of causes requires a further consideration in the light of the definition of the causal relation. A cause is defined to be the unconditional invariable antecedent. From the unconditionality it follows that the entire sum of conditions, and not one single condition, is, properly speaking, the cause. In view of the plurality of causes, an invariable antecedent must be taken to mean that any particular cause (*i.e.* assemblage of causal conditions) is invariably followed by the effect—not that the effect is invariably preceded by any particular cause.

Popularly, a single condition, say the lens or the fire-drill, is said to be a cause of fire; but, in view of the plurality of causes, this is apt to be misleading, as there is no Vyápti in this case; the lens or the fire-drill is no more a mark of fire than fire is a mark of the lens or the fire-drill.

The plurality of causes strains the definition of a cause, and undermines the relation of Vyápti between an effect and a cause. Any particular cause (causal aggregate) still indicates the effect, but not *vice versa*. The earlier Nyáya (down to Váchaspati and Jayanta) obviated the plurality, as we have seen, by introducing distinctive marks in the effect such as would indicate a single specific cause (कार्य्यवैलक्षण्य or कार्य्यभेद indicating कारणवैलक्षण्य or कारणभेद). Some, indeed, went farther and held that when the antecedent causal assemblages differ in kind, the effect-phenomena, though apparently the same, do really differ specifically (or in kind)—कारणवैजात्यात् कार्य्यवैजात्यम् । But the Nyáya discards this hypothesis; the fire is the same, though the possible causes (or causal aggregates) differ, *e.g.* the lens, the drill, etc. But the effect-phenomenon to which we attend is not the only effect; in the case of plurality of causes we must carefully examine the accompaniments of the effect, *i.e.* the sum of effects, and the examination will show some distinctive or specific circumstance or accompaniment which will enable us to definitely determine the particular assemblage of causal conditions that must have preceded in the case under examination. This is the device of the earlier Nyáya as well as of the Buddhists, as we have seen; but the later Nyáya doubts the practicability as well as the theoretical validity of such a step on an unrestricted assumption of the plurality of causes, and feels troubled by the circumstance that no effect for which more than one cause (or causal aggregate) can be assigned, can be regarded as a mark or sign (Gamaka or Vyápya) of any one of the causes in particular. Accordingly, some adherents of the later Nyáya advanced the proposition that when more than one causal aggregate can be supposed for any effect, the latter is a mark or sign (Gamaka or Vyápya) not of any one of the causal aggregates in particular, but of one or other of them; and the absence not of one such cause, but of each and every one of them, alone indicates the absence of the effect. A cause therefore should be defined to mean *one or other* of the possible alternative aggregates which, being given, the effect follows invariably and unconditionally. If we ask what is the defining mark (or quiddity) of the cause (कारणतावच्छेदक), we are told that it is *one-or-otherness* (अन्यतमत्व), and nothing else; others cut the Gordian knot by assuming that the different possible causes of the same effect possess a common power or efficiency (अतिरिक्तशक्ति), or a common "form" (जातिसौक्ष्म्य), which accounts for the production of a common effect. The latter is therefore a sign or mark of this power (शक्ति) or this form (जातिसौक्ष्म्या), which is manifested by each of the causal aggregates. This hypothesis (कल्पना), they hold, is simpler and more plausible than the hypothesis of specific differences latent in the apparently identical effect of a plurality of causes (कारणवैजात्यात् कार्य्यवैजात्यम्).

Cf. Dinakarī on the Siddhānta-Muktavali: केचित्तु वह्निं प्रति तृणफुत्कारसंयोगादीनां तृणफुत्कारसंयोगत्वादिरूपेण कारणतया व्यभिचारेण असम्भवात् अतिरिक्तशक्तिसिद्धिः । न च तृणफुत्कारयोः अरणिनिमन्योः मणितरणिकिरणयोश्च सम्बन्धस्य जन्यतावच्छेदकं बहिर्वृत्ति-वैजात्यत्रयं कल्प्यमिति न व्यभिचार इति वाच्यम् । तज्जन्यतावच्छेदकवैजात्यत्रय-कल्पनामपेक्ष्य तत्तत्सम्बन्धानां एकशक्तिमत्त्वेन कारणत्वकल्पनाया एव लघुत्वेन न्याय्यत्वात् इत्याहुः । तन्न । ... अन्यतमत्वेन कारणतासम्भवात् ... परे तु तृणादिसम्बन्धकालीनवायुसंयोगादीनां एकशक्तिमत्त्वेन हेतुतामादाय विनिगमना-विरहात् न शक्तिसिद्धिः इत्याहुः । Sloka 2; *cf.* also, तृणारणिमण्यन्यतमत्वं कारणस्य विनिगमकम् ।

Cf. Udayana, Kusumāñjali, Stavaka 1: कथं तर्हि तृणारणिमणिभ्यो भवन्नशुश्चिरेकजातीयः । एकशक्तिमत्त्वात् इति चेत् न । यदि हि विजातीयेषु अपि एकजातीयकार्य्यकारण-शक्तिः समवेयात्, न कार्य्यात् कारणविशेष क्वचित् अनुमीयेत । कारणव्यावृत्त्या च न तज्जातीयस्यैव कार्य्यस्य व्यावृत्तिरवसीयेत । ... एतेन सूक्ष्मजातीयमिति निरस्तम् । व्यवहारेऽपि तत्सौक्ष्म्यात् धूमोत्पस्यापन्नेः ।

The scientific Methods already noticed—the Joint Method of Difference (the Pañchakáraní) and the Joint Method of Agreement (Vpáptigraha with Upádhisaṅkánirasa and Tarka)—are not the only methods of ascertaining causality or concomitance, or establishing a theory (सिद्धान्त); nor are these Methods always practicable. Very often we reach the explanation of a fact (उपपत्ति) by means of a hypothesis (कल्पना) properly tested and verified (निर्णीत). A legitimate hypothesis must satisfy the following conditions :—(1) the hypothesis must explain the facts (दृष्टसिद्धि or उपपत्ति); (2) the hypothesis must not be in conflict with any observed facts or established generalisations (दृष्टसिद्धये हि अदृष्टं कल्प्यते, न दृष्टविघाताय—Jayanta, Nyáyamañjarí, Áhnika 1); (3) no unobserved agent must be assumed where it is possible to explain the facts satisfactorily by observed agencies (यदि अदृष्टमन्तरेण दृष्टं न सिद्धति काममदृष्टं कल्प्यताम्, अन्यथाऽपि तदुपपत्तौ किं तदुपकल्पनेन *ibid.*); (4) when two rival hypotheses are in the field, a crucial fact or test (विनिगमक, *ratio sufficiens*) is necessary; the absence of such a test (विनिगमनाविरह) is fatal to the establishment of either; (5) of two rival hypotheses, the simpler, *i.e.* that which assumes less, is to be preferred, *ceteris paribus* (कल्पनालाघव *versus* कल्पनागौरव); (6) of two rival hypotheses, that which is immediate or relevant to the subject-matter is to be preferred to that which is alien or remote (प्रथमोपस्थिततत्व); (7) a hypothesis that satisfies the above conditions must be capable of *verification* (निर्णय) before it can be established as a theory (सिद्धान्त). The process of verification of a hypothesis consists in showing that it can be deduced as a corollary from (or is involved by implication in) some more general proposition which is already well established (*cf.* Vatsyayana's exposition and illustration of Verification, निर्णय—including both the Deductive Method and Colligation).

This doctrine of Scientific Method, in Hindu Logic, is only a subsidiary discipline, being comprehended under the wider conception of Methodology, which aims at the ascertainment of Truth, whether scientific (Vijñána) or philosophical (Jñána) (मोक्षे धीर्ज्ञानम् स्यात् विज्ञानं शिल्पशास्त्रयो:, Amara-Kosha); the latter being the ulterior aim. In the investigation of any subject, Hindu Methodology adopts the following procedure: (1) the proposition (or enumeration) of the subject-matter (Uddesa), (2) the ascertainment of the essential characters or marks, by Perception, Inference, the Inductive Methods, etc.—resulting in definitions (by लक्षण) or descriptions (by उपलक्षण); and (3) examination and verification (परीक्षा and निर्णय). Ordinarily the first step, Uddesa, is held to include not mere Enumeration of topics, but Classification or Division proper (विभाग: उद्देशरूपानपायान्तु उद्देश एवासौ । सामान्यसंज्ञया कीर्तनमुद्देश: प्रकारभेदसंज्ञया कीर्तनं विभाग इति—Jayanta, Mañjarí); but a few recognise the latter as a separate procedure coming after Definition or Description. Any truth established by this three-fold (or four-fold) procedure is called a Siddhánta (an established theory). Now the various Pramánas, Proofs, *i.e.* sources of valid knowledge, in Hindu Logic, viz. Perception, Inference, Testimony, Mathematical Reasoning (सम्भव, including Probability in one view), are only operations subsidiary to the ascertainment of Truth (तत्त्वनिर्णय). And the Scientific Methods are merely ancillary to these Pramánas themselves.

I have explained the principles of the Hindu doctrine of Scientific Method, avoiding the technicalities of Logic as far as possible; and I cannot here enter upon the logical terminology or the logical apparatus and machinery, which would require a separate volume to themselves. For these I would refer the reader to my Paper on Hindu Logic as also for an account of the later Nyáya (नव्यन्याय), which, in spite of its arid dialectics, possesses a three-fold significance in the history of thought: (1) logical, in its conceptions of Avachchhedaka and Pratiyogi, being an attempt to introduce quantification on a connotative basis, in other words, to introduce quantitative notions of Universal and Particular, in both an affirmative and a negative aspect, into the Hindu theory of Inference and Proposition regarded connotatively as the establishment of relations among attributes or marks; (2) scientific, in its investigation of the varieties of Vyápti and Upádhi (and of अन्यथासिद्ध), being an elaboration of Scientific Method, in the attempt to eliminate the irrelevant; and (3) ontological and epistemological, in its classification and precise determinations of the various relations of Knowledge and Being, with even greater rigidity and minuteness than in Hegel's Logic of Being and Essence. I will conclude with a few observations on Applied Logic, *i.e.* the logic of the special sciences, which is such a characteristic feature of Hindu scientific investigation. What is characteristic of the Hindu scientific mind is that, without being content with the general concepts of Science and a general Methodology, it elaborated the fundamental categories and concepts of such of the special sciences as it cultivated with assiduity, and systematically adapted the general principles of Scientific Method to the requirements of the subject-matter in each case. The most signal example of applied logic (or Scientific Method) worked out with systematic carefulness is the Logic of Therapeutics in Charaka, a Logic which adapts the general concepts of cause, effect, energy, operation, etc., and the general methodology of science, to the special problems presented in the study of diseases, their causes, symptoms, and remedies (*vide* Charaka, Vimánasthána, Chap. IV.; also Sutrasthána; *vide* my Paper on Hindu Logic). Here I will give an illustration of Applied Methodology from the science of Analytical and Descriptive Grammar. Patañjali, in the Mahábháshya (*circa* 150 B.C.), is very careful as regards Methodology. I take no note now of the philosophical presuppositions of his philology (*vide* my Paper on the Hindu Science of Language), but will confine myself to his presentation of the Applied Logic of Descriptive and Analytical Grammar. The sentence is the unit of speech, as every Hindu philologer contends, but the first business of Analytical Grammar is to analyse the sentence into its significant parts and their coherent relations to one another. Assuming that articulate sounds are significant, the question is: how is the sentence, which is the unit of articulate speech, broken up into significant words and their mutual relations? Patañjali answers that this is done by an instinctive use (*cf.* Váchaspati's भूयोदर्शनजनितसंस्कारम् इन्द्रियम्) of the Joint Method of Difference (combined Addition and Subtraction), fortified by the Joint Method of Agreement (अन्वयव्यतिरेकौ). Patañjali starts with a simple case. Take the two sentence-units : Pathati (he reads) and Pachati (he cooks). Suppose you start with the assumption that these sounds are significant, and that *separate elements have separate meanings.* Then you hear Pathati, and, at the same time, a man reading is pointed at. Then the assemblage of sounds Pathati (*i.e.* Path + ati) stands for the assemblage "one reads" (*i.e.* the action reading + an individual agent). Similarly, by finger-pointing or other indication, you find that the assemblage Pachati (*i.e.* Pach + ati) stands for the assemblage "one cooks" (*i.e.* the action cooking + an individual agent, say the same agent as before).

Now look at the groupings :—

Path + ati = reading + one agent.

Pach + ati = cooking + one agent.

From repeated observation of similar groupings, one is led to conclude that Path is the invariable concomitant of the action "reading," because the disappearance of the former (the other element remaining) leads to the disappearance of the latter (a rough Method of Difference by subtraction—हीयते) ; that Pach is the invariable concomitant of the action "cooking," because the introduction of Pach (with nothing else added) leads to the introduction of the action "cooking" (a rough Method of Difference by addition—उपजायते) ; and that Ati, which is the only "common antecedent" (अन्वयी), is the invariable concomitant of "one agent," which is the only common "consequent" (अन्वयी). In fact, the last should come first by the Method of Agreement, then the other two, either by Residue or by Joint Agreement in presence and absence (अन्वयव्यतिरेकौ). So far all is plain sailing, though only very simple and very rough applications of the Methods are given. But—and this is the point—throughout the argument it is assumed that one sound is the concomitant of one idea; in other words, there is no plurality of causes to vitiate the application of the Method of Agreement in the above example. And now the objection is advanced that this basal assumption is untrue. The same sound is not the concomitant of the same idea; different words (sounds) may have the same meaning, and the same word (sound) may have different meanings. We cannot therefore by the Joint Method of Agreement (अन्वयव्यतिरेकौ) determine the meanings of words or the separate functions of roots (stems) and inflections—at least, not so simply as is pretended above. Patañjali states this difficulty in the way of applying the Scientific Methods to the problems presented by Analytical Grammar, a difficulty arising from the plurality of causes, but does not state the solution. The solution, however, depends on the Method of Subtraction and Addition (Patañjali's हीयते and उपजायते); for it will be found by extensive observation that the number of meanings of which a word (sound) may be capable is limited. So also is the number of words (sounds) expressive of a given meaning. Hence, by the Method of Difference, etc., the causal relations of words and meanings may be determined. Patañjali thus establishes the doctrine of Prakriti and Pratyaya (roots and inflections), with their separate significance, which is of course a necessary postulate in the case of an inflectional language like Sanskrit. Isolating and agglutinative languages offer less difficulty, whereas the difficulties are in some respects enhanced in the case of languages with a polysynthetic or incorporating (incapsulating) morphological structure.

कथं पुनर्ज्ञायते अयं प्रकृतयर्थः अयं प्रत्ययार्थ इति । अन्वयव्यतिरेकाभ्याम् । कोऽसौ अन्वयो व्यतिरेको वा । इह पचतीत्युक्ते कश्चित् शब्दः श्रूयते, पठतीत्युक्ते कश्चित् शब्दो हीयते (पच्), — कश्चित् उपजायते (पठ्, — कश्चित् अन्वयी (अति); — अर्थोऽपि कश्चित् हीयते (विक्लित्तिः), — कश्चित् उपजायते (पठिक्रिया), — कश्चित् अन्वयी (कर्तृत्वं चैकत्वंच) । तेन मन्यामहे यः शब्दो हीयते, तस्य असौ अर्थः योऽर्थो हीयते । यः शब्द उपजायते तस्य असौ अर्थः योऽर्थ उपजायते । यः शब्दोऽन्वयी तस्य असौ अर्थः योऽर्थोऽन्वयी ।

विषम उपन्यासः — बह्वर्थो हि शब्दा एकार्था भवन्ति । तद्यथा इन्द्रः शक्रः पुरन्दरः । एकश्च शब्दो बह्वर्थः । तद्यथा अक्षाः पादा माषा इति । अथ किं न साधीयोऽर्थवत्ता सिद्धा भवति । नापि ब्रूमोऽर्थवत्ता न सिध्यतीति । वर्णिता हि अर्थवत्ता अन्वयव्यतिरेकाभ्यामेव । तत्र कुत एतदयं प्रकृतयर्थः अयं प्रत्ययार्थ इति । (Mahábháshya, 1–3, 9.)

Patañjali not only applies the Scientific Methods to the foundations of Grammatical Analysis, but also *by their means* establishes and elaborates the fundamental categories and concepts of Grammatical (and Philological) Science, *e.g.* the concepts of action (क्रिया), agent (कर्त्ता), instrumental cause (करणं साधकतमम्), end (निमित्त), origin (हेतु), limit (अवधि), substance (द्रव्य), quality (गुण), and genus (जाति); also of the fundamental relations (at the bottom of all thought and *speech*)—the relations of time (कालिकसम्बन्ध), of space (दिग्देशसम्बन्ध), of causality (कार्य्यंकारणभाव), of inherence (समवाय), of co-inherence (सामानाधिकरख्य), of substance and attribute (विशेषणविशेष्यभाव), of the sign and the signate (संज्ञासंज्ञिभाव), of mutual dependence (इतरेतराश्रय)—an entire grammatical (and philological) apparatus, which will serve as a *point d'appui* for generations of philologists and grammarians to come.

INDEX

A. AUTHORITIES

अग्निवेश 62
अनिरुद्ध 43, 50
अमर 171, 172, 175, 289
अरुण 207
अहोबल 166
आत्रेय 206, 234, 235, 236
आत्रेय पुनर्वसु 62
आर्यभट 132, 147, 151
ईश्वरकृष्ण 51, 53, 242
उत्पल 56, 59, 83, 101, 247
उदयन 2, 51, 77, 100, 102, 110, 111, 112, 113, 114, 116, 135, 170, 173, 175, 178, 245, 248, 249, 257, 277, 281, 287
उद्योतकर 2, 45, 75, 76, 103, 104, 105, 112, 113, 116, 117, 140, 152, 154, 155, 157, 158, 159, 160, 162, 164, 255, 257, 269, 272, 274
उपवर्ष 153
उमास्वाति 93, 95, 97, 188, 192, 193, 196
कणाद 101, 146
कुमारिल 2, 151, 153, 272
कृष्णपाद 33, 36
कृष्णात्रेय 62
गङ्गाधर 69, 70, 146
गङ्गेश 110, 158, 159, 163, 164, 265
गदाधर 241
गुणरत्न 174, 180
गोतम 240

गौडपाद 50
चक्रदत्त 63, 207
चक्रपाणि 62, 66, 151, 169, 172, 175, 206, 232, 246
चरक 2, 56, 57, 58, 59, 68, 69, 70, 74, 84, 151, 169, 175, 177, 181, 184, 185, 188, 198, 205, 207, 208, 210, 212, 213, 215, 217, 218, 219, 228, 229, 232, 233, 234, 235, 236, 238, 246
चरक-दृढबल 207
जयन्त 2, 103, 104, 117, 122, 123, 134, 147, 152, 154, 155, 180, 240, 245, 252, 265, 266, 279, 280, 283, 285, 288, 289
डल्वण 59, 151, 169, 178, 180, 183, 184, 195, 196, 197, 201, 207
दामोदर 165, 166, 222
दृढबल 61, 62, 188
धन्वन्तरि 62, 173, 205, 233
नागार्जुन 62, 63
पञ्चशिख 51
पतञ्जलि 2, 13, 15, 17, 63, 178, 180, 181, 291, 292, 293, 294
पराशर 33, 37
पाणिनि 246
पार्थसारथिमिश्र 153, 271
प्रशस्तपाद 2, 52, 62, 100, 129, 130, 135, 140, 141, 142, 143, 146, 147, 156,

170, 177
ब्रह्मगुप्त 78, 80, 132
भरत 168
भानुजीदीक्षित 172
भास्कर 2, 76, 77, 78, 79, 80, 147, 149, 150
भिक्षु आत्रेय 62
मतंग 168
मथुरानाथ 110, 164, 249, 250
मल्लिषेण 95
महावीराचार्य 149
माधव 62, 257
मुकुट 172
रघुनाथ 2, 100, 122
लल्ल 151
लाड्यायन 196, 198, 200, 201
लोकाचार्य 4
वरवरमुनि 2, 36, 42, 58
वराहमिहिर 2, 56, 59, 83, 116, 124, 125, 174, 247
वर्धमान 111
वल्लभ/वल्लभाचार्य 112, 249, 250
वाग्भट 62, 205, 206, 213, 214
वाचस्पति (मिश्र) 2, 5, 7, 46, 50, 51, 52, 54, 55, 56, 75, 76, 100, 105, 111, 112, 113, 116, 117, 118, 122, 150, 154, 155, 159, 160, 161, 163, 164, 243, 245, 255, 257, 258, 264, 266, 269, 271, 272, 274, 276, 278, 282, 283, 285, 292
वात्स्यायन 114, 116, 117, 159, 160, 162, 164, 289

वार्षगण्य 51
विज्ञानभिक्षु 2, 5, 6, 14, 21, 27, 28, 38, 39, 43, 48, 49, 50, 52, 58, 114, 162, 222, 241, 242
विश्वनाथ 157, 160, 161, 264, 265
वृद्धसुश्रुत 62
वृन्द 65
वेदव्यास 51
शंकर 2, 92, 122, 181, 231, 233, 234, 242, 243
शंकरमिश्र 117, 130, 132, 145, 146, 147, 148, 152, 174, 222, 224, 225
शबर (स्वामिन्) 154, 157, 163
शिवादित्य 273
श्रीधर 2, 53, 77, 100, 101, 102, 104, 108, 135, 137, 138, 139, 140, 142, 144, 145, 147, 157, 170, 178, 181, 262
श्रीपति 247
श्रीहर्ष 245, 257, 277, 278, 281
सातवाहन 63
सिद्धनागार्जुन 62
सुश्रुत 56, 58, 59, 60, 61, 62, 84, 169, 171, 179, 180, 182, 193, 196, 199, 206, 208, 210, 213, 214, 215, 216, 217, 218, 226, 228, 229, 232, 233, 234, 250
सुश्रुत-नागार्जुन 186, 194
हेमचन्द्र 246

B. WORKS

अग्निपुराण 128, 187, 188
अर्थसालिनी 92
अनिरुद्धवृत्ति 44
अमरकोश 289
उपस्कार 132, 145, 174, 222, 224, 225
कन्दली 101, 102, 108, 170, 178, 181, 262
किरणावली 77, 102, 110, 111, 112, 113, 114, 116, 135, 170, 178, 248, 249
किरणावलीप्रकाश 111
कुसुमाञ्जलि 100, 122, 287
कौमुदी 7, 24, 46, 50, 55, 122
खड्गलक्षण 125
खण्डनखण्डखाद्य 245
गोपाल-उपनिषद् 89
चक्रपाणिसंग्रह 172
चरकसंहिता 70, 207
चिन्तामणि 158, 159, 284
छान्दोग्य-उपनिषद् 181
जल्पकल्पतरु 70, 73, 241
ज्ञानसंकलिनीतंत्र 222
तत्त्वचिन्तामणि 110, 158, 163, 250
तत्त्वत्रय 4, 24, 58
तत्त्वत्रयभाष्य 36, 42
तत्त्वत्रयविवरण 33, 36
तत्त्वनिरूपण 29, 36
तत्त्वबिन्दु 155
तत्त्ववैशारदी 5, 52, 55
तत्त्वार्थाधिगम 97, 188, 192
तर्करहस्यदीपिका 174, 180
तर्कसंग्रह 108, 115
तात्पर्यटीका 51, 75, 113, 116, 118, 155, 161, 163, 164, 258, 264, 271, 272, 283
दर्पण 65

दशकुमारचरित 65
दिनकरी 108, 265, 287
धम्मसंगनी 92
नाट्यशास्त्र 168
न्यायकन्दली 77, 100, 104, 135, 137, 139, 140
न्यायबिन्दु 253, 270
न्यायबिन्दुटीका 173
न्यायबोधिनी 108, 115
न्यायमञ्जरी 103, 123, 134, 147, 152, 154, 155, 180, 240, 245, 252, 256, 283, 288
न्यायरत्नाकर 153
न्यायवार्तिक 45, 75, 113, 155, 161, 162
न्यायसूचीनिबन्ध 51, 150
पञ्चदशी 42, 84, 87, 164, 218
परिशुद्धि 51
पुराण 41
प्रयोगचिन्तामणि 237
प्रवचनभाष्य 6, 14, 26, 28, 29, 43, 49, 50, 52, 53, 54, 162, 242
प्रशस्तपादभाष्य 53, 120, 135, 138, 139
बृहत्संहिता 56, 64, 83, 101, 124
बृहदारण्यकभाष्य 233, 234
ब्राह्मण 233
भविष्यपुराण 187, 188
भानुमती 175, 207
भामती 100, 101, 243
भावप्रकाश 172
भाषापरिच्छेद 123, 157, 161, 265
मञ्जरी 117, 176, 265, 289
महाभारत 176

महाभाष्य 178, 180, 181, 182, 291, 294
माध्यमिकसूत्रवृत्ति 62
योगरत्नाकरसमुच्चय 63
योगवार्तिक 5, 22, 27, 28, 29, 30, 33, 37, 48, 58
रसरत्नसमुच्चय 66
रसार्णव 66
रागविबोध 167
राजनिघण्टु 172, 175, 194
रुग्विनिश्चय 62
लक्षणावली 135
लीलावती 112, 249, 250
वाक्यपदीय 154, 155, 159, 164
वात्स्यायनभाष्य 114
वासवदत्ता 65
विद्वन्मनोरंजिनी 86, 92
विष्णुपुराण 29, 30, 33, 34, 37, 76, 89
वेदान्तकौस्तुभप्रभा 89
वैशेषिकसूत्र 133, 146

व्यासभाष्य 2, 5, 9, 10, 11, 13, 15, 17, 18, 21, 26, 29, 37, 45, 50, 51, 55
शबरभाष्य 154, 159
शारीरकभाष्य 92, 101, 231, 243
शेषलीलावती 166
श्लोकवार्त्तिक 151, 153, 271, 272
षड्दर्शनसमुच्चय 173
षष्टितंत्रशास्त्र 51
संगीतदर्पण 165, 166, 222, 230, 231
संगीतपारिजात 165, 166
संगीतरत्नाकर 165, 168, 222, 225, 228, 230
संगीतसमयसार 166
सप्तपदार्थी 273
सर्वदर्शनसंग्रह 261, 262
सिद्धान्तमुक्तावली 264, 265, 287
सिद्धान्तशिरोमणि 76, 80, 149
सुबाल-उपनिषद् 89
हर्षचरित 63

C. SANSKRIT WORDS

अ

अक्रव्याद 199
अजगर 186
अणु 47, 93
अण्ड 181
अण्डज 177, 178, 179, 181, 190, 191, 193, 195
अदर्शन 276
अदृष्ट 102, 132, 133, 136
अधःपातन 67
अधर्म 133
अध्यात्मवायु 243
अध्यास 250

अनन्ताणुक 94
अनस्थिक 178
अनाहतचक्र 220
अनुद्भूतवृत्तिशक्ति 3
अनुद्भूतशक्ति 90
अनुपलब्धि 254
अनुमान 250
अनुरणन 165
अनुलोमसर्ग 22
अनुवादी 167
अनूप 182, 183, 184
अन्यथासिद्ध 271
अन्यथासिद्धिशून्य 265
अन्यथासिद्धिशून्यता 279

अन्वय 256, 276, 278, 281
अन्वयी 293
अपक्षेपण 130
अपरजाति 101
अपादिक 188, 193
अपान 229
अभिघात 135, 136, 138, 139, 140, 143, 144, 146, 156
अभिभव 164
अभिसर्पण 132, 145, 146
अभ्रकविधि 63
अयस्कृति 59
अयुतसिद्ध 7
अयुतसिद्धावयवय समूह 49
अयोनिज 177, 193
अर्चिःसन्तान 151
अर्थापत्ति 274
अलम्बुषा 228
अलिङ्ग 8
अवकाशदान 25
अवकुश 185
अवच्छेदक 290
अवतान 170
अवधि 294
अवयव 130, 140, 143
अवयवसन्निवेश 90, 101, 106, 118
अवयवी 130, 140, 143
अवरोह 172
अवष्टम्भ 50, 53, 109
अवस्थापरिणाम 20
अविनाभाव 254
अविशेष 7, 10
अव्यभिचारित्व 262
असमवायिकारण 132
असाधारणधर्म 162
अस्मिता 8, 9, 10
अहङ्कार 10, 11, 12

आ

आकर्षण 132
आकाश 22, 27
आकाशपरमाणु 26
आकाशाणु 28
आकुञ्चन 130
आज्ञा 224
आज्ञाचक्र 220, 221, 223, 224
आज्ञावहा नाडी 221, 222, 223, 224, 229
आत्मन् 224
आदर्शमण्डल 186
आधारचक्र 219
आमपक्वाशय 203
आमाशय 203
आरम्भक संयोग 108
आरम्भवाद 74, 75
आलोचक पित्त 205
आवरण 36
आवरणाभाव 27
आवर्त्तकोश 183
आरोप 250
आरोहण 133, 145, 146
आश्रय 156

इ

इडा 220, 226, 227
इतरेतराश्रय 295

उ

उत्क्षेपण 130
उत्पतक 189, 194
उत्पतन 143
उदान 229, 230
उदाहरण 251, 252
उद्देश 289

उद्भिज्ज 177, 179, 181, 191, 193, 196
उद्भूतवृत्ति 13
उपचिका 189, 194
उपनय 251
उपरस 66
उपलक्षण 289
उपष्टम्भ 49, 50, 53, 109
उपष्टम्भक 75, 111
उपादान 52
उपादानकारण 49, 50, 56, 85, 108
उपाधि 275, 276, 277, 280
उपाधिविधुरता 278
उपाधिशंकानिरास 278
उरग 190, 195
उष्मज 177

ऊ

ऊर्ध्वंपातन 67
ऊह 278, 281, 282

ए

एकशफ 185

औ

औदर्य तेजस् 114
औषधि 169, 170

क

कङ्कु 197
कञ्चुक 187
कनव 196
कन्द 219, 226
कफवाहिनी 213
कम्पन 144
कम्पनसन्तानसंस्कार 151, 159, 162, 165
करण 294
कराली 188
कर्कट 184, 196
कर्णशष्कुलि 156
कर्त्ता 294
कर्पासास्थिका 189
कर्म 102, 129, 137, 159
कर्मेन्द्रिय 11
कलल 107
कला 76, 231
कल्पनागौरव 288
कल्पनालाघव 288
कादाचित्कत्व 268
कारणसामग्री 266, 283
कारणाकाश 28
कारण्डव 197
कार्यकारणभाव 166, 281, 295
कार्यसामग्री 284
कार्याकाश 28
कालरात्रि 188
कालिकसम्बन्ध 295
काष्ठदारु 171
काष्ठहारक 189
काष्ठा 76
किरणविघट्टन 116
कीट 180, 190, 194, 198, 200
कुन्थु 189, 191, 194
कुम्भीर 184, 195
कुहू 227
कूर्म 191, 195, 196, 230
कूलेचर 183, 184, 199
कृकर 230
कृकवास 191, 195
कृमि 180, 193
कृष्णल 80
कृष्णसर्प 186
कोषस्थ 183, 193, 195
क्रव्याद 185, 199

क्रिया 7
क्लोम 231
क्षण 20, 21, 76, 148, 273
क्षुद्रजन्तु 177, 178, 193, 194

ख

खरपाक 68

ग

गण्डुपद 189, 193
गतिसन्तान 159
गन्धवहा नाडी 221
गमक 274, 276, 284
गमन 130, 143
गम्य 274, 276, 284
गलगोलिक 191, 196
गवय 184
गान्धारी 227
गुडुची 172
गुण 3, 13, 21, 22, 294
गुणवैषम्य 7
गुरुत्व 132, 140, 141, 142
गुल्म 169
गुहाशय 183, 185, 199
गृहगोलिक 191, 195
गोध 191, 195
गोधेरक 191, 196
गौरसर्षप 80
ग्रहणी नाडी 203
ग्राम्य 183, 185, 199

घ

घटिका 76

च

चक्रक 253

चतुरणुक 101
चतुष्पद 190
चर्मपक्ष 192, 198
चित्तस्थान 222
चैतन्य 91, 240

ज

जघन्यगुण 96
जङ्घाल 183, 185, 199
जठरानल 114
जरायु 178
जरायुज 177, 179, 191, 198, 200
जलचर 182
जलशुक्ति 183
जलसन्तान 151
जलूका 189, 192, 193, 198
जसद 67
जशस्विनी नाडी 228
जाङ्गल 182, 183, 184
जाति 294
जीव 224
जीवज 181
जीवनयोनिप्रयत्न 224
ज्ञान 289
ज्ञानवहा नाडी 223
ज्ञानेन्द्रिय 11

त

तत्त्वनिर्णय 290
तत्पर 76
तदुत्पत्ति 253, 269, 282
तन्मात्र 9, 10, 11, 12, 18, 19, 24, 25
तमस् 3
तर्क 278, 281, 282
तात्कालिकी गति 150

तादात्म्य 166, 253, 261, 269, 282
तान्मात्रिक सृष्टि 24
तामसाहङ्कार 11, 24
तारमन्दादिभेद 162
तिमि 183, 195
तिमिंगल 183
तिर्यक्‌गमन 116
तीव्रमन्दादिभेद 162
तुबुरक 189, 194
तृण 170
तृणद्रुम 172
तृणध्वज 172
तृणपत्र 189, 194
तेजोधातु 238
तैलकीट 194
त्रपुसबिज 189
त्रसरेणु 148
त्रिवृत्करण 88
त्रुटि 76, 148
त्र्यणुक 101

द

दंश 190, 194
दर्वीकर 186
दर्शन 245
दर्शनादर्शन 276
दिक् 21
दिग्‌देशसम्बन्ध 295
दूर्वा 169
दृग्‌गणितैक्य 247
दृष्टसिद्धि 288
देवदत्त (वायु) 230
देश 21, 22
दैव 237
दोष 250
द्व्यणुक 52, 94, 99
द्रवत्व 132
द्रव्य 93, 294
द्रव्यान्तरसंयोग 90

ध

धनञ्जय (वायु) 230
धमनी 208, 210, 213, 214, 215, 217, 219
धर्म 133, 266
धर्मपरिणाम 20
धातु 205
धातुविष 69
ध्वनि 153

न

नकुल 191
नक्र 191, 196
नन्द्यावर्त 190, 194
नाग (जन्तु) 187
नाग (वायु) 230
नाडी 219
नाद 153, 155
नादवृद्धि 163
नाभिकन्द 220, 226
नाभिचक्र 226
निगमन 251
निमित्त 16, 294
निमित्तकारण 14, 15, 50, 52, 75, 132, 156
निमेष 76
नियतसाहचर्य 276
निर्णय 288, 289
निर्विष 186
नूपुरक 189, 193
नोदन 134, 135, 136, 138, 139, 140, 144, 146

प

पक्षिविराल 192, 198
पक्षी 190
पञ्चकरणी 258, 259, 260, 261, 267, 288

पञ्चीकरण 86, 91
पतन 131
पतंग 190, 194
पद्म 186, 219
पयस्विनी 227
परममहत् 48
परमाणु 9, 11, 12
परिच्छिन्न 28
परिच्छिन्नत्व 3
परिणाम 7, 22, 55, 74, 85, 89, 93, 166
परिणामवाद 74
परिस्पन्द 7, 26, 29, 30, 31, 91, 93, 100, 121
परिमाण 3, 47
परीक्षा 289
पर्णमृग 183, 185, 199
पर्पटितान्न 66
पर्याय 93
पाक 231
पाकजोत्पत्ति 99, 102
पाकनिष्ठ औषधि 173
पाचकाख्य पित्त 205
पादिन 183, 184, 195, 196
पारिमाण्डल्य 83, 117
पिङ्गला 220, 226, 227
पिठरपाक 103
पित्ताशय 203, 205
पिपीलिका 179, 189, 194
पिलुपाक 103
पुतिघस 185
पुत्तिका 190, 194
पुद्गल 93
पुरुष 6
पुषा 227
पोतज 191, 192, 197, 198, 200
प्रकाण्ड 171
प्रकृति 2, 8, 10, 11, 294
प्रचय 154, 159

प्रतान 214
प्रतिज्ञा 251
प्रतिध्वनि 161
प्रतिबन्ध 146, 253
प्रतिबिम्ब 161
प्रतिषेध 254
प्रतियोगी 290
प्रतुद 182, 183, 184, 197
प्रत्यक्ष 252
प्रत्यय 294
प्रधान 3
प्रयत्न 131, 224
प्रसह 182, 183, 184, 197, 198
प्रसारण 130
प्राण 91, 228, 229, 241, 242, 245
प्राणवहा 224, 225
प्राणवायु 203
प्रेरण 135
प्लव 183, 184, 197

फ

फेणीभूत कफ 203

ब

बीज 234, 235
ब्रह्म 85
ब्रह्मग्रन्थि 219, 226
ब्रह्मनाडी 269
ब्रह्मरन्ध्र 219
ब्रह्माण्ड 219

भ

भरण्ड 198
भस्मीकरण 67
भानुभवन 220, 226

भारतीभवन 220
भावना 136
भुजंग 190, 195, 196
भूतादि 24, 27, 31, 34, 40
भूयोदर्शन 277, 278
भूशय 182
भ्रम 250
भ्रमण 130, 131, 144
भ्रमर 189, 194

म

मकर 180, 183, 195
मकरी 188
मक्षिका 190, 194
मञ्जिष्ठा 65
मणिपूरक 220
मण्डली 186
मत्स्य 183, 190, 191, 195
मद्गुमूषिक 185
मध्यमपाक 68
मध्ययव 80
मनश्चक्र 221, 223, 224
मनस् 11, 91, 224
मनोवहा नाडी 219, 221, 222, 223, 224
मशक 190, 194
महत् 8, 9, 10, 11, 12, 47
महत्त्व 163
महाकृष्ण 186
महान् 163
महापद्म 186
महाभूत 57, 86
महास्रोतस् 203
मांसाद 185
माक्षिक 67
मिलितद्रव्य 49, 52
मुखसन्दंश 200
मुहूर्त 77
मूर्च्छन 116

मूषिक 192
मृगपक्षी 198
मृगेवरु 185
मृदुपाक 68

य

यन्त्रज्ञ 64
यन्त्रविद् 64
यमदूतिका 188
युतिसिद्ध 7
योगचूर्ण 65
योगवर्त्तिका 65
योनय: 233
योनिज 177, 193
योनिसंकर 179
यौगपद्याभिमान 272

र

रक्तवाहिनी 213, 214
रञ्जकाख्य पित्त 205
रजस् 3
रजिमत् 186
रश्मिपरावर्तन 116
रस 66, 174, 203
रसक 67
रसतन्मात्र 32
रसवहा नाडी 221
रसवाहिनी 213, 214
रसामृतचूर्ण 65
रागगन्धयुक्तिविद: 64
राजसिक अहंकार 11
राजिसर्षप 80
रुह 197
रोहिणिका 189, 194
रूक्षत्व 96
रूपतन्मात्र 31
रूपवहा नाडी 221

ल

लक्षण 289

लक्षणपरिणाम 20
लज्जावती लता 174
लता 169, 170
ललनाचक्र 220
लव 77
लापक 191
लिङ्ग 8, 9, 10
लिङ्गव्यपदेश 251
लूता 194
लोमपक्ष 191, 197
लोहशास्त्र 62, 63

व

वज्राभ 67
वज्रलेप 64, 125
वनस्पति 169, 170
वरट 189, 194
वल्गुलि 192, 198
वल्लुक 183
वानर 199
वानस्पत्य 169
वायु 107, 228, 229, 232
वायुसन्तान 154, 155
वारना (नाडी) 228
वारिशय 182
विकिरण 32
विजातीय संयोग 54
विजातीयोत्पत्ति 90
विज्ञान 289
विड 63, 68
विधारक प्रयत्न 132
विनिगमक 288
विभागज 158
विभु 27, 48
विमल 67
विलेशय (बिलेशय) 182, 183, 185, 198
विलोमसर्ग 22
विवर्त 85

विवर्त्तन 166
विवादी 167
विशेष 7, 9, 11
विशेषणविशेष्यभाव 295
विश्वोदरा (नाडी) 228
विषमव्याप्ति 274
विष्किर 182, 183, 184, 197
विष्टम्भ 50, 53, 109, 111
विसंवादि ज्ञान 244
विसदृशपरिणाम 10, 22
वीचितरङ्ग 151
वीचितरङ्गन्याय 155
वीरुध् 169
वृक 185
वृक्ष 11, 170
वृक्षशायिक 185
वृक्षायुर्वेद 174
वृक्षेशय 186
वृश्चिक 190, 194
वेग 129, 132, 136, 137, 143, 160, 165
वेगाख्यसंस्कार 137
वेंकरञ्ज 186
वैषम्य 7
वोडिक 183, 194
व्यजन 166
व्यतिरेक 256, 276, 277, 278, 281
व्यभिचार 276
व्यभिचारादर्शन 276
व्याघात 267, 277
व्यान (वायु) 204, 229
व्यापक 274, 284
व्याप्ति 250, 252, 253, 266, 273, 275, 279, 281
व्याप्तिग्रहोपाय 269, 276
व्याप्य 274, 284
व्याल 200
व्यूह 45, 101, 106, 118
व्यूहन 53

श

शक्ति 122, 263, 265, 266
शंकितोपाधि 277
शंख 183, 189, 193
शंखन 183
शंखपाली 186
शंखिनी (नाडी) 228
शतपदी 189, 191, 194, 196
शब्दजशब्द 158
शब्दतन्मात्र 29, 30
शब्दवहा नाडी 221
शब्दसन्तान 151, 155, 156, 158, 159
शयिक 191
शरीर 11
शल्लक 191
शस्त्रपान 124
शिफा 172
शिरा 208, 209, 214, 215, 219
शिलादारण 124
शिल्पशास्त्र 148
शिशुमार 184, 191, 195, 196
शुक्ति 183
शुक्तिक 189, 194
शेवल 172
श्रुति 165
श्रुतिभेद 162
श्रोतस् 208, 209, 232
श्ववित् 191

स

संयुक्तसंयोग 139
संयोग 96, 134
संयोगज 158
संयोगजसंयोग 119
संवाद 245
संवादि ज्ञान 244
संवादी 167
संसृष्टविवेक 7
संस्कार 135, 136, 140, 142, 144, 159, 160, 250
संस्थान 90
संस्वेदज 178
संहतक्रिया 103
संहतभूतधर्म 90
संहतभूतार्थ 49, 52
संकलित गति 149
सजातीय संयोग 49
सजातीयोपष्टम्भ 49
संज्ञासंज्ञिभाव 295
सत्त्व 3
सदृशपरिणाम 10, 22, 23, 122
सप्ततवच: 231
समवाय 295
समवायिकारण 108
समव्याप्ति 274
समष्टिबुद्धि 4
समान 229
समानवायु 203
समानजातीयोत्पत्ति 90
समूह 48
सम्प्रयोग 250
सम्बुक 183, 189, 194
सम्भव 289
सम्भूयक्रिया 90, 103
संमूर्च्छन 145
सरस्वती 227
सरीसृप 178, 180
सर्प 191 195
सविकल्पकज्ञान 223
सहकारिशक्ति 14
सहस्रार चक्र 221, 223, 224
सहायक 36
साध्यनिर्देश 251
साध्यसमव्याप्ति 281
सामानाधिकरण्य 295
साम्यावस्था 6, 7, 10, 28
सारंग 189, 194

सिद्धान्त 288
सुप्ति 225
सुषुप्ति 225
सुषुम्ना 219, 223, 226, 227
सूक्ष्मगति 79
सूक्ष्मभूत 9, 53
सूक्ष्मशरीर 53
सूर्यपाक 114
सोमचक्र 221
स्कन्ध 93
स्तम्भन 67
स्थितिस्थापकत्व 135
स्थितिस्थापक संस्कार 136, 160
स्थूलगति 79, 149
स्थूलभूत 9, 11, 12
स्थूलभूतपरमाणु 24
स्निग्धत्व 96
स्पन्दन 130, 131, 132, 144, 145, 151, 152
स्पर्शतन्मात्र 31
स्पर्शवहा नाडी 221

स्फोट 153
स्वप्न 225
स्वप्नवहा नाडी 223
स्वभाव 252, 253, 261
स्वभावप्रतिबन्ध 281
स्वर 165
स्वाधिष्ठानचक्र 220
स्वाप 225
स्वाभाविक 134
स्वाभाविक परिणाम 89
स्वाभाविक सम्बन्ध 276
स्वार्थानुमान 251
स्वेदज 177, 179, 193
स्वेदन 67

ह

हस्त 148
हस्तिजिह्वा (नाडी) 227
हस्ती 191
हेतु 251, 294

D. ENGLISH

Acoustics 153 ff
After-sound 161
Agreement in absence 256, 278
Agreement in presence 256, 278
Ākāśa compound 202
Ākāśa, two stages 121
Alimentary canal 203
Anaesthetic drugs 65
Analysis of motion 129
Analysis of vibratory motion 159 ff
Animals 190
Animals with four senses 189
Animals with three senses 189
Animals with two senses 188
Antithesis 8
Ap-compound 202
Ap-substances, simple and compound 60

Archimedes 77
Aristotelian syllogism 251
Aristotle 218, 259
Ascertainment of inseparableness 254
Atomic theory, of the Buddhists 92; of the Jainas, 93
Atoms, structure of 34 ff
Automatic & reflex activity 228ff
Bacon 263
Balloons 135
Bamboo 171
Bapudeva Sastri 78
Bhautic quasi-compounds 111
Bhūtas, characters of 57
Brain 219
Buddhist analysis of inference 253
Calcination 67

Capillary motion 132, 146
Carbo-hydrates 202
Cardiac plexus 220
Casting 67
Catalytic agent 36
Causal efficiency 260
Causality 277
Causation 13
Causation, Sāṅkhya view 13 ff
Cause and effect 13
Cause and effect, synchronousness of 272
Causes 131
Caustic alkalis 59
Cererbo-spinal system 219
Change, two kinds of 89
Chārvāka view of inference 252
Chemical action 113
Chemical combination 103
Chemical composition and decomposition 66
Chemical industries 64 ff
Chemical technology 124
Chemistry in the medical schools 56 ff
Chemistry of colours 70
Chyle 203
Circulation 206
Circulatory system 208 ff
Classification by series 188
Classification of animals 177 ff; in Patañjali, 178; in Charaka, 177; in Praśastapāda, 177; in Śaṅkara, 181; in Suśruta, 178; in Umāsvāti, 188 ff
Classification of plants 169 ff
Coagulated mercury 65
Co-effects 263, 271
Collocation 13, 15
Colour-potential 31
Colours of metallic flames 66
Colour-Tanmātra 34
Combination of forces 139
Complexion of offspring 238
Composition of gravity with momentum 141
Compounds 57, 59
Consciousness 175

Consciousness, Chārvāka explanation, 240; Sāṅkhya view, 240
Conservation 13
Continued pressure 136
Correspondence 261
Cosmic dissolution 22 ff
Cosmic evolution 8, 10, 22; stages 8 ff
Cosmic vibratory motion 121
Cosmo-genesis 40
Cranial nerves 217
Creation, Vedāntic view 85 ff
Creative transformation 6
Crucial test 288
Current motion 145
Curvilinear motion 130 143
Darwin's "gemmule" 234
Decimal notation 51
Descartes 150
Determinants of sex 237 ff
Devala 166, 167
Diatonic scale 166
Dietary animals 182
Differential calculus 77; applied to computation of motion 150
Differentiation 7, 9
Differentiation in integration 7
Dissection of dead bodies, 246
Distillation 67
Disturbance of equilibrium 5
Diurnal revolution of the earth 151
Drying 67
Earth-compounds 202
Echo 161 ff
Elasticity 135, 160
Elements, physical characters of 57 f
Elements and compounds 48 ff
Empirical ego 8
Empirical intuition 21
Empirical recipes 124
Energy (rajas) 3, 12, 13
Energy, conservation of 12; and transformation of, 14
Equilibrium 6, 8

Essence (sattva) 3
Evolution 6, 7
Evolutionary process 89
Experiment 248 ff
Extensity 3
Extraction 67
Fallacies of observation 250
Fertilization of ovum 237
Filing 67
Fluidity 136
Foetal development 231 ff
Foetus, composition of 69
Force, kinds of 136
Force of gravity 132
Forces, composition of 142
Functions of the Śirās 212
Ganglionic centres and plexuses 219 ff
Gemmule 234, 236
General properties of matter 94
Genesis, of the Tanmātras etc. 29; of an atom 30; of matter 24; of the bhūtas 39
Germ-plasm theory 236
Glass, making and polishing of 248
Gravity 3, 136
Hardening of steel 124
Heart 225
Heart as seat of consciousness 211, 218
Heat 113
Heat-potential 31
Hegel 290
Heliotropic movement 173
Heredity 233 ff
Hetero-bhautic quasi-compounds 109
Hindu Materia Medica 172
Hindu musical scale 166
Homogeneity 7
Hydro-carbon 202
Hypothesis 288
Identity of essence 261, 279
Ids 234, 236
Impact 136, 143
Incineration 67
Inductive generalization 252

Inertia 3
Infinite time 18
Infra-atomic particles 18, 25, 27
Infra-atomic unit potentials 28 ff
Inorganic and organic compounds 56
Inseparableness 254
Instantaneous motion 78
Integration 77
Intellectual intuition 21
Intelligence stuff 3
Intensity (of sounds) 162
Invariable and unconditional antecedence 123
Invariable concomitance, 252, 261
Joint agreement in presence and absence 293
Joint method of agreement 288, 293
Joint method of difference 259, 288, 292
Killing 67
Kinetics 129 ff
Laplace's Table 247
Law of Karma 133
Legitimate hypothesis, conditions of 288
Liberation of energy 15
Life 239 ff
  Sāṅkhya view 241
Lumbar plexus 220
Mass 3, 12
Massiveness 163
Material evolution 8
Materialists 252
Matter 3
Matter, evolution of 24 ff
Matter-rudiment 27
Matter-stuff 11
Measures of capacity 82
Measures of time & space 76
Melting 67
Menstruum 36
Mental impression of parents 238
Merit and demerit 133

Metabolism 202 ff
Metallurgic processes 66
Method of agreement 279
Method of difference 259, 279
Method of subtraction 257, 269
Methodology 289
Mill, J.S. 252, 259, 265, 278, 281
Mill's view of major premise 252
Mill's induction 251
Mill's joint method 281
Mind stuff 11
Mineral kingdom 66
Mixtures 112
Molecular qualities in chemical compounds 70
Moment, definition of 19
Momentum 129, 136, 159, 160
Mono-bhautic compounds of higher order 106
Mono-bhautic compounds of the first order 104
Mono-bhautic Earth compound 59
Mono-bhautic Earth substances 59
Motion 3, 131, 137
Motion, kinds of 131 ff
Motion ascribed to adṛṣṭa 147 ff
Motion of a particle 142
Motion of fluids 132
Motions produced by contact 134
Musical intervals 167 ff
Musical sounds 165 ff
Neo-Platonic quaternion 88
Nervous cords and fibres 225 ff
Nervous system in Charaka 217 ff
Nervous system in Tantras 218 f
Newton 77
Nitrogen compounds 202
Notion of three axes 150 ff
Nourishment 126
Nyāya analysis of the causal relation 271 ff
Nyāya doctrine of inference 262
Nyāya objection to the Buddhist method of difference 367 ff
Nyāya-Vaiśeṣika chemical theory 98
Object-series (of evolution) 9
Obscuration of sounds 164
Observation 245
Obstetric surgery 246
Ovum, influences of nutrition on 237
Offspring, sexual character of 237
Oleaginous substances 111
Organic compounds 68
Original constituents (of Cosmos) 4 ff
Original equilibrium 28
Overtones 162
Palingenesis 233
Parasitical plants 172
Perfumery 64
Pitch 162
Plant life, characteristics of 173
Plant physiology 173 ff
Plurality of causes 255, 273, 284, 285
Poison 69
Post-mortem operation 246
Potential energy 3
Powdering 67
Precious stones 59
Precipitation 67
Preparation of cements 64, 125; of chemical compounds 62; of fast dyes 64; of mercury 63
Pressure 135
Pressure and impact, causes of 138 ff
Primary qualities 58
Principle of causality 252
Proto-atom 27
Purification 67
Purity of gold 249
Qualities of compounds 61
Quantum 3
Quaternion 88
Quintuplication 86 ff
Rain-gauge 247

Reals 3, 8
Reals, collocation of 6
Reasoning in a circle 253
Rebounding 143
Reeds 172
Reflection of sound 161
Relative motion 151 ff
Repeated observation 277
Rinsing 67
Rotatory motion 130, 144
Rudiment-matter 29, 30, 31, 40
Sacro-coccygeal plexus 219
Salts 59
Sceptics 252
Scientific method 244 ff
Searing of hard rocks 124
Seeds, treatment of 126
Sensible qualities 95
Serial motion 151 f
Sex, modification by food & drinks 238
Sexual characters of plants 174
Sivadas Sen 63
Size of atoms 76
Sleep 173
Sleep & waking, phenomena of 174
Small intestine 203
Smell-Tanmātra 34
Snakes 186; in Purāṇas 187 f; in Suśruta-Nāgārjuna 186
Solid (coordinate) Geometry 118, 150
Solutions 67, 112
Sound-potential 29, 30
Sound-Tanmātra 34
Space 21 f
Specific characters, inheritance of 234
Spencer's "ids" 234
Spontaneous generation 239
Spottiswoode 78, 79, 150
Stadia of cosmic evolution 8
Steaming, 67

Subject-series of evolution 8
Surgical knowledge 62
Suspected upādhi 277
Synthesis 8
Taste-potential 32
Taste-Tanmātra 34
Tejas compounds 202
Theory 288
Theory of atomic combination 99
Thesis 8
Timbre 162
Time continuum 20
Tones 162
Touch-potential 31
Touch-Tanmātra 34
Transformation 13, 20
Transmitted force 136
Triplication 88
Truth, test of 244
Typical sounds 87
Unconditional invariable concomitance 253
Unconditionality 278
Uniformity of coexistence 253, 261
Uniformity of nature 253, 277
Uniformity of succession 253
Unity of space & time 148 ff
Unity of apperception 8
Unknown agencies 133
Upward motion 146
Vascular system 213 ff
Vāyu-compounds 202
Velocity 149
Verification 288
Vibration-potential 31
Vibratory motion 130, 144
Volition 136
Vortical motion 143
Water-atom 32
Weight and capacity 80
Weight of air 248